# Tales And Sketches: The Shepherd's Calendar (continued) Emigration. The Two Highlanders. The Watchmaker. A Story Of The Forty-six. A Tale Of The Martyrs. Adam Scott. The Baron St. Gio. The Mysterious Bride. Nature's Magic Lantern...

James Hogg

NEWARK CASTLE

BY

# THE ETTRICK SHEPHERD.

## VOL. IV.

Moffat

*James Hogg*

# TALES AND SKETCHES,

BY

## THE ETTRICK SHEPHERD.

INCLUDING

THE BROWNIE OF BODSBECK, WINTER EVENING TALES,
SHEPHERD'S CALENDAR, &c., &c.

AND SEVERAL PIECES NOT BEFORE PRINTED,

WITH ILLUSTRATIVE ENGRAVINGS,

CHIEFLY FROM REAL SCENES.

BY D. O. HILL, Esq., S. A.

VOL. IV.

BLACKIE & SON, QUEEN STREET, GLASGOW;
SOUTH COLLEGE STREET, EDINBURGH;
AND WARWICK SQUARE, LONDON.

MDCCCXXXVII.

GLASGOW:
PRINTED BY GEORGE BROOKMAN.

# CONTENTS OF VOL. IV.

THE

# SHEPHERD'S CALENDAR.

---

## CHAP. IX.

### TIBBY HYSLOP'S DREAM.

In the year 1807, when on a jaunt through the valleys of Nith and Annan, I learned the following story on the spot where the incidents occurred, and even went and visited all those connected with it, so that there is no doubt with regard to its authenticity.

In a cottage called Knowe-back, on the large farm of Drumlochie, lived Tibby Hyslop, a respectable spinster, about the age of forty I thought when I saw her, but, of course, not so old when the first incidents occurred which this singular tale relates. Tibby was represented to me as being a good Christian, not in name and profession only, but in word and in deed; and I believe I may add, in heart and in soul. Nevertheless, there was something in her manner and deportment different from other people——a sort of innocent simplicity, bordering on silliness, together with an instability of thought, that, in the eyes of many, approached to abstraction.

But then Tibby could repeat the book of the Evangelist Luke by heart, and many favourite chapters both of the Old and New Testaments; while there was scarcely one in the whole country so thoroughly acquainted with those Books from beginning to end; for, though she had read a portion every day for forty years, she had never perused any other books but the Scriptures. They were her week-day books, and her Sunday books, her books of amusement, and books of devotion. Would to God that all our brethren and sisters of the human race—the poor and comfortless, as well as the great and wise—knew as well how to estimate these books as Tibby Hyslop did!

Tibby's history is shortly this : Her mother married a sergeant of a recruiting party. The year following he was obliged to go to Ireland, and from thence nobody knew whither ; but neither he nor his wife appeared again in Scotland. On their departure, they left Tibby, then a helpless babe, with her grandmother, who lived in a hamlet somewhere about Tinwald ; and with that grandmother was she brought up, and taught to read her Bible, to card, spin, and work at all kinds of country labour to which women are accustomed. Jane Hervey was her grandmother's name, a woman then scarcely past her prime, certainly within forty years of age ; with whom lived her elder sister, named Douglas ; and with these two were the early years of Tibby Hyslop spent, in poverty, contentment, and devotion.

At the age of eighteen, Tibby was hired at the Candlemas fair, for a great wage, to be a byre-woman to Mr Gilbert Forret, then farmer at Drumlochie. Tibby had then acquired a great deal of her mother's dangerous bloom—dangerous, when attached to poverty and so much simplicity of heart ; and when she came home and told what she had done, her mother and aunt, as she always denominated the two, marvelled much at the extravagant conditions, and began to express some fears regarding her new master's designs, till Tibby put them all to rest by the following piece of simple information :

" Dear, ye ken, ye needna be feared that Mr Forret has ony design o' courting me, for dear, ye ken, he has a wife already, and five bonnie bairns ; and he'll never be sae daft as fa' on and court anither ane. I'se warrant he finds ane enow for him, honest man !"

" Oh, then, you are safe enough, since he is a married man, my bairn," said Jane.

The truth was, that Mr Forret was notorious for debauching young and pretty girls, and was known in Dumfries market by the name of Gibby Gledger, from the circumstance of his being always looking slyly after them. Perceiving Tibby so comely, and at the same time so simple, he hired her at nearly double wages, and moreover gave her a crown as arle-money.

Tibby went home to her service, and being a pliable, diligent creature, she was beloved by all. Her master commended her for her neatness, and whenever a quiet opportunity offered, would pat her rosy cheek, and say kind things. Tibby took all these in good part, judging them tokens of approbation of her good services, and was proud of them ; and if he once or twice whispered a place and an hour of assignation, she took it for a joke, and paid no further attention to it. A whole year passed over without the worthy farmer having accomplished his cherished purpose regarding poor Tibby. He hired her to remain with him, still on the former high conditions, and moreover he said to her : " I wish your grandmother and grand-aunt would take my pleasant cottage of Knowe-back. They should have it for a mere trifle—a week's shearing or so—so long as you remain in my service ; and as it is likely to be a long while before you and I part, it would be better to have them near you, that you might see them often, and attend to their wants. I could give them plenty of work through the whole year, on the best conditions. What think you of this proposal, Rosy ?"—a familiar name he often called her by.

" O, I'm sure, sir, I think ye are the kindest man that ever existed. What a blessing is it when riches open up the heart to acts of charity and benevolence ! My poor auld mother and aunty will be blythe to grip at the kind offer ; for they sit under a hard master yonder. The Almighty will bestow a blessing on you for this, sir !"

Tibby went immediately with the joyful news to her poor mother and aunt. Now, they had of late found themselves quite easy in their circumstances, owing to the large wages Tibby received, every farthing of which was added to the common stock; and though Tibby displayed a little more finery at the meeting-house, it was her grandmother who purchased it for her, without any consent on her part. "I am sure," said her grandmother, when Tibby told the story of her master's kindness and attention, "I am sure it was the kindest intervention o' Providence that ever happened to poor things afore, when ye fell in wi' that kind worthy man, i' the mids o' a great hiring market, where ye might just as easily hae met wi' a knave, or a niggard, as wi' this man o' siccan charity an' mercy."

> " Ay; the wulcat maun hae his collop,
>    And the raven maun hae his part,
> And the tod will creep through the heather,
>    For the bonny moor-hen's heart,"

said old Douglas Hervey, poking the fire all the while with the tongs, and speaking only as if speaking to herself—"Hech-wow, and lack-a-day! but the times are altered sair since I first saw the sun! Poor, poor Religion, wae's me for her! She was first driven out o' the lord's castle into the baron's ha,' out o' the baron's ha' into the farmer's bien dwelling; and at last out o' that into the poor cauldrife shiel, where there's nae ither comfort but what she brings wi' her."

"What has set ye onna thae reflections the day, aunty?" cried Tibby aloud at her ear; for she was half deaf, and had so many flannel mutches on, besides a blue napkin, which she always wore over them all, that her deafness was nearly completed altogether.

"Oogh! what's the lassie saying?" said she, after listening a good while, till the sounds penetrated to the interior of her ear, "what's the young light-head saying about the defections o' the day? what kens she about them?—oogh! Let me see your face, dame, and find your hand, for I hae neither seen the ane, nor felt the tither, this lang and mony a day." Then taking her grandniece by the hand, and looking close into her face through the spectacles, she added,—"Ay, it is a weel-faured sonsy face, very like the mother's that bore ye ; and hers was as like *her* mother's ; and there was never as muckle common sense amang a' the three as to keep a brock out o' the kail-yard. Ye hae an unco good master, I hear —oogh ! I'm glad to hear't—hoh-oh-oh-oh !—verra glad. I hope it will lang continue, this kindness. Poor Tibby!—as lang as the heart disna gang wrang, we maun excuse the head, for it'll never since gang right. I hope they were baith made for a better warld, for nane o' them were made for this."

When she got this length, she sat hastily down, and began her daily and hourly task of carding wool for her sister's spinning, abstracting herself from all external considerations.

" I think aunty's unco parabolical the day," said Tibby to her grandmother ; " what makes her that gate ?"

" O dear, hinny, she's aye that gate now. She speaks to naebody but hersell," said Jane. " But—lownly be it spoken—I think whiles there's ane speaks till her again that my een canna see."

" The angels often conversed wi' good folks langsyne. I ken o' naething that can hinder them to do sae still, if they're sae disposed," said Tibby ; and so the dialogue closed for the present.

Mr Forret sent his carts at the term, and removed the old people to the cottage of Knoweback, free of all charge, like a gentleman as he was ; and things went on exceedingly well. Tibby had a sincere regard for her master ; and as he continued to speak to her, when alone, in a kind and playful manner, she had several times ventured to broach religion to him, trying to discover the state of his soul. Then he would shake his head, and look demure in mockery, and repeat some grave, becoming words. Poor Tibby thought he *was* a righteous man.

But in a short time his purposes were divulged in such a manner as to be no more equivocal. That morning immediately preceding the development of this long-cherished atrocity, Jane Hervey was awaked at an early hour by the following unintelligible dialogue in her elder sister's bed.

"Have ye seen the news o' the day, kerlin?"

"Oogh?"

"Have ye seen the news o' the day?"

"Ay, that I hae, on a braid open book, without clasp or seal.    Whether will you or the deil win?"

"That depends on the citadel.    If it stand out, a' the powers o' hell winna shake the fortress, nor sap a stane o' its foundation."

"Ah, the fortress is a good ane, and a sound ane; but the poor head captain!—ye ken what a sweet-lipped, turnip-headit brosey he is.    O, lack-a-day, my poor Tibby Hyslop!—my innocent, kind, thowless Tibby Hyslop!"

Jane was frightened at hearing such a colloquy, but particularly at that part of it where her darling child was mentioned.  She sprung from her own bed to that of her sister, and cried in her ear with a loud voice,—"Sister, sister, Douglas, what is that you are saying about our dear bairn?"

"Oogh?   I was saying naething about your bairn. She lies in great jeopardy yonder; but nane as yet. Gang away to your bed—wow, but I was sound asleep."

"There's naebody can make aught out o' her but non-sense," said Jane.

After the two had risen from their scanty breakfast, which Douglas had blessed with more fervency than ordinary, she could not settle at her carding, but always stopped short, and began mumbling and speaking to her-self.   At length, after a long pause, she looked over her shoulder, and said,—"Jeanie, warna ye speaking o' ganging ower to see our bairn the day?   Haste thee and gang away, then; and stay nouther to put on clean bus-sing, kirtle, nor barrie, else ye may be an antrin meenut or twa ower lang."

Jane made no reply, but, drawing the skirt of her gown over her shoulders, she set out for Drumlochie, a distance of nearly a mile; and as she went by the corner of the byre, she imagined she heard her grandchild's voice, in great passion or distress, and ran straight into the byre, crying, " What's the matter wi' you, Tibby? what ails you, my bairn?" but receiving no answer, she thought the voice must have been somewhere without, and slid quietly away, looking everywhere, and at length went down to the kitchen.

Mr Forret, *alias* Gledging Gibby, had borne the brunt of incensed kirk-sessions before that time, and also the unlicensed tongues of mothers, roused into vehemence by the degradation of beloved daughters; but never in his life did he bear such a rebuke as he did that day from the tongue of one he had always viewed as a mere simpleton. It was a lesson—a warning of the most sublime and terrible description, couched in the pure and emphatic language of Scripture. Gibby cared not a doit for these things, but found himself foiled, and exposed to his family and the whole world, if this fool chose to do it. He was, therefore, glad to act a part of deep hypocrisy, pretending the sincerest contrition, regretting, with tears, his momentary derangement. Poor Tibby readily believed and forgave him; and thinking it hard to ruin a repentant sinner in his worldly and family concerns, she promised never to divulge what had passed; and he, knowing well the value of her word, was glad at having so escaped.

Jane found her grand-daughter apparently much disturbed; but having asked if she was well enough, and receiving an answer in the affirmative, she was satisfied, and only added, " Your crazed aunty wad gar me believe ye war in some jeopardy, and hurried me away to see you, without giving me leave to change a steek." One may easily conceive Tibby's astonishment at hearing this, considering the moment at which her grandmother arrived. As soon as the latter was gone, she kneeled before her Maker, and poured out her soul in grateful thanksgiving for her deliverance; and, in particular, for such a manifest interference of some superior intelligence in her behalf.

" How did you find our poor bairn the day, titty Jean?
Did she no tell you ony thing?" asked Douglas, on Jane's
return.

" She tauld me naething, but said she was weel."

" She's ae fool, and ye're another! If I had been her
I wad hae blazed it baith to kirk and council;—to his
wife's ear, and to his minister's! She's very weel, is
she?—Oogh! Ay. Hoh—oh—oh—oh!—silly woman
—silly woman—Hoh—oh—oh!"

In a few weeks Mr Forret's behaviour to his simple
dairymaid altered very materially. He called her no
more by the endearing name of Rosy; poor idiot was
oftener the term; and finding he was now safe from
accusation, his malevolence towards her had scarcely any
bounds. She made out her term with difficulty, but he
refused to pay the stipulated wage on pretence of her
incapacity; and as she had by that time profited well at
his hand, she took what he offered, thanked him, and
said no more about it. She was no more hired as a
servant, but having at the first taken a long lease of the
cottage, she continued, from year to year, working on
the farm by the day, at a very scanty allowance. Old
Douglas in a few years grew incapable of any work,
through frailty of person, being constantly confined to
bed, though in mind as energetic and mysterious as ever.

Jane wrought long, till at length a severe illness in
1799 rendered her unfit to do any thing farther than
occasionally knit a stocking; and Tibby's handywork was
all that herself and the two old women had to depend
upon. They had brought her up with care and kindness
amid the most pinching poverty, and now, indeed, her
filial affection was severely put to the proof; but it was
genuine, and knew no bounds. Night and day she
toiled for her aged and feeble relatives, and a murmur or
complaint never was heard from her lips. Many a
blessing was bestowed on her as they raised their palsied
heads to partake of her hard-earned pittance; and many
a fervent prayer was poured out, when no mortal heard
it.

Times grew harder and harder. Thousands yet living remember what a period that was for the poor, while meal, for seasons, was from four to five shillings a-stone, and even sometimes as high as seven. Tibby grew fairly incapable of supporting herself and her aged friends. She stinted herself for their sakes, and that made her still more incapable; yet often with tears in her eyes did she feed these frail beings, her heart like to melt because she had no more to give them. There are no poor-rates in that country. Knoweback is quite retired —nobody went near it, and Tibby complained to none, but wrought on, night and day, in sorrow and anxiety, but still with a humble and thankful heart.

In this great strait, Mrs Forret was the first who began, unsolicited, to take compassion on the destitute group. She could not conceive how they existed on the poor creature's earnings. So she went privately to see them, and when she saw their wretched state, and heard their blessings on their dear child, her heart was moved to pity, and she determined to assist them in secret; for her husband was such a churl that she durst not venture to do it publicly. Accordingly, whenever she had an opportunity, she made Tibby come into the kitchen, and get a meal for herself; and often the considerate lady slid a small loaf, or a little tea and sugar, into her lap, for the two aged invalids;—for gentle woman is always the first to pity, and the first to relieve.

Poor Tibby! how her heart expanded with gratitude on receiving these little presents! for her love for the two old dependent creatures was of so pure and sacred a sort, as scarcely to retain in it any thing of the common feelings of humanity. There was no selfish principle there—they were to her as a part of her own nature.

Tibby never went into the kitchen unless her mistress desired her, or sent her word by some of the other day-labourers to come in as she went home. One evening, having got word in this last way, she went in, and the lady of the house, with her own hand, presented her with a little bowl of beat potatoes and some milk. This was all; and one would have thought it was an aliment so humble and plain that scarcely any person would have grudged it to a hungry dog. It so happened, however, that as Tibby was sitting behind backs enjoying the meal, Mr Forret chanced to come into the kitchen to give some orders; and perceiving Tibby so comfortably engaged, he, without speaking a word, seized her by the neck with one hand, and by the shoulder with the other, and hurrying her out at the back-door into the yard, flung her with all his might on a dunghill. "Wha the devil bade you come into my house and eat up the meat that was made for others?" cried he, in a demoniac voice, choking with rage; and then he swore a terrible oath, which I do not choose to set down, that "if he found her again at such employment, he would cut her throat and fling her to the dogs."

Poor Tibby was astounded beyond the power of utterance, or even of rising from the place where he had thrown her down, until lifted by two of the maid-servants, who tried to comfort her as they supported her part of the way home; and bitterly did they blame their master, saying it would have been a shame to any one who had the feelings of a man to do such an act; but as for their master he scarcely had the feelings of a beast. Tibby never opened her mouth, neither to blame nor complain, but went on her way crying till her heart was like to break.

She had no supper for the old famishing pair that night. They had tasted nothing from the time that she left them in the morning; and as she had accounted herself sure of receiving something from Mrs Forret that night, she had not asked her day's wages from the grieve, glad to let a day run up now and then, when able to procure a meal in any other honest way. She had nothing to give them that night, so what could she do? She was obliged, with a sore heart, to kiss them and tell them so; and then, as was her custom, she said a prayer over their couch, and laid herself down to sleep, drowned in tears.

She had never so much as mentioned Mr Forret's name, either to her grandmother or grand-aunt that night, or by the least insinuation given them to understand that he had used her ill; but no sooner were they composed to rest, and all the cottage quiet, than old Douglas began abusing him with great vehemence. Tibby, to her astonishment, heard some of his deeds spoken of with great familiarity, which she was sure never had been whispered to the ear of flesh. But what shocked her most of all, was the following terrible prognostication, which she heard repeated three several times:—" Na, na, I'll no see it, for I'll never see aught earthly again beyond the wa's o' this cottage; but Tibby will live to see it;—ay, ay, she'll see it." Then a different voice asked—" What will *she* see, kerlin?"—" She'll see the craws picking his banes at the back o' the dyke."

Tibby's heart grew cold within her when she heard this terrible announcement, because, for many years bygone, she had been convinced, from sensible demonstration, that old Douglas Hervey had commerce with some superior intelligence; and after she had heard the above sentence repeated again and again, she shut her ears, that she might hear no more; committed herself once more to the hands of a watchful Creator, and fell into a troubled sleep.

The elemental spirits that weave the shadowy tapestry of dreams, were busy at their aerial looms that night in the cottage of Knowe-back, bodying forth the destinies of men and women in brilliant and quick succession. One only of these delineations I shall here set down, precisely as it was related to me, by my friend the worthy clergyman of that parish, to whom Tibby told it the very next day. There is no doubt that her grand-aunt's disjointed prophecy formed the ground-work of the picture; but be that as it may, this was her dream; and it was for the sake of telling it, and tracing it to its fulfilment, that I begin this story:

Tibby Hyslop dreamed, that on a certain spot which she had never seen before, between a stone-dyke and the verge of a woody precipice, a little, sequestered, inaccessible corner, of a triangular shape,—or, as she called it to the minister, "a three-neukit crook o' the linn," she saw Mr Forret lying without his hat, with his throat slightly wounded, and blood running from it; but he neither appeared to be dead, nor yet dying, but in excellent spirits. He was clothed in a fine new black suit, had full boots on, which appeared likewise to be new, and gilt spurs. A great number of rooks and hooded crows were making free with his person;—some picking out his eyes, some his tongue, and some tearing out his bowels. In place of being distressed by their voracity, he appeared much delighted, encouraging them all that he could, and there was perfectly good understanding between the parties. In the midst of this horrible feast, a large raven dashed down from a dark cloud, and driving away all the meaner birds, fell a-feasting himself;—opened the breast of his victim, who was still alive, and encouraging him on; and after praying on his vitals for some time, at last picked out his heart, and devoured it; and then the mangled wretch, after writhing for a short time in convulsive agonies groaned his last.

This was precisely Tibby's dream as it was told to me, first by my friend Mr Cunningham of Dalswinton, and afterwards by the clergyman to whom she herself had related it next day. But there was something in it not so distinctly defined; for though the birds which she saw devouring her master, were rooks, blood-crows, and a raven, still each individual of the number had a likeness, by itself, distinguishing it from all the rest; a certain character, as it were, to support; and these particular likenesses were so engraven on the dreamer's mind, that she never forgot them, and she could not help looking for them both among "birds and bodies," as she expressed it, but never could distinguish any of them again; and the dream like many other distempered visions, was forgotten, or only remembered now and then with a certain tremor of antecedent knowledge.

Days and seasons passed over, and with them the

changes incident to humanity. The virtuous and indefatigable Tibby Hyslop was assisted by the benevolent,
who had heard of her exertions and patient sufferings;
and the venerable Douglas Hervey had gone in peace to
the house appointed for all living, when one evening in
June, John Jardine, the cooper, chanced to come to
Knowe-back, in the course of his girding and hooping
peregrinations. John was a living and walking chronicle
of the events of the day, all the way from the head of
Glen-Breck to the Bridge of Stony-Lee. He knew every
man, and every man's affairs—every woman, and every
woman's failings; and his intelligence was not like that
of many others, for it was generally to be depended on.
How he got his information so correctly, was a mystery
to many, but whatever John the cooper told as a fact,
was never disputed, and any woman, at least, might have
ventured to tell it over again.

"These are hard times for poor folks, Tibby. How
are you and auld granny coming on?"

"Just fechtin on as we hae done for mony a year.
She is aye contentit, poor body, and thankfu,' whether I
hae little to gie her, or muckle. This life's naething but
a fecht, Johnnie, frae beginning to end."

"It's a' true ye say, Tibby," said the cooper, interrupting her, for he was afraid she was about to enter
upon religious topics, a species of conversation that did
not accord with John's talents or dispositions; "It's a'
rtue ye say, Tibby; but your master will soon be sic a
rich man now, that we'll a' be made up, and you amang
the lave will be made a lady."

"If he get his riches honestly, and the blessing o' the
Almighty wi' them, John, I shall rejoice in his prosperity;
but neither me nor ony ither poor body will ever be
muckle the better o' them. What way is he gaun to get
siccan great riches? If a' be true that I hear, he is gaun
to the wrang part to seek them."

"Aha, lass, that's a' that ye ken about it. Did ye no
hear that he had won the law-plea on his laird, whilk has
been afore the Lords for mair than seven years? And

did ye no hear that he had won ten pleas afore the courts
o' Dumfries, a' rising out o' ane anither, like ash girder-
ings out o' ae root, and that he's to get, on the haill,
about twenty thousand punds worth o' damages?"

" That's an unco sight o' siller, John. How muckle
is that?"

" Aha, lass, ye hae fixed me now; but they say it
will come to as muckle gowd as six men can carry on
their backs. And we're a' to get twenties, and thirties,
and forties o' punds for bribes, to gar us gie faithfu' and
true evidence at the great concluding trial afore the
Lords; and you are to be bribit amang the rest, to gar ye
tell the haill truth, and nothing but the truth."

" There needs nae waste o' siller to gar me do that.
But, Johnnie, I wad like to ken whether that mode o'
taking oaths,—solemn and saucred oaths,—about the
miserable trash o' this warld, be according to the tenor o'
Gospel revelation, and the third o' the Commands?"

" Aha, lass, ye *hae* fixed me now! That's rather a
kittle point; but I believe it's a' true that ye say, However, ye'll get the offer of a great bribe in a a few days;
and take ye my advice, Tibby—Get haud o' the bribe
aforehand; for if ye lippen to your master's promises,
you will never finger a bodle after the job's done."

" I'm but a poor simple body, Johnnie, and canna manage
ony siccan things. But I shall need nae fee to gar me
tell the truth, and I winna tell an untruth for a' my master's estate, and his sax backfu's o' gowd into the bargain. If the sin o' the soul, Johnnie——"

" Ay, ay, that's very true, Tibby, very true, indeed,
about the sin o' the soul! But as ye were saying about
being a simple body—What wad ye think if I were to
cast up that day Gledging Gibby came here to gie you
your lesson—I could maybe help you on a wee bit—
What wad ye gie me if I did?"

" Alack, I hae naething to gie you but my blessing;
but I shall pray for the blessing o' God on ye."

" Ay, ay, as ye say. I daresay there might be waur
things. But could ye think o' naething else to gie a

body wha likes as weel to be paid aff-hand as to gie credit? That's the very thing I'm cautioning you against."

"I dinna expect ony siller frae that fountain-head, Johnnie: It is a dry ane to the puir and the needy, and an unco sma' matter wad gar me make over my rights to a pose that I hae neither faith nor hope in. But ye're kenn'd for an auld-farrant man; if ye can bring a little honestly my way, I sall gie you the half o't; for weel I ken it will never come by ony art or shift o' mine."

"Ay, ay, that's spoken like a sensible and reasonable woman, Tibby Hyslop, as ye are and hae always been. But think you that nae way could be contrived"—and here the cooper gave two winks with his left eye—"by the whilk ye could gie me it a', and yet no rob yoursell of a farthing?"

"Na, na, Johnnie Jardine, that's clean aboon my comprehension: But ye're a cunning draughty man, and I leave the haill matter to your guidance."

"Very weel, Tibby, very weel. I'll try to ca' a gayan substantial gird round your success, if I can hit the width o' the chance, and the girth o' the gear. Gude day to you the day; and think about the plan o' equal-aqual that I spake o'."

Old maids are in general very easily courted, and very apt to take a hint. I have, indeed, known a great many instances in which they took hints very seriously, before ever they were given. Not so with Tibby Hyslop. So heavy a charge had lain upon her the greater part of her life, that she had never turned her thoughts to any earthly thing beside, and she knew no more what the cooper aimed at, than if the words had not been spoken. When he went away, her grandmother called her to the bedside, and asked if the cooper had gone away. Tibby answered in the affirmative; on which granny said, " What has he been havering about sae lang the day? I thought I heard him courting ye."

"Courting me! Dear granny, he was courting nane o' me; he was telling me how Mr Forret had won as muckle siller at the law as sax men can carry on their backs, and how we are a' to get a part of it."

"Dinna believe him, hinny; the man that can win siller at the law, will lose it naewhere. But, Tibby, I heard the cooper courting you, and I thought I heard you gie him your consent to manage the matter as he likit. Now you hae been a great blessing to me. I thought you sent to me in wrath, as a punishment of my sins, but I have found that you were indeed sent to me in love and in kindness. You have been the sole support of my old age, and of hers wha is now in the grave, and it is natural that I should like to see you put up afore I leave you. But, Tibby Hyslop, John Jardine is not the man to lead a Christian life with. He has nae mair religion than the beasts that perish—he shuns it as a body would do a loathsome or poisonous draught: And besides, it is weel kenn'd how sair he neglected his first wife. Hae naething to do wi' him, my dear bairn, but rather live as you are. There is neither sin nor shame in being unwedded; but there may be baith in joining yourself to an unbeliever."

Tibby was somewhat astonished at this piece of information. She had not conceived that the cooper meant any thing in the way of courtship; but found that she rather thought the better of him for what it appeared he had done. Accordingly she made no promises to her grandmother, but only remarked, that "it was a pity no to gie the cooper a chance o' conversion, honest man."

The cooper kept watch about Drumlochie and the hinds' houses, and easily found out all the farmer's movements, and even the exact remuneration he could be prevailed on to give to such as were pleased to remember according to his wishes. Indeed it was believed that the most part of the hinds and labouring people recollected nothing of the matter in dispute farther than he was pleased to inform them, and that in fact they gave evidence to the best of their knowledge or remembrance, although that evidence might be decidedly wrong.

One day Gibby took his gun, and went out towards Knowe-back. The cooper also, guessing what his purpose was, went thither by a circuitous route, in order to come in as it were by chance. Ere he arrived, Mr Forret had begun his queries and instructions to Tibby. —The two could not agree by any means; Tibby either could not recollect the yearly crops on each field on the farm of Drumlochie, or recollected wrong. At length, when the calculations were at the keenest, the cooper came in, and at every turn he took Mr Forret's side, with the most strenuous asseverations, abusing Tibby for her stupidity and want of recollection.

"Hear me speak, Johnnie Jardine, afore ye condemn me aff-loof: Mr Forret says that the Crooked Holm was pease in the 96, and corn in the 97: I say it was corn baith the years. How do ye say about that?"

"Mr Forret's right—perfectly right. It grew pease in the 96, and aits, good Angus aits, in the 97. Poor gowk! dinna ye think that he has a' thae things merkit down in black and white? and what good could it do to him to mislead you? Depend on't, he is right there."

"Could ye tak your oath on that, Johnnie Jardine?"

"Ay, this meenint,—sax times repeated, if it were necessary."

"Then I yield—I am but a poor silly woman, liable to mony errors and ortcomings—I maun be wrang, and I yield that it is sae. But I am sure, John, you cannot but remember this sae short while syne,—for ye shure wi' us that har'st,—Was the lang field niest Robie Johnston's farm growing corn in the dear year, or no? I say it was."

"It was the next year, Tibby," said Mr Forret; "you are confounding one year with another again; and I see what is the reason. It was oats in 99, grass in 1800, and oats again in 1801; now you never remember any of the intermediate years, but only those that you shore on these fields. I cannot be mistaken in a rule I never break."

The cooper had now got his cue.   He perceived that the plea ultimately depended on proof relating to the proper cropping of the land throughout the lease : and he supported the farmer so strenuously, that Tibby, in her simplicity, fairly yielded, although not convinced ; but the cooper assured the farmer that he would put all to rights, provided she received a handsome acknowledgment ; for there was not the least doubt that Mr Forret was right in every particular.

This speech of the cooper's gratified the farmer exceedingly, as his whole fortune now depended upon the evidence to be elicited in the court at Dumfries, on a day that was fast approaching, and he was willing to give any thing to secure the evidence on his side ; so he made a long set speech to Tibby, telling her how necessary it was that she should adhere strictly to the truth—that, as it would be an awful thing to make oath to that which was false, he had merely paid her that visit to instruct her remembrance a little in that which was the truth, it being impossible, on account of his jottings, that he could be mistaken ; and finally it was settled, that for thus telling the truth, and nothing but the truth, Tibby Hyslop, a most deserving woman, was to receive a present of £15, as wages for time bygone.   This was all managed in a very sly manner by the cooper, who assured Forret that all should go right, as far as related to Tibby Hyslop and himself.

The day of the trial arrived, and counsel attended from Edinburgh for both parties, to take full evidence before the two Circuit Lords and Sheriff.   The evidence was said to have been unsatisfactory to the Judges, but upon the whole in Mr Forret's favour.   The cooper's was decidedly so, and the farmer's counsel were crowing and bustling immoderately, when at length Tibby Hyslop was called to the witnesses' box.   At the first sight of her master's counsel, and the Dumfries writers and notaries that were hanging about him, Tibby was struck dumb with amazement, and almost bereaved of sense.   She at once recognized them all and severally, as the birds that she saw, in her dream, devouring her master, and picking the flesh from his bones; while the great lawyer from Edinburgh was, in feature, eye, and beak, the identical raven which at last devoured his vitals and heart.

This singular coincidence brought reminiscences of such a nature over her spirit, that, on the first questions being put, she could not answer a word. She knew from thenceforward that her master was a ruined man, and her heart failed, on thinking of her kind mistress and his family. The counsel then went, and whispering Mr Forret, inquired what sort of a woman she was, and if her evidence was likely to be of any avail. As the cooper had behaved in a very satisfactory way, and had answered for Tibby, the farmer was intent on not losing her evidence, and answered his counsel that her was a worthy honest woman, who would not swear to a lie for the king's dominions, and that her evidence was of much consequence. This intelligence the lawyer announced to the bench with great pomposity, and the witness was allowed a little time to recover her spirits.

Isabella Hyslop, spinster, was again called, answered to her name, and took the oath distinctly, and without hesitation, until the official querist came to the usual question, " Now, has any one instructed you what to say, or what you are to answer ?" when Tibby replied with a steady countenance, " Nobody, except my master." The counsel and client stared at one another, while the Court could hardly maintain their gravity of deportment. The querist went on——

" What ? Do you say your master instructed you what to say ?"

" Yes."

" And did he give, or promise to give you, any reward for what you were to say ?"

" Yes."

" How much did he give, or promise you, for answering as he directed you ?"

" He gave me fifteen pound-notes."

Here Mr Forret and his counsel, losing all patience at

seeing the case take this unexpected turn, interrupted the proceedings, the latter addressing the Judges, with vehemence, to the following purport :—

" My Lords, in my client's name, and in the names of justice and reason, I protest against proceeding with this woman's evidence, it being manifest that she is talking through a total derangement of intellect. At first she is dumb, and cannot answer nor speak a word, and now she is answering in total disregard of all truth and propriety. I appeal to your Lordships if such a farrago as this can be at all inferential or relevant ?"

" Sir, it was but the other minute," said the junior Judge, " that you announced to us with great importance, that this woman was a person noted for honesty and worth, and one who would not tell a lie for the king's dominions. Why not then hear her evidence to the end ? For my own part, I perceive no tokens of discrepancy in it, but rather a scrupulous conscientiousness. Of that, however, we shall be better able to judge when we have heard her out. I conceive that, for the sake of both parties, this woman ought to be strictly examined."

" Proceed with the evidence, Mr Wood," said the senior Lord, bowing to his assistant.

Tibby was reminded that she was on her great oath, and examined over again; but she adhered strictly to her former answers.

" Can you repeat any thing to the Court that he desired you to say ?"

" Yes ; he desired me, over and over again, to tell the whole truth, and nothing but the truth."

" And, in order that you should do this, he paid you down fifteen pounds sterling ?"

" Yes."

" This is a very singular transaction : I cannot perceive the meaning of it. You certainly must be sensible that you made an advantageous bargain ?"

" Yes."

" But you depone that he charged you to tell only the truth ?"

" **Yes**, he did, and before witnesses, too."

Here Mr Forret's counsel began to crow amain, as if the victory had been his own; but the junior Judge again took him short by saying, " Have patience, sir.—My good woman, I esteem your principles and plain simplicity very highly. We want only to ascertain the truth, and you say your master charged you to tell that only. Tell me this, then—did he not inform you what the truth was ?"

" Yes. It was for that purpose he came over to see me, to help my memory to what was the truth, for fear I should hae sworn wrang; which wad hae been a great sin, ye ken."

" Yes, it would so. I thought that would be the way. —You may now proceed with your questions regularly, Mr Wood."

" Are you quite conscious, now, that those things he brought to your remembrance were actually the truth ?"

" No."

" Are you conscious they were *not* the truth ?"

" Yes ; at least some of them, I am sure, were not."

" Please to condescend on one instance."

" He says he has it markit in his buik, that the Crookit Houm, that lies at the back o' the wood, ye ken, grew pease in the ninety-sax, and corn in the ninety-se'en ; now, it is unco queer that he should hae settin't down wrang, for the Houm was really and truly aits baith the years."

" It is a long time since ; perhaps your memory may be at fault."

" If my master had not chanced to mention it, I could not have been sure, but he set me a-calculating and comparing ; and my mother and me have been consulting about it, and have fairly settled it."

" And are you absolutely positive it was oats both years ?"

" Yes."

" Can you mention any circumstance on which you rest your conclusions ?"

" Yes ; there came a great wind ae Sabbath day, in
the ninety-sax, and that raised the shearers' wages, at
Dumfries, to three shillings the day.   We began to the
Crookit Houm on a Monanday's morning, at three shillings a-day, and that very day twalmonth, we began till't
again at tenpence.   We had a gude deal o' speaking
about it, and I said to John Edie, ' What need we grum-
ble? I made sae muckle at shearing, the last year, that
it's no a' done yet.'   And he said, ' Ah, Tibby, Tibby,
but wha can hain like you ;' "

" Were there any others that you think your master
had marked down wrong?"

" There was ane, at ony rate—the lang field neist
Robie Johnston's march : He says it was clover in the
drouthy dear year, and aits the neist ; but that's a year
I canna forget ; it was aits baith years.   I lost a week's
shearing on it the first year, waiting on my aunty, and
the neist year she was dead ; and I shore the lang field
neist Robie Johnston's wi' her sickle-heuk, and black rib-
bons on my mutch."

The whole of Tibby's evidence went against Mr Forret's interest most conclusively, and the Judges at last
dismissed her, with high compliments on her truth and
integrity.   The cause was again remitted to the Court
of Session for revisal after this evidence taken ; and the
word spread over all the country that Mr Forret had won.
Tibby never contradicted this, nor disputed it ; but she
was thoroughly convinced, that in place of winning, he
would be a ruined man.

About a month after the examination at Dumfries he
received a letter from his agents in Edinburgh, buoying
him up with hopes of great and instant success, and urging the utility of his presence in town at the final decision of the cause on which all the minor ones rested.
Accordingly he equipped himself, and rode into Dumfries
in the evening, to be ready to proceed by the mail the
following morning, saying to his wife, as he went away,
that he would send home his mare with the carrier, and
that as he could not possibly name the day on which he

would be home, she was to give herself no uneasiness.
The mare was returned the following night, and put up
in her own stall, nobody knew by whom; but servants
are such sleepy, careless fellows, that few regarded the
circumstance.    This was on a Tuesday night.    A whole
week passed over, and still Mrs Forret received no news
of her husband, which kept her very uneasy, as their
whole fortune, being, and subsistence, now depended on
the issue of this great lawsuit, and she suspected that
the case still continued dubious, or was found to be going
against him.

A more unhappy result followed than that she anticipated.    On the arrival of the Edinburgh papers next
week, the whole case, so important to farmers, was de-
tailed; and it was there stated, that the great farmer and
improver, Mr Forret of Drumlochie, had not only for-
feited his whole fortune by improper husbandry, and
manifest breaches of the conditions on which he held his
lease, but that criminal letters had been issued against
him for attempts to pervert justice, and rewards offered
for his detention or seizure.    This was terrible news for
the family at Drumlochie; but there were still sanguine
hopes entertained that the circumstances were mis-stated,
or, if the worst should prove true, that perhaps the husband and father might make his escape; and as there
was no word from him day after day, this latter sentiment began to be cherished by the whole family as their
only remaining and forlorn hope.

But one day, as poor Tibby Hyslop was going over to
the Cat Linn, to gather a burden of sticks for firewood,
she was surprised, on looking over the dike, to see a great
body of crows collected, all of which were so intent on
their prey, that they seemed scarcely to regard her
presence as a sufficient cause for their desisting; she
waved her burden-rope at them over the dike, but they
refused to move.    Her heart nearly failed her, for she
remembered of having before seen the same scene, with
some fearful concomitants.    But pure and unfeigned religion, the first principle of which teaches a firm reliance on

divine protection, can give courage to the weakest of human beings.    Tibby climbed over the dike, drove the vermin away, and there lay the corpse of her late unfortunate master, wofully mangled by these voracious birds of prey.    He had bled himself to death in the jugular vein, was lying without the hat, and clothed in a fine new black suit of clothes, top-boots, which appeared likewise to be new, and gilt spurs; and the place where he lay was a little three-cornered sequestered spot, between the dike and the precipice, and inaccessible by any other way than through the field.    It was a spot that Tibby had never seen before.

A letter was found in Mr Forret's pocket, which had blasted all his hopes, and driven him to utter distraction; he had received it at Dumfries, returned home, and put up his mare carefully in the stable, but not having courage to face his ruined family, he had hurried to that sequestered spot, and perpetrated the deed of self-destruction.

The only thing more I have to add is, that the Lord President, having made the remark that he paid more regard to that poor woman, Isabella Hyslop's evidence, than to all the rest elicited at Dumfries, the gainers of the great plea became sensible that it was principally in consequence of her candour and invincible veracity that they were successful, and sent her a present of twenty pounds.    She was living comfortably at Knoweback when I saw her, a contented and happy old maiden.

---

# CHAP. X.

### MARY BURNET.

THE following incidents are related as having occurred at a shepherd's house, not a hundred miles from St Mary's Loch; but, as the descendants of one of the families still reside in the vicinity, I deem it requisite to use names which cannot be recognised, save by those who have heard the story.

John Allanson, the farmer's son of Inverlawn, was a handsome, roving, and incautious young man, enthusiastic, amorous, and fond of adventure, and one who could hardly be said to fear the face of either man, woman, or spirit. Among other love adventures, he fell a-courting Mary Burnet, of Kirkstyle, a most beautiful and innocent maiden, and one who had been bred up in rural simplicity. She loved him, but yet she was afraid of him; and though she had no objection to meeting with him among others, yet she carefully avoided meeting him lone, though often and earnestly urged to it. One day, the young man, finding an opportunity, at Our Lady's Chapel, after mass, urged his suit for a private meeting so ardently, and with so many vows of love and sacred esteem, that Mary was so far won as to promise, that *perhaps* she would come and meet him.

The trysting place was a little green sequestered spot, on the very verge of the lake, well known to many an angler, and to none better than the writer of this old tale; and the hour appointed, the time when the King's Elwand (now foolishly termed the Belt of Orion) set his first golden knob above the hill. Allanson came too early; and he watched the sky with such eagerness and devotion, that he thought every little star that arose in the south-east the top knob of the King's Elwand. At last the Elwand did arise in good earnest, and then the youth, with a heart palpitating with agitation, had nothing for it but to watch the heathery brow by which bonny Mary Burnet was to descend. No Mary Burnet made her appearance, even although the King's Elwand had now measured its own equivocal length five or six times up the lift.

Young Allanson now felt all the most poignant miseries of disappointment; and, as the story goes, uttered in his heart an unhallowed wish——he wished that some witch or fairy would influence his Mary to come to him in spite of her maidenly scruples. This wish was thrice repeated with all the energy of disappointed love. It was thrice repeated, and no more, when, behold, Mary appeared on the brae, with wild and eccentric motions, speeding to the appointed place. Allanson's excitement seems to have been more than he was able to bear, as he instantly became delirious with joy, and always professed that he could remember nothing of their first meeting, save that Mary remained silent, and spoke not a word, either good or bad. In a short time she fell a-sobbing and weeping, refusing to be comforted, and then, uttering a piercing shriek, sprung up, and ran from him with amazing speed.

At this part of the loch, which, as I said, is well known to many, the shore is overhung by a precipitous cliff, of no great height, but still inaccessible, either from above or below. Save in a great drought, the water comes to within a yard of the bottom of this cliff, and the intermediate space is filled with rough unshapely pieces of rock fallen from above. Along this narrow and rude space, hardly passable by the angler at noon, did Mary bound with the swiftness of a kid, although surrounded with darkness. Her lover, pursuing with all his energy, called out, "Mary! Mary! my dear Mary, stop and speak with me. I'll conduct you home, or anywhere you please, but do not run from me. Stop, my dearest Mary—stop!"

Mary would not stop; but ran on, till, coming to a little cliff that jutted into the lake, round which there was no passage, and, perceiving that her lover would there overtake her, she uttered another shriek, and plunged into the lake. The loud sound of her fall into the still water rung in the young man's ears like the knell of death; and if before he was crazed with love, he was now as much so with despair. He saw her floating lightly away from the shore towards the deepest part of the loch; but, in a short time, she began to sink, and gradually disappeared, without uttering a throb or a cry. A good while previous to this, Allanson had flung off his bonnet, shoes, and coat, and plunged in. He swam to the place where Mary disappeared; but there was neither boil nor gurgle on the water, nor even a bell of departing breath, to mark the place where his beloved had sunk. Being strangely impressed, at that trying moment, with a determination to live or die with her, he tried to dive, in hopes either to bring her up or to die in her arms ; and he thought of their being so found on the shore of the lake, with a melancholy satisfaction ; but by no effort of his could he reach the bottom, nor knew he what distance he was still from it. With an exhausted frame, and a despairing heart, he was obliged again to seek the shore, and, dripping wet as he was, and half naked, he ran to her father's house with the woful tidings. Every thing there was quiet. The old shepherd's family, of whom Mary was the youngest, and sole daughter, were all sunk in silent repose ; and oh how the distracted lover wept at the thoughts of wakening them to hear the doleful tidings ! But waken them he must ; so, going to the little window close by the goodman's bed, he called, in a melancholy tone, " Andrew ! Andrew Burnet, are you waking ?"

" Troth, man, I think I be : or, at least, I'm half-and half. What hast thou to say to auld Andrew Burnet at this time o' night ?"

" Are you waking, I say ?"

" Gudewife, am I waking ? Because if I be, tell that stravaiger sae. He'll maybe tak your word for it, for mine he winna tak."

" O Andrew, none of your humour to-night ;—I bring you tidings the most woful, the most dismal, the most heart-rending, that ever were brought to an honest man's door."

" To his window, you mean," cried Andrew, bolting out of bed, and proceeding to the door. " Gude sauff us, man, come in, whaever you be, and tell us your tidings face to face ; and then we'll can better judge of the truth of them. If they be in concord wi' your voice, they are melancholy indeed. Have the reavers come, and are our kye driven ?"

" Oh, alas ! waur than that—a thousand times waur

than that! Your daughter—your dear beloved and only daughter, Mary—"

"What of Mary?" cried the goodman. "What of Mary?" cried her mother, shuddering and groaning with terror; and at the same time she kindled a light.

The sight of their neighbour, half-naked, and dripping with wet, and madness and despair in his looks, sent a chillness to their hearts, that held them in silence, and they were unable to utter a word, till he went on thus— "Mary is gone; your darling and mine is lost, and sleeps this night in a watery grave,—and I have been her destroyer!"

"Thou art mad, John Allanson," said the old man, vehemently, "raving mad; at least I hope so. Wicked as thou art, thou hadst not the heart to kill my dear child. O yes, you are mad—God be thanked, you are mad. I see it in your looks and demeanour. Heaven be praised, you are mad! You *are* mad; but you'll get better again. But what do I say?" continued he, as recollecting himself,—"We can soon convince our own senses. Wife, lead the way to our daughter's bed."

With a heart throbbing with terror and dismay, old Jean Linton led the way to Mary's chamber, followed by the two men, who were eagerly gazing, one over each of her shoulders. Mary's little apartment was in the farther end of the long narrow cottage; and as soon as they entered it, they perceived a form lying on the bed, with the bedclothes drawn over its head; and on the lid of Mary's little chest, that stood at the bedside, her clothes were lying neatly folded, as they wont to be. Hope seemed to dawn on the faces of the two old people when they beheld this, but the lover's heart sunk still deeper in despair. The father called her name, but the form on the bed returned no answer; however, they all heard distinctly sobs, as of one weeping. The old man then ventured to pull down the clothes from her face; and, strange to say, there indeed lay Mary Burnet, drowned in tears, yet apparently nowise surprised at the ghastly appearance of the three naked figures. Allanson gasped

for breath, for he remained still incredulous. He touched
her clothes—he lifted her robes one by one,—and all of
them were dry, neat, and clean, and had no appearance
of having sunk in the lake.

There can be no doubt that Allanson was confounded
by the strange event that had befallen him, and felt like
one struggling with a frightful vision, or some energy
beyond the power of man to comprehend. Nevertheless
the assurance that Mary was there in life, weeping although she was, put him once more beside himself with
joy; and he kneeled at her bedside, beseeching permission but to kiss her hand. She, however, repulsed him
with disdain, saying with great emphasis—" You are a
bad man, John Allanson, and I entreat you to go out of
my sight. The sufferings that I have undergone this
night have been beyond the power of flesh and blood to
endure; and by some cursed agency of yours have these
sufferings been brought about. I therefore pray you, in
His name, whose law you have transgressed, to depart
out of my sight."

Wholly overcome by conflicting passions, by circumstances so contrary to one another, and so discordant with
every thing either in the works of Nature or Providence,
the young man could do nothing but stand like a rigid
statue, with his hands lifted up, and his visage like that
of a corpse, until led away by the two old people from
their daughter's apartment. They then lighted up a fire
to dry him, and began to question him with the most
intense curiosity; but they could elicit nothing from
him, but the most disjointed exclamations—such as,
" Lord in Heaven, what can be the meaning of this!"
And at other times—" It is all the enchantment of the
devil; the evil spirits have got dominion over me!"

Finding they could make nothing of him, they began
to form conjectures of their own. Jean affirmed that it
had been the Mermaid of the loch that had come to him
in Mary's shape, to allure him to his destruction; but
Andrew Burnet, setting his bonnet to one side, and
raising his left hand to a level with it, so that he might

c 2

have full scope to motion and flourish, suiting his action to his words, thus began, with a face of sapience never to be excelled :—

"Gudewife, it doth strike me that thou art very wide of the mark. It must have been a spirit of a great deal higher quality than a meer-maiden, who played this this extra-ōrdinary prank. The meer-maiden is not a spirit, but a beastly sensitive creature, with a malicious spirit within it. Now, what influence could a cauld clatch of a creature like that, wi' a tail like a great saumont-fish, hae ower our bairn, either to make her happy or unhappy? Or where could it borrow her claes, Jean? Tell me that. Na, na, Jean Linton, depend on it, the spirit that courtit wi' poor sinfu' Jock there, has been a fairy; but whether a good ane or an ill ane, it is hard to determine."

Andrew's disquisition was interrupted by the young man falling into a fit of trembling that was fearful to look at, and threatened soon to terminate his existence. Jean ran for the family cordial, observing by the way, that "though he was a wicked person, he was still a fellow-creature, and might live to repent;" and influenced by this spark of genuine humanity, she made him swallow two horn-spoonfuls of strong aquavitæ. Andrew then put a piece of scarlet thread round each wrist, and taking a strong rowan-tree staff in his hand, he conveyed his trembling and astonished guest home, giving him at parting this sage advice :—

"I'll tell you what it is, Jock Allanson,—ye hae run a near risk o' perdition, and, escaping that for the present. o' losing your right reason. But tak an auld man's advice——never gang again out by night to beguile ony honest man's daughter, lest a worse thing befall thee."

Next morning Mary dressed herself more neatly than usual, but there was manifestly a deep melancholy settled on her lovely face, and at times the unbidden tear would start into her eye. She spoke no word, either good or bad, that ever her mother could recollect, that whole morning; but she once or twice observed her

daughter gazing at her, as with an intense and melancholy
interest. About nine o'clock in the morning, she took
a hay-raik over her shoulder, and went down to a meadow at the east end of the loch, to coil a part of her
father's hay, her father and brother engaging to join her
about noon, when they came from the sheepfold. As
soon as old Andrew came home, his wife and he, as was
natural, instantly began to converse on the events of the
preceding night; and in the course of their conversation
Andrew said, "Gudeness be about us, Jean, was not
yon an awfu' speech o' our bairn's to young Jock Allanson last night?"

"Ay, it was a downsetter, gudeman, and spoken like
a good Christian lass."

"I'm no sae sure o' that, Jean Linton. My good woman, Jean Linton, I'm no sae sure o' that. Yon speech
has gi'en me a great deal o' trouble o' heart; for d'ye ken,
an take my life,—ay, an take your life, Jean,—nane o'
us can tell whether it was in the Almighty's name or the
devil's that she discharged her lover."

"O fy, Andrew, how can ye say sae? How can ye
doubt that it was in the Almighty's name?"

"Couldna she have said sae then, and that wad hae
put it beyond a' doubt? And that wad hae been the
natural way too; but instead of that she says, 'I pray
you, in the name of him whose law you have transgressed, to depart out o' my sight.' I confess I'm terrified when I think about yon speech, Jean Linton.
Didna she say too that 'her sufferings had been beyond
what flesh and blood could have endured?' What was
she but flesh and blood? Didna that remark infer that
she was something mair than a mortal creature? Jean
Linton, Jean Linton! what will you say if it should turn
out that our daughter is drowned, and that yon was the
fairy we had in the house a' the night and this morning?"

"O haud your tongue, Andrew Burnet, and dinna
make my heart cauld within me. We hae aye trusted
in the Lord yet, and he has never forsaken us, nor will
he yet gie the Wicked One power ower us or ours.'

" Ye say very weel, Jean, and we maun e'en hope for the best," quoth old Andrew ; and away he went, accompanied by his son Alexander, to assist their beloved Mary on the meadow.

No sooner had Andrew set his head over the bents, and come in view of the meadow, than he said to his son, " I wish Jock Allanson maunna hae been east-the-loch fishing for geds the day, for I think my Mary has made very little progress in the meadow."

" She's ower muckle ta'en up about other things this while to mind her wark," said Alexander : " I wadna wonder, father, if that lassie gangs a black gate yet."

Andrew uttered a long and a deep sigh, that seemed to ruffle the very fountains of life, and, without speaking another word, walked on to the hay field.   It was three hours since Mary had left home, and she ought at least to have put up a dozen coils of hay each hour.   But, in place of that, she had put up only seven altogether, and the last was unfinished.   Her own hay-raik, that had an M and a B neatly cut on the head of it, was leaning on the unfinished coil, and Mary was wanting.   Her brother, thinking she had hid herself from them in sport, ran from one coil to another, calling her many bad names, playfully ; but after he had turned them all up, and several deep swathes besides, she was not to be found. This young man, who slept in the byre, knew nothing of the events of the foregoing night, the old people and Allanson having mutually engaged to keep them a profound secret, and he had therefore less reason than his father to be seriously alarmed.   When they began to work at the hay Andrew could work none ; he looked this way and that way, but in no way could he see Mary approaching ; so he put on his coat and went away home, to pour his sorrows into the bosom of his wife ; and, in the mean time, he desired his son to run to all the neighbouring farming-houses and cots, every one, and make inquiries if any body had seen Mary.

When Andrew went home and informed his wife that their darling was missing, the grief and astonishment of the aged couple knew no bounds. They sat down and wept together, and declared over and over that this act of Providence was too strong for them, and too high to be understood. Jean besought her husband to kneel instantly, and pray urgently to God to restore their child to them; but he declined it, on account of the wrong frame of his mind, for he declared, that his rage against John Allanson was so extreme as to unfit him for approaching the throne of his Maker. "But if the profligate refuses to listen to the entreaties of an injured parent," added he, "he shall feel the weight of an injured father's arm."

Andrew went straight away to Inverlawn, though without the least hope of finding young Allanson at home; but, on reaching the place, to his amazement, he found the young man lying ill of a burning fever, raving incessantly of witches, spirits, and Mary Burnet. To such a height had his frenzy arrived, that when Andrew went there, it required three men to hold him in the bed. Both his parents testified their opinions openly, that their son was bewitched, or possessed of a demon, and the whole family was thrown into the greatest consternation. The good old shepherd, finding enough of grief there already, was obliged to confine his to his own bosom, and return disconsolate to his little family circle, in which there was a woful blank that night.

His son returned also from a fruitless search. No one had seen any traces of his sister but an old crazy woman, at a place called Oxcleuch, said that she had seen her go by in a grand chariot with young Jock Allanson, toward the Birkhill Path, and by that time they were at the Cross of Dumgree. The young man said he asked her what sort of a chariot it was, as there was never such a thing in that country as a chariot, nor yet a road for one. But she replied that he was widely mistaken, for that a great number of chariots sometimes passed that way, though never any of them returned. These words appearing to be merely the ravings of superannuation, they were not regarded; but when no other traces of Mary could be found, old Andrew went up to consult this crazy dame once more, but he was not able to bring any such thing to her recollection. She spoke only in parables, which to him were incomprehensible.

Bonny Mary Burnet was lost. She left her father's house at nine o'clock on a Wednesday morning, the 17th of September, neatly dressed in a white jerkin and green bonnet, with her hay-raik over her shoulder; and that was the last sight she was doomed ever to see of her native cottage. She seemed to have had some presentiment of this, as appeared from her demeanour that morning before she left it. Mary Burnet of Kirkstyle was lost, and great was the sensation produced over the whole country by the mysterious event. There was a long ballad extant at one period on the melancholy catastrophe, which was supposed to have been composed by the chaplain of St Mary's; but I have only heard tell of it, without ever hearing it sung or recited. Many of the verses concluded thus :—

> " But Bonny Mary Burnet
> We will never see again."

The story soon got abroad, with all its horrid circumstances, (and there is little doubt that it was grievously exaggerated,) and there was no obloquy that was not thrown on the survivor, who certainly in some degree deserved it, for, instead of growing better, he grew ten times more wicked than he was before. In one thing the whole country agreed, that it had been the real Mary Burnet who was drowned in the loch, and that the being which was found in her bed, lying weeping and complaining of suffering, and which vanished the next day, had been a fairy, an evil spirit, or a changeling of some sort, for that it never spoke save once, and that in a mysterious manner; nor did it partake of any food with the rest of the family. Her father and mother knew not what to say or what to think, but they wandered through this weary world like people wandering in a dream. Every thing that belonged to Mary Burnet was kept by her parents as the most sacred relics, and many a tear did her aged mother shed over them. Every article of her dress brought the once comely wearer to mind. Andrew often said, "That to have lost the darling child of their old age in any way would have been a great trial, but to lose her in the way that they had done, was really mair than human frailty could endure."

Many a weary day did he walk by the shores of the loch, looking eagerly for some vestige of her garments, and though he trembled at every appearance, yet did he continue to search on. He had a number of small bones collected, that had belonged to lambs and other minor animals, and, haply, some of them to fishes, from a fond supposition that they might once have formed joints of her toes or fingers. These he kept concealed in a little bag, in order, as he said, " to let the doctors see them." But no relic, besides these, could he ever discover of Mary's body.

Young Allanson recovered from his raging fever scarcely in the manner of other men, for he recovered all at once, after a few days' raving and madness. Mary Burnet, it appeared, was by him no more remembered. He grew ten times more wicked than before, and hesitated at no means of accomplishing his unhallowed purposes. The devout shepherds and cottagers around detested him ; and, both in their families and in the wild, when there was no ear to hear but that of Heaven, they prayed protection from his devices, as if he had been the Wicked One ; and they all prophesied that he would make a bad end.

One fine day about the middle of October, when the days begin to get very short, and the nights long and dark, on a Friday morning, the next year but one after Mary Burnet was lost, a memorable day in the fairy annals, John Allanson, younger of Inverlawn, went to a great hiring fair at a village called Moffat in Annandale, in order to hire a housemaid. His character was so notorious, that not one young woman in the district would serve in his father's house ; so away he went to the fair at Moffat, to hire the prettiest and loveliest girl he could there find, with the intention of ruining her as soon as she came home. This is no supposititious accusation, for he acknowledged his plan to Mr David Welch of Cariferan, who rode down to the market with him, and seemed to boast of it, and dwell on it with delight. But the maidens of Annandale had a guardian angel in the fair that day, of which neither he nor they were aware.

Allanson looked through the hiring market, and through the hiring market, and at length fixed on one young woman, which indeed was not difficult to do, for there was no such form there for elegance and beauty. Mr Welch stood still and eyed him. He took the beauty aside. She was clothed in green, and as lovely as a new-blown rose.

"Are you to hire, pretty maiden?"

"Yes, sir."

"Will you hire with me?"

"I care not though I do. But if I hire with you, it must be for the long term."

"Certainly. The longer the better. What are your wages to be?"

"You know, if I hire, I must be paid in kind. I must have the first living creature that I see about Inverlawn to myself."

"I wish it may be me, then. But what do you know about Inverlawn?"

"I think I *should* know about it."

'Bless me! I know the face as well as I know my own, and better. But the name has somehow escaped me. Pray, may I ask your name?"

Hush! hush!" said she solemnly, and holding up her hand at the same time; "Hush, hush, you had better say nothing about that here."

"I am in utter amazement!" he exclaimed. "What is the meaning of this? I conjure you to tell me your name?"

"It is Mary Burnet," said she, in a soft whisper;

and at the same time she let down a green veil over her face.

If Allanson's death-warrant had been announced to him at that moment, it could not have deprived him so completely of sense and motion. His visage changed into that of a corpse, his jaws fell down, and his eyes became glazed, so as apparently to throw no reflections inwardly. Mr Welch, who had kept his eye steadily on them all the while, perceived his comrade's dilemma, and went up to him. "Allanson?—Mr Allanson? What is the matter with you, man?" said he. "Why, the girl has bewitched you, and turned you into a statue!"

Allanson made some sound in his throat, as if attempting to speak, but his tongue refused its office, and he only jabbered. Mr Welch, conceiving that he was seized with some fit, or about to faint, supported him into the Johnston Arms; but he either could not, or would not, grant him any explanation. Welch being, however, resolved to see the maiden in green once more, persuaded Allanson, after causing him to drink a good deal, to go out into the hiring-market again, in search of her. They ranged the market through and through, but the maiden in green was gone, and not to be found. She had vanished in the crowd the moment she divulged her name, and even though Welch had his eye fixed on her, he could not discover which way she went. Allanson appeared to be in a kind of stupor as well as terror, but when he found that she had left the market, he began to recover himself, and to look out again for the top of the market.

He soon found one more beautiful than the last. She was like a sylph, clothed in robes of pure snowy white, with green ribands. Again he pointed this new flower out to Mr David Welch, who declared that such a perfect model of beauty he had never in his life seen. Allanson, being resolved to have this one at any wages, took her aside, and put the usual question; "Do you wish to hire, pretty maiden?"

"Yes, sir."

" Will you hire with me ?"

" I care not though I do."

" What, then, are your wages to be ? Come—say ? And be reasonable ; I am determined not to part with you for a trifle."

" My wages must be in kind ; I work on no other conditions.——Pray, how are all the good people about Inverlawn ?"

Allanson's breath began to cut, and a chillness to creep through his whole frame, and he answered, with a faltering tongue,—" I thank you,—much in their ordinary way."

" And your aged neighbours," rejoined she, " are they still alive and well ?"

" I—I—I think they are," said he, panting for breath. ' But I am at a loss to know whom I am indebted to for these kind recollections."

" What," said she, " have you so soon forgot Mary Burnet of Kirkstyle ?"

Allanson started as if a bullet had gone through his heart. The lovely sylph-like form glided into the crowd, and left the astounded libertine once more standing like a rigid statue, until aroused by his friend, Mr Welch. He tried a third fair one, and got the same answers, and the same name given. Indeed, the first time ever I heard the tale, it bore that he tried *seven,* who all turned out to be Mary Burnets of Kirkstyle ; but I think it unlikely that he would try so many, as he must long ere that time have been sensible that he laboured under some power of enchantment. However, when nothing else would do, he helped himself to a good proportion of strong drink. While he was thus engaged, a phenomenon of beauty and grandeur came into the fair, that caught the sole attention of all present. This was a lovely dame, riding in a gilded chariot, with two liverymen before, and two behind, clothed in green and gold ; and never sure was there so splendid a meteor seen in a Moffat fair. The word instantly circulated in the market, that this was the Lady Elizabeth Douglas, eldest daughter to the

Earl of Morton, who then sojourned at Auchincastle, in the vicinity of Moffat, and which lady at that time was celebrated as a great beauty all over Scotland. She was afterwards Lady Keith; and the mention of this name in the tale, as it were by mere accident, fixes the era of it in the reign of James the Fourth, at the very time that fairies, brownies, and witches, were at the rifest in Scotland.

Every one in the market believed the lady to be the daughter of the Earl of Morton; and when she came to the Johnston Arms, a gentleman in green came out bareheaded, and received her out of the carriage. All the crowd gazed at such unparalleled beauty and grandeur, but none was half so much overcome as Allanson. He had never conceived aught half so lovely either in earth, or heaven, or fairyland; and while he stood in a burning fever of admiration, think of his astonishment, and the astonishment of the countless crowd that looked on, when this brilliant and matchless beauty beckoned him towards her! He could not believe his senses, but looked this way and that to see how others regarded the affair; but she beckoned him a second time, with such a winning courtesy and smile, that immediately he pulled off his beaver cap and hasted up to her; and without more ado she gave him her arm, and the two walked into the hostel.

Allanson conceived that he was thus distinguished by Lady Elizabeth Douglas, the flower of the land, and so did all the people of the market; and greatly they wondered who the young farmer could be that was thus particularly favoured; for it ought to have been mentioned that he had not one personal acquaintance in the fair save Mr David Welch of Cariferan. The first thing the lady did was to inquire kindly after his health. Allanson thanked her ladyship with all the courtesy he was master of; and being by this time persuaded that she was in love with him, he became as light as if treading on the air. She next inquired after his father and mother.——Oho! thought he to himself, poor creature, she is terribly in for it! but her love shall not be thrown

away upon a backward or ungrateful object.——He answered her with great politeness, and at length began to
talk of her noble father and young Lord William, but
she cut him short by asking if he did not recognise her.

"Oh, yes! He knew who her ladyship was, and remembered that he had seen her comely face often before,
although he could not, at that particular moment, recall
to his memory the precise time or places of their meeting."

She next asked for his old neighbours of Kirkstyle,
and if they were still in life and health!

Allanson felt as if his heart were a piece of ice. A
chillness spread over his whole frame; he sank back on
a seat, and remained motionless; but the beautiful and
adorable creature soothed him with kind words, till he
again gathered courage to speak.

"What!" said he; "and has it been your own lovely
self who has been playing tricks on me this whole day?"

"A first love is not easily extinguished, Mr Allanson,"
said she. "You may guess from my appearance, that I
have been fortunate in life; but, for all that, my first
love for you has continued the same, unaltered and unchanged, and you must forgive the little freedoms I used
to-day to try your affections, and the effects my appearance would have on you."

"It argues something for my good taste, however,
that I never pitched on any face for beauty to-day but
your own," said he. "But now that we have met once
more, we shall not so easily part again. I will devote
the rest of my life to you, only let me know the place
of your abode."

"It is hard by," said she, "only a very little space
from this; and happy, happy, would I be to see you
there to-night, were it proper or convenient. But my
lord is at present from home, and in a distant country."

"I should not conceive that any particular hinderance
to my visit," said he.

With great apparent reluctance she at length consented to admit of his visit, and offered to leave one of
her gentlemen, whom she could trust, to be his conductor;

but this he positively refused. It was his desire, he said, that no eye of man should see him enter or leave her happy dwelling. She said he was a self-willed man, but should have his own way; and after giving him such directions as would infallibly lead him to her mansion, she mounted her chariot and was driven away.

Allanson was uplifted above every sublunary concern. Seeking out his friend, David Welch, he imparted to him his extraordinary good fortune, but he did not tell him that she was not the Lady Elizabeth Douglas. Welch insisted on accompanying him on the way, and refused to turn back till he came to the very point of the road next to the lady's splendid mansion; and in spite of all that Allanson could say, Welch remained there till he saw his comrade enter the court gate, which glowed with lights as innumerable as the stars of the firmament.

Allanson had promised to his father and mother to be home on the morning after the fair to breakfast. He came not either that day or the next; and the third day the old man mounted his white pony, and rode away towards Moffat in search of his son. He called at Cariferan on his way, and made inquiries at Mr Welch. The latter manifested some astonishment that the young man had not returned; nevertheless he assured his father of his safety, and desired him to return home; and then with reluctance confessed that the young man was engaged in an amour with the Earl of Morton's beautiful daughter; that he had gone to the castle by appointment, and that he, David Welch, had accompanied him to the gate, and seen him enter, and it was apparent that his reception had been a kind one, since he had tarried so long.

Mr Welch, seeing the old man greatly distressed, was persuaded to accompany him on his journey, as the last who had seen his son, and seen him enter the castle. On reaching Moffat they found his steed standing at the hostel, whither it had returned on the night of the fair, before the company broke up; but the owner had not been heard of since seen in company with Lady Elizabeth Douglas. The old man set out for Auchincastle,

D 2

taking Mr David Welch along with him; but long ere they reached the place, Mr Welch assured him he would not find his son there, as it was nearly in a different direction that they rode on the evening of the fair. However, to the castle they went, and were admitted to the Earl, who, after hearing the old man's tale, seemed to consider him in a state of derangement. He sent for his daughter Elizabeth, and questioned her concerning her meeting with the son of the old respectable countryman—of her appointment with him on the night of the preceding Friday, and concluded by saying he hoped she had him still in some safe concealment about the castle.

The lady, hearing her father talk in this manner, and seeing the serious and dejected looks of the old man, knew not what to say, and asked an explanation. But Mr Welch put a stop to it by declaring to old Allanson that the Lady Elizabeth was not the lady with whom his son made the appointment, for he had seen her, and would engage to know her again among ten thousand; nor was that the castle towards which he had accompanied his son, nor any thing like it. "But go with me," continued he, "and, though I am a stranger in this district, I think I can take you to the very place."

They set out again; and Mr Welch traced the road from Moffat, by which young Allanson and he had gone, until, after travelling several miles, they came to a place where a road struck off to the right at an angle. "Now I know we are right," said Welch; "for here we stopped, and your son intreated me to return, which I refused, and accompanied him to yon large tree, and a little way beyond it, from whence I saw him received in at the splendid gate. We shall be in sight of the mansion in three minutes."

They passed on to the tree, and a space beyond it; but then Mr Welch lost the use of his speech, as he perceived that there was neither palace nor gate there, but a tremendous gulf, fifty fathoms deep, and a dark stream foaming and boiling below.

"How is this?" said old Allanson. "There is neither mansion nor habitation of man here!"

Welch's tongue for a long time refused its office, and he stood like a statue, gazing on the altered and awful scene. "He only, who made the spirits of men," said he, at last, "and all the spirits that sojourn in the earth and air, can tell how this is. We are wandering in a world of enchantment, and have been influenced by some agencies above human nature, or without its pale; for here of a certainty did I take leave of your son—and there, in that direction, and apparently either on the verge of that gulf, or the space above it, did I see him received in at the court gate of a mansion, splendid beyond all conception. How can human comprehension make any thing of this?"

They went forward to the verge, Mr Welch leading the way to the very spot on which he saw the gate opened, and there they found marks where a horse had been plunging. Its feet had been over the brink, but it seemed to have recovered itself, and deep, deep down, and far within, lay the mangled corpse of John Allanson; and in this manner, mysterious beyond all example, terminated the career of that wicked and flagitious young man.— What a beautiful moral may be extracted from this fairy tale!

But among all these turnings and windings, there is no account given, you will say, of the fate of Mary Burnet; for this last appearance of hers at Moffat seems to have been altogether a phantom or illusion. Gentle and kind reader, I can give you no account of the fate of that maiden; for though the ancient fairy tale proceeds, it seems to me to involve her fate in ten times more mystery than what we have hitherto seen of it.

The yearly return of the day on which Mary was lost, was observed as a day of mourning by her aged and disconsolate parents,—a day of sorrow, of fasting, and humiliation. Seven years came and passed away, and the seventh returning day of fasting and prayer was at hand. On the evening previous to it, old Andrew was moving along the sands of the loch, still looking for some relic of his beloved Mary, when he was aware of a little shrivelled old man, who came posting towards him. The creature was not above five spans in height, and had a face scarcely like that of a human creature; but he was, nevertheless, civil in his deportment, and sensible in speech. He bade Andrew a good evening, and asked him what he was looking for. Andrew answered, hat he was looking for that which he should never find.

"Pray, what is your name, ancient shepherd?" said the stranger; "for methinks I should know something of you, and perhaps have a commission to you."

"Alas! why should you ask after my name?" said Andrew. "My name is now nothing to any one."

"Had not you once a beautiful daughter, named Mary?" said the stranger.

"It is a heart-rending question, man," said Andrew; "but certes, I had once a beloved daughter named Mary."

"What became of her?" asked the stranger.

Andrew shook his head, turned round, and began to move away; it was a theme that his heart could not brook. He sauntered along the loch sands, his dim eye scanning every white pebble as he passed along. There was a hopelessness in his stooping form, his gait, his eye, his features,—in every step that he took there was a hopeless apathy. The dwarf followed him, and began to expostulate with him. "Old man, I see you are pining under some real or fancied affliction," said he. "But in continuing to do so, you are neither acting according to the dictates of reason nor true religion. What is man that he should fret, or the son of man that he should repine, under the chastening hand of his Maker?"

"I am far frae justifying mysell," returned Andrew, surveying his shrivelled monitor with some degree of astonishment. "But there are some feelings that neither reason nor religion can o'ermaster; and there are some that a parent may cherish without sin."

"I deny the position," said the stranger, "taken either absolutely or relatively. All repining under the Supreme decree is leavened with unrighteousness. But, subtleties aside, I ask you, as I did before, What became of your daughter?"

"Ask the Father of her spirit, and the framer of her body," said Andrew, solemnly; "ask Him into whose hands I committed her from childhood. He alone knows what became of her, but I do not."

"How long is it since you lost her?"

"It is seven years to-morrow."

"Ay! you remember the time well. And have you mourned for her all that while?"

"Yes; and I will go down to the grave mourning for my only daughter, the child of my age, and of all my affection. O, thou unearthly-looking monitor, knowest thou aught of my darling child? for if thou dost, thou wilt know that she was not like other women. There was a simplicity and a purity about my Mary, that was hardly consistent with our frail nature."

"Wouldst thou like to see her again?" said the dwarf.

Andrew turned round, his whole frame shaking as with a palsy, and gazed on the audacious imp. "See her again, creature!" cried he vehemently—"Would I like to see her again, sayest thou?"

"I said so," said the dwarf, "and I say further, Dost thou know this token? Look, and see if thou dost?"

Andrew took the token, and looked at it, then at the shrivelled stranger, and then at the token again; and at length he burst into tears, and wept aloud; but they were tears of joy, and his weeping seemed to have some breathings of laughter intermingled in it. And still as he kissed the token, he called out in broken and convulsive sentences,—"Yes, auld body, I *do* know it!—I *do* know it!—I *do* know it! It is indeed the same golden Edward, with three holes in it, with which I presented my Mary on her birth-day, in her eighteenth year, to buy a new suit for the holidays. But when she took it

she said—ay, I mind weel what my bonny woman said,
—' It is sae bonny and sae kenspeckle,' said she, ' that
I think I'll keep it for the sake of the giver.'   O dear,
dear!—Blessed little creature, tell me how she is, and
where she is?  Is she living, or is she dead?"

"She is living, and in good health," said the dwarf;
"and better, and braver and happier, and lovelier than
ever; and if you make haste, you will see her and her
family at Moffat to-morrow afternoon.   They are to pass
there on a journey, but it is an express one, and I am sent
to you with that token, to inform you of the circumstance, that you may have it in your power to
see and embrace your beloved daughter once before you
die."

"And am I to meet my Mary at Moffat?  Come away,
little, dear, welcome body, thou blessed of heaven, come
away, and taste of an auld shepherd's best cheer, and I'll
gang foot for foot with you to Moffat, and my auld wife
shall gang foot for foot with us too.   I tell you, little,
blessed, and welcome crile, come along with me."

" I may not tarry to enter your house, or taste of your
cheer, good shepherd," said the being.   " May plenty
still be within your walls, and a thankful heart to enjoy
it!   But my directions are neither to taste meat nor
drink in this country, but to haste back to her that sent
me.   Go—haste, and make ready, for you have no time
to lose."

" At what time will she be there?" cried Andrew,
flinging the plaid from him to run home with the tidings.

" Precisely when the shadow of the Holy Cross falls
due east," cried the dwarf; and turning round, he hasted
on his way.

When old Jean Linton saw her husband coming hob-
bling and running home without his plaid, and having his
doublet flying wide open, she had no doubt that he had
lost his wits; and, full of anxiety, she met him at the
side of the kail-yard.   " Gudeness preserve us a' in our
right senses, Andrew Burnet what's the matter wi'you,
Andrew Burnet?"

"Stand out o' my gate, wife, for, d'ye see, I am rather in a haste, Jean Linton."

"I see that indeed, gudeman; but stand still, and tell me what has putten you *in* sic a haste. Ir ye dementit?"

"Na, na; gudewife, Jean Linton, I'm no dementit— I'm only gaun away till Moffat."

"O, gudeness pity the poor auld body! How can ye gang to Moffat, man? Or what have ye to do at Moffat? Dinna ye mind that the morn is the day o' our solemnity?"

"Haud out o' my gate, auld wife, and dinna speak o solemnities to me. I'll keep it at Moffat the morn. Ay, gudewife, and ye shall keep it at Moffat, too. What d'ye think o' that, woman? Too-whoo! ye dinna ken the metal that's in an auld body till it be tried."

"Andrew—Andrew Burnet!'

"Get awa' wi' your frightened looks, woman; and haste ye, gang and fling me out my Sabbath-day claes. And, Jean Linton, my woman, d'ye hear, gang and pit on your bridal gown, and your silk hood, for ye maun be at Moffat the morn too; and it is mair nor time we were awa'. Dinna look sae surprised, woman, till I tell ye, that our ain Mary is to meet us at Moffat the morn."

"O, Andrew! dinna sport wi' the feelings of an auld forsaken heart!"

"Gude forbid, my auld wife, that I should ever sport wi' feeling o' yours," cried Andrew, bursting into tears; "they are a' as saacred to me as breathings frae the Throne o' Grace. But it is true that I tell ye; our dear bairn is to meet us at Moffat the morn, wi' a son in every hand; and we maun e'en gang and see her since again, and kiss her and bless her afore we dee."

The tears now rushed from the old woman's eyes like fountains, and dropped from her sorrow-worn cheeks to the earth, and then, as with a spontaneous movement, she threw her skirt over her head, kneeled down at her husband's feet, and poured out her soul in thanksgiving to her Maker. She then rose up, quite deprived of her senses through joy, and ran crouching away on the road

towards Moffat, as if hasting beyond her power to be at
it.    But Andrew brought her back; and they prepared
themselves for their journey.

Kirkstyle being twenty miles from Moffat, they set out
on the afternoon of Tuesday, the 16th of September;
slept that night at a place called Tnrnbery Shiel, and
were in Moffat next day by noon.    Wearisome was the
remainder of the day to that aged couple; they wandered
about conjecturing by what road their daughter would
come, and how she would come attended.    "I have
made up my mind on baith these matters," said Andrew;
" at first I thought it was likely that she would come out
of the east, because a' our blessings come frae that airt;
but finding now that would be o'er near to the very road
we hae come oursells, I now take it for granted she'll
come frae the south; and I just think I see her leading
a bonny boy in every hand, and a servant lass carrying a
bit bundle ahint her."

The two now walked out on all the southern roads,
in hopes to meet their Mary, but always returned to
watch the shadow of the Holy Cross; and, by the time
it fell due east, they could do nothing but stand in the
middle of the street, and look round them in all directions.    At length, about half a mile out on the Dumfries
road, they perceived a poor beggar woman approaching
with two children following close to her, and another
beggar a good way behind.    Their eyes were instantly
riveted on these objects; for Andrew thought he perceived
his friend the dwarf in the one that was behind; and now
all other earthly objects were to them nothing, save
these approaching beggars.    At that moment a gilded
chariot entered the village from the south, and drove by
them at full speed, having two livery-men before, and
two behind, clothed in green and gold.    "Ach-wow!
the vanity of worldly graandeur!" ejaculated Andrew,
as the splendid vehicle went thundering by; but neither
he nor his wife deigned to look at it farther, their whole
attention being fixed on the group of beggars.    "Ay, it
is just my woman," said Andrew, "it is just hersell; I

ken her gang yet, sair pressed down wi' poortith although she be. But I dinna care how poor she be, for baith her and hers sall be welcome to my fireside as lang as I hae ane."

While their eyes were thus strained, and their hearts melting with tenderness and pity, Andrew felt something embracing his knees, and, on looking down, there was his Mary, blooming in splendour and beauty, kneeling at his feet. Andrew uttered a loud hysterical scream of joy, and clasped her to his bosom; and old Jean Linton stood trembling, with her arms spread, but durst not close them on so splendid a creature, till her daughter first enfolded her in a fond embrace, and then she hung upon her and wept. It was a wonderful event—a restoration without a parallel. They indeed beheld their Mary, their long-lost darling; they held her in their embraces, believed in her identity, and were satisfied. Satisfied, did I say? They were happy beyond the lot of mortals. She had just alighted from her chariot; and, perceiving her aged parents standing together, she ran and kneeled at their feet. They now retired into the hostel, where Mary presented her two sons to her father and mother. They spent the evening in every social endearment; and Mary loaded the good old couple with rich presents, watched over them till midnight, when they both fell into a deep and happy sleep, and then she remounted her chariot, and was driven away. If she was any more seen in Scotland, I never heard of it; but her parents rejoiced in the thoughts of her happiness till the day of their death.

---

## CHAP. XI.

### THE LAIRD OF WINEHOLM.

" HAVE you heard any thing of the apparition which has been seen about Wineholm Place?" said the Dominie.

" Na, I never heard of sic a thing as yet," quoth the smith; "but I wadna wonder muckle that the news should turn out to be true."

The Dominie shook his head, and uttered a long "h'm-h'm-h'm," as if he knew more than he was at liberty to tell.

" Weel, that beats the world," said the smith as he gave over blowing the bellows, and looked anxiously in the Dominie's face.

The Dominie shook his head again.

The smith was now in the most ticklish quandary; eager to learn particulars, that he might spread the astounding news through the whole village, and the rest of the parish to boot, but yet afraid to press the inquiry, for fear the cautious Dominie should take the alarm of being reported as a tattler, and keep all to himself. So the smith, after waiting till the wind-pipe of the great bellows ceased its rushing noise, covered the gloss neatly up with a mixture of small coals, culm, and cinders; and then, perceiving that nothing more was forthcoming from the Dominie, he began blowing again with more energy than before—changed his hand—put the other sooty one in his breeches-pocket—leaned to the horn—looked in a careless manner to the window, or rather gazed on vacancy, and always now and then stole a sly look at the Dominie's face. It was quite immovable. His cheek was leaned on his open hand, and his eyes fixed on the glowing fire. It was very teasing this for poor Clinkum the smith. But what could he do? He took out his glowing iron, and made a shower of fire sweep through the whole smithy, whereof a good part, as intended, sputtered upon the Dominie; but that imperturbable person only shielded his face with his elbow, turned his shoulder half round, and held his peace. Thump, thump! clink, clink! went the hammer for a space; and then when the iron was returned to the fire, " Weel, that beats the world!" quoth the smith.

" What is this that beats the world, Mr Clinkum?" asked the Dominie, with the most cool and provoking indifference.

"This story about the apparition," quoth the smith.

"What story?" said the Dominie.

Now really this perversity was hardly to be endured, even in a learned Dominie, who, with all his cold indifference of feeling, was sitting toasting himself at a good smithy fire. The smith felt this, (for he was a man of acute feeling,) and therefore he spit upon his hand and fell a-clinking and pelting at the stithy with both spirit and resignation, saying within himself, "These dominie bodies just beat the world!"

"What story?" reiterated the Dominie. "For my part, I related no story, nor have ever given assent to a belief in such a story that any man has heard. Nevertheless, from the results of ratiocination, conclusions may be formed, though not algebraically, yet corporately, by constituting a quantity, which shall be equivalent to the difference, subtracting the less from the greater, and striking a balance in order to get rid of any ambiguity or paradox."

At the long adverb, *nevertheless*, the smith gave over blowing, and pricked up his ears; but the definition went beyond his comprehension.

"Ye ken, that just beats the whole world for deepness," said the smith; and again began blowing the bellows.

"You know, Mr Clinkum," continued the Dominie, "that a proposition is an assertion of some distinct truth, which only becomes manifest by demonstration. A corollary is an obvious, or easily inferred consequence *of* a proposition; while an hypothesis is a *sup*-position, or concession made, during the process of demonstration. Now do you take me along with you? Because, if you do not, it is needless to proceed."

"Yes, yes, I understand you middling weel; but I wad like better to hear what other folks say about it than you."

"And why so? Wherefore would you rather hear another man's demonstration than mine?" said the Dominie, sternly.

"Because, ye ken, ye just beat the whole world for words," quoth the smith.

" Ay, ay! that is to say, words without wisdom," said the Dominie, rising and stepping away. "Well, well, every man to his sphere, and the smith to the bellows."

" Ye're quite mista'en, master," cried the smith after him; "it isna the want o' wisdom in you that plagues me, it is the owerplush o't."

This soothed the Dominie, who returned and said mildly—"By the by, Clinkum, I want a leister of your making; for I see there is no other tradesman makes them so well. A five-grained one make it; at your own price."

" Very weel, sir. When will you be needing it?"

" Not till the end of close-time."

" Ay, ye may gar the three auld anes do till then."

"'What do you wish to insinuate, sir? Would you infer, because I have three leisters, that therefore I am a breaker of the laws? That I, who am placed here as a pattern and monitor of the young and rising generation, should be the first to set them an example of insubordination?"

" Na, but, ye ken, that just beats the world for words! but we ken what we ken, for a' that, master."

" You had better take a little care what you say, Mr Clinkum; just a little care. I do not request you to take particular care, for of that your tongue is incapable, but a very little is necessary. And mark you—don't go to say that I said this or that about a ghost, or mentioned such a ridiculous story."

" The crabbitness o' that body beats the world!" said the smith to himself, as the Dominie went halting homeward.

The very next man that entered the smithy door was no other than John Broadcast, the new Laird's hind, who had also been hind to the late laird for many years, and who had no sooner said his errand than the smith addressed him thus:—" Have *you* ever seen this ghost that there is such a noise about?"

" Ghost! Na, goodness be thankit, I never saw a

ghost in my life, save aince a wraith. What ghost do you mean?"

" So you never saw nor heard tell of any apparition about Wineholm Place lately?"

" No, I hae reason to be thankfu' I have not."

" Weel that beats the world! Whow, man, but ye are sair in the dark! Do you no think there are siccan things in nature as folk no coming fairly to their right ends, John ?"

" Goodness be wi' us! Ye gar a' the hairs o' my head creep, man. What's that you're saying?"

" Had ye never ony suspicions o' that kind, John ?"

" No ; I canna say that I had."

" None in the least ? Weel, that beats the world !"

" O, haud your tongue, haud your tongue ! We hae great reason to be thankfu' that we are as we are !"

" How as we are ?"

" That we arena stocks or stones, or brute beasts, as the Minister o' Traquair says. But I hope in God there is nae siccan a thing about my master's place as an unearthly visitor."

The smith shook his head, and uttered a long hem, hem, hem ! He had felt the powerful effect of that himself, and wished to make the same appeal to the feelings and longings after information of John Broadcast. The bait took ; for the latent spark of superstition, not to say any thing about curiosity, was kindled in the heart of honest John, and there being no wit in the head to counteract it, the portentous hint had its full sway. John's eyes stelled in his head, and his visage grew long, assuming something of the hue of dried clay in winter. " Hech, man, but that's an awsome story !" exclaimed he. " Folks hae great reason to be thankfu' that they are as they are. It is truly an awsome story."

" Ye ken, it just beats the world for that," quoth the smith.

" And is it really thought that this Laird made awav wi' our auld master ?" said John.

The smith shook his head again, and gave a strait wink with his eyes.

" Weel, I hae great reason to be thankfu' that I never heard siccan a story as that !" said John.    " Wha was it tauld you a' about it ?"

" It was nae less a man than our mathewmatical Dominie," said the smith ; " he that kens a' things, and can prove a proposition to the nineteenth part of a hair. But he is terrified the tale should spread ; and therefore ye maunna say a word about it."

" Na, na ; I hae great reason to be thankfu' I can keep a secret as weel as the maist feck o' men, and better than the maist feck o' women.    What did he say ? Tell us a' that he said."

" It is not so easy to repeat what he says, for he has sae mony lang-nebbit words, which just beat the world. But he said, though it was only a supposition, yet it was easily made manifest by positive demonstration."

" Did you ever hear the like o' that !    Now, havena we reason to be thankful that we are as we are ?    Did he say that it was by poison that he was taken off, or that he was strangled ?"

" Na ; I thought he said it was by a collar, or a collary, or something to that purpose."

" Then, it wad appear there is no doubt of it ?    I think the Doctor has reason to be thankfu' that he's no taken up.    Is not that strange ?"

" O, ye ken, it just beats the world !"

" He deserves to be torn at young horses' tails," said the ploughman.

" Ay, or nippit to death with red-hot pinchers," quoth the smith.

" Or harrowed to death, like the children of Ammon," continued the ploughman.

" Na, I'll tell you what should be done wi' him—he should just be docked and fired like a farcied horse," quoth the smith.    " Od help ye, man, I could beat the world for laying on a proper poonishment."

John Broadcast went home full of terror and dismay.

He told his wife the story in a secret—she told the dairymaid with a tenfold degree of secrecy; and so ere long it reached the ears of Dr Davington himself, the New Laird, as he was called. He was unusually affected at hearing such a terrible accusation against himself; and the Dominie being mentioned as the propagator of the report, a message was forthwith dispatched to desire him to come up to the Place, and speak with the Laird. The Dominie suspected there was bad blood a-brewing against him; and as he had too much self-importance to think of succumbing to any man alive, he sent an impertinent answer to the Laird's message, bearing, that if Dr Davington had any business with him, he would be so good as attend at his class-room when he dismissed his scholars.

When this message was delivered, the Doctor, being almost beside himself with rage, instantly dispatched two village constables with a warrant to seize the Dominie, and bring him before him; for the Doctor was a justice of the peace. Accordingly, the poor Dominie was seized at the head of his pupils, and dragged away, crutch and all, up before the new Laird, to answer for such an abominable slander. The Dominie denied every thing concerning it, as indeed he might, save having asked the smith the simple question, "if he had heard ought of a ghost at the Place?" But he refused to tell why he asked that question. He had his own reasons for it, he said, and reasons that to him were quite sufficient; but as he was not obliged to disclose them, neither would he.

The smith was then sent for, who declared that the Dominie had told him of the ghost being seen, and a murder committed, which he called a *rash assassination*, and said it was obvious and easily inferred that it was done by a collar.

How the Dominie did storm! He even twice threatened to knock down the smith with his crutch; not for the slander,—he cared not for that nor the Doctor a pin, but for the total subversion of his grand illustration from geometry; and he therefore denominated the smith's head *the logarithm to number one*, a reproach of which I do not understand the gist, but the appropriation of it pleased the Dominie exceedingly, made him chuckle, and put him in better humour for a good while. It was in vain that he tried to prove that his words applied only to the definition of a problem in geometry,—he could not make himself understood; and the smith maintaining his point firmly, and apparently with conscientious truth, appearances were greatly against the Dominie, and the Doctor pronounced him a malevolent and dangerous person.

"O, ye ken, he just beats the world for that," quoth the smith.

"I a malevolent and dangerous person, sir!" said the Dominie, fiercely, and altering his crutch from one place to another of the floor, as if he could not get a place to set it on. "Dost thou call me a malevolent and dangerous person, sir? What then art thou? If thou knowest not I will tell thee. Add a cipher to a ninth figure, and what does that make? Ninety you will say. Ay, but then put a cipher *above* a nine, and what does that make? ha—ha—ha—I have you there. Your case exactly in higher geometry! for say the chord of sixty degrees is radius, then the sine of ninety degrees is equal to the radius, so the secant of 0, that is nihil-nothing, as the boys call it, is radius, and so is the co-sine of 0. The versed sine of 90 degrees is radius, (that is nine with a cipher added, you know,) and the versed sine of 180 degrees is the diameter; then of course the sine increases from 0 (that is cipher or nothing) till it becomes radius, and then it decreases till it becomes nothing. After this you note it lies on the *contrary* side of the diameter, and consequently, if positive before, is negative now, so that it must end in 0, or a cipher above a nine at most.

"This unintelligible jargon is out of place here, Mr Dominie; and if you can show no better reasons for raising such an abominable falsehood, in representing me as an incendiary and murderer, I shall procure you a lodging in the house of correction."

"Why, sir, the long and short of the matter is this—. I only asked at that fellow there, that logarithm of stupidity! if he had heard aught of a ghost having been seen about Wineholm Place. I added nothing farther either positive or negative. Now, do you insist on my reasons for asking such a question?"

"I insist on having them."

"Then what will you say, sir, when I inform you, and declare my readiness to depone to the truth of it, that I saw the ghost myself?—yes, sir—that I saw the ghost of your late worthy father-in-law myself, sir; and though I said no such thing to that decimal fraction, yet it told me, sir—yes, the spirit of your father-in-law told me, sir, that you are a murderer."

"Lord, now, what think ye o' that?" quoth the smith. "Ye had better hae letten him alane; for od, ye ken, he's the deevil of a body that ever was made! He just beats the world!"

The Doctor grew as pale as death, but whether from fear or rage, it was hard to say. "Why, sir, you are mad! stark, raving mad," said the Doctor; "therefore, for your own credit, and for the peace and comfort of my wife and myself, and our credit among our retainers, you must unsay every word that you have now said."

"I'll just as soon say that the parabola and the ellipsis are the same," said the Dominie; "or that the diameter is not the longest line that can be drawn in the circle. And now, sir, since you have forced me to divulge what I was much in doubt about, I have a great mind to have the old Laird's grave opened to-night, and have the body inspected before witnesses."

"If you dare disturb the sanctuary of the grave," said the Doctor vehemently, "or with your unhallowed hands touch the remains of my venerable and revered predecessor, it had been better for you, and all who make the attempt, that you never had been born. If not then for my sake, for the sake of my wife, the sole daughter of the man to whom you have all been obliged, let this abominable and malicious calumny go no farther, but put

it down ; I pray of you to put it down, as you would
value your own advantage.

"I have seen him, and spoke with him—that I aver,"
said the Dominie. "And shall I tell you what he said
to me ?"

"No, no! I'll hear no more of such absolute and disgusting nonsense," said the Laird.

"Then, since it hath come to this, I will declare it in
the face of the whole world, and pursue it to the last,"
said the Dominie, "ridiculous as it is, and I confess that
it is even so. I have seen your father-in-law within the
last twenty hours; at least a being in his form and habil-
iments, and having his aspect and voice. And he told
me, that he believed you were a very great scoundrel,
and that you had helped him off the stage of time in a
great haste, for fear of the operation of a will, which he
had just executed, very much to your prejudice. I was
somewhat aghast, but ventured to remark, that he must
surely have been sensible whether you murdered him or
not, and in what way. He replied, that he was not
absolutely certain, for at the time you put him down, he
was much in his customary way of nights,—very drunk;
but that he greatly suspected you had hanged him, for,
ever since he had died, he had been troubled with a severe crick in his neck. Having seen my late worthy
patron's body deposited in the coffin, and afterwards
consigned to the grave, these things overcame me, and a
kind of mist came over my senses ; but I heard him saying as he withdrew, what a pity it was that my nerves
could not stand this disclosure. Now, for my own satisfaction, I am resolved that to-morrow, I shall raise the
village, with the two ministers at the head of the multitude, and have the body, and particularly the neck of
the deceased, minutely inspected."

"If you do so, I shall make one of the number," said
the Doctor. "But I am resolved that in the first place
every mean shall be tried to prevent a scene of madness
and absurdity so disgraceful to a well-regulated village,
and a sober community.

"There is but one direct line that can be followed, and any other would either form an acute or obtuse angle," said the Dominie; "therefore I am resolved to proceed right forward, on mathematical principles;" and away he went, skipping on his crutch, to arouse the villagers to the scrutiny.

The smith remained behind, concerting with the Doctor, how to controvert the Dominie's profound scheme of unshrouding the dead; and certainly the smith's plan, viewed professionally, was not amiss. "O, ye ken, sir, we maun just gie him another heat, and try to saften him to reason, for he's just as stubborn as Muirkirk ir'n. He beats the world for that."

While the two were in confabulation, Johnston, the old house-servant, came in and said to the Doctor—"Sir, your servants are going to leave the house, every one, this night, if you cannot fall on some means to divert them from it. The old Laird is, it seems, risen again, and come back among them, and they are all in the utmost consternation. Indeed, they are quite out of their reason. He appeared in the stable to Broadcast, who has been these two hours dead with terror, but is now recovered, and telling such a tale down stairs, as never was heard from the mouth of man."

"Send him up here," said the Doctor. "I will silence him. What does the ignorant clown mean by joining in this unnatural clamour?"

John came up, with his broad bonnet in his hand, shut the door with hesitation, and then felt twice with his hand if it really was shut. "Well, John," said the Doctor, "what absurd lie is this that you are vending among your fellow servants, of having seen a ghost?" John picked some odds and ends of threads out of his bonnet, and said nothing. "You are an old superstitious dreaming dotard," continued the Doctor; "but if you propose in future to manufacture such stories, you must, from this instant, do it somewhere else than in my service, and among my domestics. What have you to say for yourself?"

" Indeed, sir, I hae naething to say but this, that we hae a' muckle reason to be thankfu' that we are as we are."

" And whereon does that wise saw bear ? What relation has that to the seeing of a ghost ? Confess then this instant, that you have forged and vended a deliberate lie."

" Indeed, sir, I hae muckle reason to be thankfu' "——

" For what ?"

" That I never tauld a deliberate lee in my life. My late master came and spake to me in the stable ; but whether it was his ghaist or himsell—a good angel or a bad ane, I hae reason to be thankfu' I never said ; for I *do—not—ken*."

" Now, pray let us hear from that sage tongue of yours, so full of sublime adages, what this doubtful being said to you ?"

" I wad rather be excused, an it were your honour's will, and wad hae reason to be thankfu'."

" And why should you decline telling this ?"

" Because I ken ye wadna believe a word o't, it is sic-can a strange story. O sirs, but folks hae muckle reason to be thankfu' that they are as they are !"

" Well, out with this strange story of yours. I do not promise to credit it, but shall give it a patient hearing, provided you swear that there is no forgery in it."

" Weel, as I was suppering the horses the night, I was dressing my late kind master's favourite mare, and I was just thinking to mysell, An he had been leeving, I wadna hae been my lane the night, for he wad hae been standing over me cracking his jokes, and swearing at me in his good-natured hamely way. Aye, but he's gane to his lang account, thinks I, and we poor frail dying creatures that are left ahind hae muckle reason to be thankfu' that we are as we are ; when I looks up, and behold there's my auld master standing leaning against the trivage, as he used to do, and looking at me. I canna but say my heart was a little astoundit, and maybe lap up through my midriff into my breath-bellows—I couldna say ; but in the strength o' the Lord I was enabled to retain my senses for a good while. 'John Broadcast,' said he, with a deep and angry tone,—" John Broadcast, what the d—l are you thinking about? You are not currying that mare half. What a d—d lubberly way of dressing a horse is that?"

" ' L—d make us thankfu', master! ' says I, 'are you there?'

" ' Where else would you have me to be at this hour of the night, old blockhead?' says he.

" ' In another hame than this, master,' says I; 'but I fear me it is nae good ane, that ye are sae soon tired o't.'

" ' A d—d bad one, I assure you,' says he.

" ' Ay, but, master,' says I, ' ye hae muckle reason to be thankfu' that ye are as ye are.'

" ' In what respects, dotard?' says he.

" ' That ye hae liberty to come out o't a start now and then to get the air,' says I; and oh, my heart was sair for him when I thought o' his state! and though I was thankfu' that I was as I was, my heart and flesh began to fail me, at thinking of my being speaking face to face wi' a being frae the unhappy place. But out he briks again wi' a grit round o' swearing about the mare being ill keepit; and he ordered me to cast my coat and curry her weel, for that he had a lang journey to take on her the morn.

" ' You take a journey on her!' says I, ' I fear my new master will dispute that privilege with you, for he rides her himsell the morn.'

" ' He ride her!' cried the angry spirit; and then it burst out into a lang string of imprecations, fearsome to hear, against you, sir; and then added, ' Soon, soon shall he be levelled with the dust! The dog! the parricide! first to betray my child, and then to put down myself! —But he shall not escape! he shall not escape!' cried he with such a hellish growl, that I fainted, and heard no more."

" Weel, that beats the world!" quoth the smith; " I wad hae thought the mare wad hae luppen ower yird and stane, or fa'en down dead wi' fright."

" Na, na," said John, " in place o' that, whenever she heard him fa' a-swearing, she was sae glad that she fell a-nichering."

" Na, but that beats the hail world a'thegither !" quoth the smith. " Then it has been nae ghaist ava, ye may depend on that."

" I little wat what it was," said John, " but it was a being in nae good or happy state o' mind, and is a warning to us a' how muckle reason we hae to be thankfu' that we are as we are."

The Doctor pretended to laugh at the absurdity of John's narrative, but it was with a ghastly and doubtful expression of countenance, as though he thought the story far too ridiculous for any clodpole to have contrived out of his own head ; and forthwith he dismissed the two dealers in the marvellous, with very little ceremony, the one protesting that the thing beat the world, and the other that they had both reason to be thankfu' that they were as they were.

The next morning the villagers, small and great, were assembled at an early hour to witness the lifting of the body of their late laird, and headed by the established and dissenting clergymen, and two surgeons, they proceeded to the tomb, and soon extracted the splendid coffin, which they opened with all due caution and ceremony. But instead of the murdered body of their late benefactor, which they expected in good earnest to find, there was nothing in the coffin but a layer of gravel, of about the weight of a corpulent man !

The clamour against the new laird then rose all at once into a tumult that it was impossible to check, every one declaring aloud that he had not only murdered their benefactor, but, for fear of the discovery, had raised the body, and given, or rather sold it, for dissection. The thing was not to be tolerated ! so the mob proceeded in a body up to Wineholm Place, to take out their poor deluded lady, and burn the Doctor and his basely acquired habitation to ashes. It was not till the multitude had surrounded the house, that the ministers and two or three other gentlemen could stay them, which they only did by assuring the mob that they would bring out the Doctor before their eyes, and deliver him up to justice. This pacified the throng ; but on inquiry at the hall, it was found that the Doctor had gone off early that morning, so that nothing further could be done for the present. But the coffin, filled with gravel, was laid up in the aisle, and kept open for inspection.

Nothing could now exceed the consternation of the simple villagers of Wineholm at these dark and mysterious events. Business, labour, and employment of every sort, were at a stand, and the people hurried about to one another's houses, and mingled their conjectures together in one heterogeneous mass. The smith put his hand to the bellows, but forgot to blow till the fire went out ; the weaver leaned on his beam, and listened to the legends of the ghastly tailor. The team stood in mid furrow, and the thrasher agaping over his flail ; and even the Dominie was heard to declare that the geometrical series of events was increasing by no *common* ratio, and therefore ought to be calculated rather arithmetically than by logarithms ; and John Broadcast saw more and more reason for being thankful that he was as he was, and neither a stock, nor a stone, nor a brute beast.

Every new thing that happened was more extraordinary than the last : and the most puzzling of all was the circumstance of the late Laird's mare, saddle, bridle, and all, being off before day the next morning : so that Dr Davington was obliged to have recourse to his own, on which he was seen posting away on the road towards Edinburgh. It was thus but too obvious that the ghost of the late Laird had ridden off on his favourite mare, the Lord only knew whither ! for as to that point none of the sages of Wineholm could divine. But their souls grew chill as an iceberg, and their very frames rigid, at the thoughts of a spirit riding away on a brute beast to the place appointed for wicked men. And had not John Broadcast reason to be thankful that he was as he was ?

However, the outcry of the community became so outrageous, of murder, and foul play in so many ways, that
the officers of justice were compelled to take note of it;
and accordingly the Sheriff-substitute, the Sheriff-clerk,
the Fiscal, and two assistants, came in two chaises to
Wineholm to take a precognition; and there a court was
held which lasted the whole day, at which Mrs Davington, the late Laird's only daughter, all the servants, and
a great number of the villagers, were examined on oath.
It appeared from the evidence that Dr Davington had
come to the village and set up as a surgeon—that he had
used every endeavour to be employed in the Laird's
family in vain, as the latter detested him.   That he,
however, found means of inducing his only daughter to
elope with him, which put the Laird quite beside himself,
and from thenceforward he became drowned in dissipa-
tion.    That such, however, was his affection for his
daughter, that he caused her to live with him, but would
never suffer the Doctor to enter his door—that it was
nevertheless quite customary for the Doctor to be sent
for to his lady's chamber, particularly when her father
was in his cups; and that on a certain night, when the
Laird had had company, and was so overcome that he
could not rise from his chair, he had died suddenly of
apoplexy; and that no other skill was sent for, or near
him, but this his detested son-in-law, whom he had by
will disinherited, though the legal term for rendering that
will competent had not expired.   The body was coffined
the second day after death, and locked up in a low
room in one of the wings of the building; and nothing
farther could be elicited.   The Doctor was missing,
and it was whispered that he had absconded; indeed
it was evident, and the Sheriff acknowledged, that according to the evidence taken, the matter had a very
suspicious aspect, although there was no direct proof
against the Doctor.   It was proved that he had attempted to bleed the patient, but had not succeeded,
and that at that time the old Laird was black in the
face.

When it began to wear nigh night, and nothing farther could be learned, the Sheriff-clerk, a quiet considerate gentleman, asked why they had not examined
the wright who made the coffin, and also placed the body
in it? The thing had not been thought of; but he was
found in court, and instantly put into the witness's box,
and examined on oath. His name was James Sanderson,
a stout-made, little, shrewd-looking man, with a very pe-
culiar squint. He was examined thus by the Procura-
tor-fiscal.

" Were you long acquainted with the late Laird of
Wineholm, James ?"

" Yes, ever since I left my apprenticeship ; for I suppose about nineteen years."

" Was he very much given to drinking of late ?"

" I could not say. He took his glass geyan heartily."

" Did you ever drink with him ?"

" O yes, mony a time."

" You must have seen him very drunk then ? Did you
ever see him so drunk that he could not rise, for instance ?"

" O never ! for, lang afore that, I could not have
kenn'd whether he was sitting or standing."

" Were you present at the corpse-chesting ?"

" Yes, I was."

" And were you certain the body was then deposited
in the coffin ?"

" Yes ; quite certain."

" Did you screw down the coffin-lid firmly then as you
do others of the same make ?"

" No, I did not."

" What were your reasons for that ?"

" They were no reasons of mine—I did what I was
ordered. There were private reasons, which I then wist
not of. But, gentlemen, there are some things connected with this affair, which I am bound in honour not to
reveal—I hope you will not compel me to divulge them
at present."

" You are bound by a solemn oath, James, which is the highest of all obligations; and for the sake of justice, you must tell every thing you know; and it would be better if you would just tell your tale straight forward, without the interruption of question and answer."

" Well then, since it must be so: That day, at the chesting, the Doctor took me aside, and says to me, 'James Sanderson, it will be necessary that something be put into the coffin to prevent any unpleasant flavour before the funeral; for, owing to the corpulence, and inflamed state of the body by apoplexy, there will be great danger of this.'

" ' Very well, sir,' says I, ' what shall I bring?'

" ' You had better only screw down the lid lightly at present, then,' said he, ' and if you could bring a bucketful of quicklime, a little while hence, and pour it over the body, especially over the face, it is a very good thing, an excellent thing for preventing any deleterious effluvia from escaping.'

" ' Very well, sir,' says I; and so I followed his directions. I procured the lime; and as I was to come privately in the evening to deposit it in the coffin, in company with the Doctor alone, I was putting off the time in my workshop, polishing some trifle, and thinking to myself that I could not find in my heart to choke up my old friend with quicklime, even after he was dead, when, to my unspeakable horror, who should enter my workshop but the identical Laird himself, dressed in his dead-clothes in the very same manner in which I had seen him laid in the coffin, but apparently all streaming in blood to the feet. I fell back over against a cart-wheel, and was going to call out, but could not; and as he stood straight in the door, there was no means of escape. At length the apparition spoke to me in a hoarse trembling voice, enough to have frightened a whole conclave of bishops out of their senses; and it says to me, ' Jamie Sanderson! O, Jamie Sanderson! I have been forced to appear to you in a d——d frightful guise!' These were the very first words it spoke,—and they were far frae being a lie; but I hafflins thought to mysell, that a being in such circumstances might have spoke with a little more caution and decency. I could make no answer, for my tongue refused all attempts at articulation, and my lips would not come together; and all that I could do, was to lie back against my new cart-wheel, and hold up my hands as a kind of defence. The ghastly and blood-stained apparition, advancing a step or two, held up both its hands, flying with dead ruffles, and cried to me in a still more frightful voice, ' O my faithful old friend ! I have been murdered ! I am a murdered man, Jamie Sanderson ! and if you do not assist me in bringing upon the wretch due retribution, you will be d——d to hell, sir.' "

" This is sheer raving, James," said the Sheriff, interrupting him. " These words can be nothing but the ravings of a disturbed and heated imagination. I entreat you to recollect, that you have appealed to the great Judge of heaven and earth for the truth of what you assert here, and to answer accordingly."

" I know what I am saying, my Lord Sheriff," said Sanderson ; " and I am telling naething but the plain truth, as nearly as my state of mind at the time permits me to recollect. The appalling figure approached still nearer and nearer to me, breathing threatenings if I would not rise and fly to its assistance, and swearing like a sergeant of dragoons at both the Doctor and myself. At length it came so close on me, that I had no other shift but to hold up both feet and hands to shield me, as I had seen herons do when knocked down by a goshawk, and I cried out ; but even my voice failed, so that I only cried like one through his sleep.

" ' What the devil are you lying gaping and braying at there ?' said he, seizing me by the wrists, and dragging me after him. ' Do you not see the plight I am in, and why won't you fly to succour me ?'

" I now felt to my great relief, that this terrific apparition was a being of flesh, blood, and bones like myself ; that, in short, it was indeed my kind old friend the Laird popped out of his open coffin, and come over to pay me an evening visit, but certainly in such a guise as earthly visit was never paid. I soon gathered up my scattered senses, took my old friend into my room, bathed him all over, and washed him well in lukewarm water; then put him into a warm bed, gave him a glass or two of warm punch, and he came round amazingly. He caused me to survey his neck a hundred times I am sure; and I had no doubt he had been strangled, for there was a purple ring round it, which in some places was black, and a little swollen; his voice creaked like a door hinge, and his features were still distorted. He swore terribly at both the Doctor and myself; but nothing put him half so mad as the idea of the quicklime being poured over him, and particularly over his face. I am mistaken if that experiment does not serve him for a theme of execration as long as he lives."

"So he is then alive, you say?" asked the Fiscal.

"O yes, sir! alive and tolerably well, considering. We two have had several bottles together in my quiet room; for I have still kept him concealed, to see what the Doctor would do next. He is in terror for him somehow, until sixty days be over from some date that he talks of, and seems assured that that dog will have his life by hook or crook, unless he can bring him to the gallows betimes, and he is absent on that business to-day. One night lately, when fully half seas over, he set off to the schoolhouse, and frightened the Dominie; and last night he went up to the stable, and gave old Broadcast a hearing for not keeping his mare well enough.

"It appeared that some shaking motion in the coffining of him had brought him to himself, after bleeding abundantly both at mouth and nose; that he was on his feet ere he knew how he had been disposed of, and was quite shocked at seeing the open coffin on the bed, and himself dressed in his grave-clothes, and all in one bath of blood. He flew to the door, but it was locked outside; he rapped furiously for something to drink; but the room was far removed from any inhabited part of the house, and none regarded. So he had nothing for it but to open the window, and come through the garden and the back loaning to my workshop. And as I had got orders to bring a bucketful of quicklime, I went over in the forenight with a bucketful of heavy gravel, as much as I could carry, and a little white lime sprinkled on the top of it; and being let in by the Doctor, I deposited that in the coffin, screwed down the lid, and left it, and the funeral followed in due course, the whole of which the Laird viewed from my window, and gave the Doctor a hearty day's cursing for daring to support his head and lay it in the grave.——And this, gentlemen, is the substance of what I know concerning this enormous deed, which is, I think, quite sufficient. The Laird bound me to secrecy until such time as he could bring matters to a proper bearing for securing of the Doctor; but as you have forced it from me, you must stand my surety, and answer the charges against me."

The Laird arrived that night with proper authority, and a number of officers, to have the Doctor, his son-in-law, taken into custody; but the bird had flown; and from that day forth he was never seen, so as to be recognised, in Scotland. The Laird lived many years after that; and though the thoughts of the quicklime made him drink a great deal, yet from that time he never suffered himself to get *quite* drunk, lest some one might have taken it into his head to hang him, and he not know any thing about it. The Dominie acknowledged that it was as impracticable to calculate what might happen in human affairs as to square the circle, which could only be effected by knowing the ratio of the circumference to the radius. For shoeing horses, vending news, and awarding proper punishments, the smith to this day just beats the world. And old John Broadcast is as thankful to Heaven as ever that things are as they are.

## CHAP. XII.

### WINDOW WAT'S COURTSHIP.

GREAT have been the conquests, and grievous the deray, wrought in the hearts of the rustic youth by some mountain nymphs. The confusion that particular ones have sometimes occasioned for a year or two almost exceeds credibility. When any young woman has obtained a great reputation for beauty, every young man in the bounds is sure either to be in love with her, or to believe that he is so ; and as all these run on a Friday's evening to woo her, of course the pride and vanity of the fair is raised to such a height, that she will rarely yield a preference to any, but is sure to put them all off with jibes and jeers. This shyness, instead of allaying, never fails to increase, the fervour of the flame ; an emulation, if not a rivalship, is excited among the younkers, until the getting a single word exchanged with the reigning beauty becomes a matter of thrilling interest to many a tender-hearted swain ; but, generally speaking, none of these admired beauties are married till they settle into the more quiet vale of life, and the current of admiration has turned towards others. Then do they betake themselves to sober reflection, listen to the most rational, though not the most youthful, of their lovers, and sit down, contented to share through life the toils, sorrows, and joys of the humble cot.

I am not now writing of ladies, nor of "farmers' bonny daughters ;" but merely of country maidens, such as ewe-milkers, hay-workers, har'st-shearers, the healthy and comely daughters of shepherds, hinds, country tradesmen, and small tenants ; in short, all the rosy, romping, and light-hearted dames that handle the sickle, the hoe, the hay-raik, and the fleece. And of these I can say, to their credit, that rarely an instance happens of a celebrated beauty turning out a bad, or even an indifferent wife. This is perhaps owing to the circumstance of their never marrying very young, (for a youthful marriage of a pair who have nought but their exertions and a good name to depend on for the support of a family, is far from being a prudent or highly commendable step,) or that these belles, having had too much experience in the follies and flippancies of youthful love, and youthful lovers, make their choice at last on principles of reason; or it may be owing to another reason still, namely, that among the peasantry young men never flock about, or make love to a girl who is not noted for activity as well as beauty. Cleverness is always the first recommendation; and consequently, when a young woman so endowed chooses to marry, it is natural to suppose that the good qualities, which before were only occasionally called into exercise, will then be exerted to the utmost. Experience is the great teacher among the labouring class, and her maxims are carried down from father to son in all their pristine strength. Seldom are they violated in any thing, and never in this. No young man will court a beautiful daw, unless he be either a booby or a rake.

In detailing a signal instance of the power of country beauty, I shall make use of fictitious names; and as I have not been an eye-witness to the scenes I mean to detail, I judge it best to give them in the colloquial style, exactly in the same manner as they have been rehearsed to me. Without adopting this mode, I might make a more perfect arrangement in my present story, but could not give it any degree of the interest it appeared to me to possess; nor could the characters be exhibited so well in any way as by letting them speak for themselves.

------

" Wat, what was the matter wi' you, that ye never keepit your face to the minister the last Sabbath day ? Yon's an unco unreverend gate in a kirk, man. I hae seen you keep a good ee on the preacher, and take good tent to what was gaun, too; and troth I'm wae to see ye altered to the waur."

"I kenna how I might chance to be looking, but I hope I was listening as weel as you, or ony that was there!—Heighow! It's a weary warld this!"

"What has made it siccan a weary warld, Wat? I'm sure it wasna about the ills o' life that the minister was preaching that day, that has gart ye change sae sair? Now, Wat, I tentit ye weel a' the day, and I'll be in your debt for a toop lamb at Michaelmass, gin ye'll just tell me ae distinct sentence o' the sermon on Sabbath last."

"Hout, Jock, man! ye ken I dinna want to make a jest about ony saacred thing; and as for your paulie toop lamb, what care I for it?"

"Ye needna think to win aff that gate, callant. Just confess the truth, that ye never heard a word the good man said, and that baith your heart and your ee war fixed on some object in the contrair direction. And I may be mista'en, but I think I could guess what it was."

"Whisht, lad, and let us alane o' your sinfu' sur-meeses. I might turn my back on the minister during the time o' the prayer; but that was for getting a lean on the seat, and what ill was in that?"

"Ay and ye might likewise hirsel yoursell up to the corner o' the seat a' the time o' baith the sermons, and lean your head on your hand, and look through your fingers too. Can ye deny this? or that your een were fixed the haill day on ae particular place?"

"Aweel, I winna gie a friend the lee to his face. But this I will say—that an you had been gieing a' the attention to the minister, that ane should do wha takes it upon him to lecture his neighbours at this rate, ye wadna hae been so weel aveesed with respect to my behaviour in the kirk. Take that for your share o' blame. And mair than that, if I'm nae waur than you, neither am I waur than other folk; for an ye had lookit as weel at a' the rest as it seems ye did at me, ye wad dae seen that a' the men in the kirk were looking the same gate."

"And a' at the same object too? And a' as deeply interested in it as you? Isna that what ye're thinking? Ah, Wat, Wat! love winna hide! I saw a pair o' slae-black een that threw some geyán saucy disdainfu' looks up the kirk, and I soon saw the havock they were making, and had made, i' your simple honest heart. Wow, man! but I fear me you are in a bad predickiment."

'Weel, weel, murder will out, and I confess between twa friends, Jock, there never was a lad in sic a predickiment as I am. I needna keep ought frae you; but for the life that's i' your bouk, dinna let a pater about it escape frae atween your lips. I wadna that it were kenn'd how deeply I am in love, and how little it is like to be requited, for the haill warld! But I am this day as miserable a man as breathes the breath o' life. For I like yon lass as man never likit another, and a' that I get is scorn, and gibes, and mockery in return. O Jock, I wish I was dead in an honest natural way, and that my burial day were the morn!"

"Weel, after a', I daresay that is the best way o' winding up a hopeless love concern. But only it ought surely to be the last resource. Now, will ye be candid, and tell me gin ye hae made all lawful endeavours to preserve your ain life, as the commandment requires us to do, ye ken? Hae ye courtit the lass as a man ought to court her who is in every respect her equal?"

."Oh, yes, I have! I have told her a' my love, and a' my sufferings; but it has been only to be mockit, and dismissed about my business."

"And for that ye whine and make wry faces, as yo are doing just now? Na, na, Wat, that's no the gate o't;—a maid maun just be wooed in the same spirit she shows; and when she shows sauciness, there's naething for is but taking a step higher than her in the same humour, letting her always ken, and always see, that you are naturally her superior, and that you havena forgotten that you are even stooping from your dignity when you condescend to ask her to become your equal. If she refuse to be your joe at the fair, never either whine or look disappointed, but be sure to wale the bonniest lass you can get in the market, and lead her to the same party where your saucy dame is. Take her to the top o' the dance, the top o' the table at dinner, and laugh, and sing; and aye between hands, whisper your bonny partner; and if your ain lass disna happen to be unco weel buckled, it is ten to ane she will find an opportunity of offering you her company afore night. If she look angry or offended at your attention to others, you are sure o' her. They are queer creatures the lasses, Wat, and I rather dread ye haena muckle skill or experience in their bits o' wily gates. For, to tell you the truth, there's naething pleases me sae weel as to see them begin to pout, and prim their bits o' gabs, and look sulky out frae the wick o' the ee, and gar ilka feather and flower-knot quiver wi' their angry capers; for let me tell you, it is a great matter to get them to take offence—it lets a man see they are vexed for the loss o' him."

"If you had ever loved as I do, Jock, ye wad hae found little comfort in their offence. For my part every disdainfu' word that yon dear lovely lassie says, gangs to my heart like a red-hot spindle. My life is bound up in her favour. It is only in it that I can live, move, or breathe; and whenever she says a severe or cutting word to me, I feel as if ane o' my members were torn away, and I am glad to escape as lang as I am ony thing ava; for I find, if I war to remain, a few mae siccan sentences wad soon annihilate me."

"Ou ay! you're a buirdly chield, to be sure; but I have nae doubt ye wad melt away like snaw off a dike, or a dead sheep weel pykit by the corbies! Wow, man, but it maks me wae to think o't! and sae, to save you frae sic a melancholy end, I shall take in hand to bring her to your ain terms, in three months' time, if you will take my advice."

"O man, speak; for ye are garring a' the blood in my

veins rin up to my head, as gin it war a thousand ants galloping like mad, running races."

"Weel, Wat, in the first place, I propose to gang down yonder a night by mysell, and speak baith to her father and her, to find how the land lies; and after that we can gang down baith thegither, and gie her a fair broadside.—The deil's in't, if we sanna bring her to reason."

Wat scratched his head, and pulled the grass (that was quite blameless in the affair) furiously up by the roots, but made no answer. On being urged to declare his sentiments, he said, "I dinna ken about that way o' ganging down your lane; I wish you maunna stick by the auld fisher's rule, 'Every man for his ain hand.' For I ken weel, that nae man alive can see her, and speak to her, and no be in love wi' her."

• "It is a good thing in love affairs, Wat, that there are hardly two in the world wha think the same way."

"Ay, but this is a particular case; for a' the men in the country think the same gate here, and rin the same gate to the wooing. It is impossible to win near the house on a Friday night without knocking your head against that of some rival. Na, na, John, this plan o' ganging down by yoursell winna do. And now when I think on't, ye had better no gang down ava; for if we gang down friends, we'll come up enemies; and that wadna be a very agreeable catastroff."

"Now shame fa' me, gin ever I heard sic nonsense! To think that a' the warld see wi' your een! Hear ye, Wat—I wadna gie that snap o' my fingers for her. I never saw her till Sunday last, when I came to your kirk ance errand for that purpose, and I wadna ken her again gin I war to meet her here come out to the glen wi' your whey—what ails you, ye fool, that you're dighting your een?"

"Come out to the glen wi' *my* whey! Ah, man! the words gaed through me like the stang of a bumbee. Come out to the glen wi' my whey! Gude forgie my sin, what is the reason I canna thole that thought? That

were a consummation devoutly to be wussed, as the sol-
oquy in the Collection says.   I fear I'll never see that
blessed sight ! But, Jock, take my advice ; stay at hame,
and gangna near her, gin ye wad enjoy ony peace o' conscience."

"Ye ken naething about women, Wat, and as little
about me.   If I gang near her, it will only be to humble
her a wee, and bring her to reason, for your sake.  Jock
the Jewel wadna say 'Wae's me !' for the best lass's
frown in a' the Kingdom o' Britain—whatever some of
them might do for his."

Jock the Jewel went down in all his might and high
experience, to put every thing to rights between his
friend Wat and the bonny Snaw-fleck, as this pink of a
mountain damsel was called : For be it understood, that
every girl in the parish was named after one of the birds
of the air ; and every man, too, young and old, had his
by-name, by which we shall distinguish them all for the
present.   Thus the Snaw-fleck's father was called Tod-
Lowrie, (the fox ;) his eldest daughter, the Eagle ; the
second, the Sea-maw ; and his only son was denominated
the Foumart, (polecat,) on account of a notable hunt he
once had with one of these creatures in the middle of the
night, in a strange house ;—and it was the worst name I
ever heard for a young man.   Our disconsolate lover was
called Window Wat, on account of his bashful nature,
and, as was alleged, because he was in the habit of hanging about the windows when he went a-courting, and
never venturing in.   It was a good while after this first
rencounter before the two shepherds met again with the
opportunity of resuming the discussion of their love affairs.
But at length an occasion offered, and then——But we
must suffer every man to tell his own tale, else the sport
will be spoilt

"Weel, Wat, hae ye been ony mair down at Lowrie's
Lodge, sin' I saw you ?"

"And if I hae, I hae been little the better o' you.   I
heard that you were there before me—and sinsyne too."

"Now, Wat, that's mere jealousy and suspicion, for

ye didna see the lass to ken whether I was there or not.
I ken ye wad be hinging about the window-soles as usual,
keeking in, feasting your een, seeing other woosters
beiking their shins at the ingle; but for a' that, durstna
venture ben. Come, I dinna like siccan sachless gates
as thae. I *was* down, I'se no deny't, but I gaed to wark
in a manner different from yours. Unco cauldrife wark
that o' standing peenging about windows, man! Come,
tell me a' your expedition, and I'll tell you mine,—like
friends, ye ken."

" Mine's no ill to tell. I gaed down that night after
I saw you, e'en though Wednesday be the widower's
night. More than I were there, but I was fear'd ye had
got there afore me, and then, wi' your great skill o' the
ways o' women, ye might hae left me nae chance at a'.
I was there, but I might as weel hae staid at hame, for
there were sae mony o' the out-wale wallie-tragle kind o'
wooers there, like mysell, a' them that canna win forret
on a Friday night, that I got the back o' the hallan to
keep; but there's ae good thing about the auld Tod's
house,—they never ditt up their windows. Ane sees
aye what's gaun on within doors. They leave a' their
actions open to the ee o' man, yon family; and I often
think it is nae ill sign o' them. Auld Tod-Lowrie himsell
sometimes looks at the window in a kind o' considering
mood, as if doubtful that at that moment he is both overheard and overseen; but, or it is lang, he cocks up his
bonnet and cracks as crouse as ever, as if he thought
again. There's aye ae ee that sees me at a' times, and a
ear that hears me; and when that's the case, what need
I care for a' the birkies o' the land!—I like that open
independent way that the family has. But O, they are
surely sair harassed wi' wooers!"

" The wooers are the very joy o' their hearts, except-
ing the Foumart's; he hates them a' unless they can tell
him hunders o' lies about battles, bogles, and awfu' murders, and persecutions. And the leaving o' the windows
open too is not without an aim. The Eagle is beginning
to weary for a husband; and if ye'll notice how dink she

dresses hersell ilka night, and jinks away at the muckle
wheel as she war spinning for a wager.    They hae found
out that they are often seen at night, yon lasses ; and
though they hae to work the foulest work o' the bit farm
a' the day when naebody sees them, at night they are a'
dressed up like pet-ewes for a market, and ilka ane is
acting a part.    The Eagle is yerking on at the wheel,
and now and then gieing a smirk wi' her face to the window.    The snaw-fleck sits busy in the neuk, as sleek as
a kinnen, and the auld clocker fornent her admiring and
misca'ing her a' the time.    The white Sea-maw flees up
and down the house, but and ben, ae while i' the spence,
ane i' the awmrie, and then to the door wi' a soap-suds.
Then the Foumart, he sits knitting his stocking, and
quarrelling wi' the haill o' them.    The feint a haet he
minds but sheer ill nature.    If there be a good body i'
the house, the auld Tod is the ane.    He is a geyan honest, downright carle, the Tod."

"It is hardly the nature o' a tod to be sae; and there's
no ae bit o' your description that I gang in wi'! It is a
fine douse family.

> 'But O the Snaw-fleck!
> The bonny bonny Snaw-fleck!
> She is the bird for me, O!'"

"If love wad make you a poeter, Wat, I wad say it
had wrought miracles.    Ony mair about the bonny Snaw-
fleck, eh? I wonder how you can make glowing love-sangs
standing at a cauld window—No the way that, man.  Tell
me plainly, did ye ever get a word o' the bonny lass ava?"

"Hey how me!—I can hardly say that I did ; and
yet I hae been three times there sin' I saw you."

"And gat your travel for your pains a' the times?"

"No sae bad as that, neither.   I had the pleasure o'
seeing her, bonny, braw, innocent, and happy, busy working her mother's wark.    I saw her smile at her brother's
crabbit words, and I saw the approving glances beam frae
the twa auld folk's een.    When her father made family-
worship, she took her Bible, and followed devoutly wi'

her ee the words o' holy writ, as the old man read them;
and her voice in singing the psalm was as mellow and as
sweet as the flute playing afar off. Ye may believe me,
Jock, when I saw her lift up her lovely face in sweet devotion, I stood on the outside o' the window and grat like
a bairn. It was mair than my heart could thole; and
gin it warna for shame, I wad gang every night to enjoy
the same heavenly vision."

"As I'm a Christian man, Wat, I believe love *has*
made a poeter of you. Ye winna believe me, man, that
very woman is acting her part. Do you think she didna
ken that ye saw her, and was making a' thae fine mur-
geons to throw glamour in your een, and gar you trow
she was an angel? I managed otherwise; but it is best
to tell a' plain out, like friends, ye ken. Weel, down I
goes to Lowrie's Lodge, and, like you, keeks in at the
window; and the first thing I saw was the auld Tod
toving out tobacco-reek like a moorburn. The haill big-
gin was sae chokefu' o' the vapour, it was like a dark
mist, and I could see naething through it but his ain
braid bonnet moving up and down like the tap o' the
smith's bellows, at every poogh he gave. At length he
handit by the pipe to the auld wife, and the reek soon
turned mair moderate. I could then see the lasses a'
dressed out like dolls, and several young boobies o' hinds,
thrashers, and thrum-cutters, sitting gashing and glowr-
ing among them.——I shall soon set your backs to the
wa', thinks I, if I could get ony possible means o' introduction.——It wasna lang till ane offered; out comes a
lass wi' a cog o' warm water, and she gars it a' clash on
me. 'Thanks t'ye for your kindness, my woman,' says
I. 'Ye canna say I hae gi'en ye a cauld reception,' says
she. 'But wha are ye, standing like a thief i' the mirk?'
——'Maybe kenn'd folk, gin it war daylight,' quo' I. 'Ye
had better come in by, and see gin candle-light winna
beet the mister,' says she. 'Thanks t'ye,' says I; 'but
I wad rather hae you to come *out by*, and try gin stern-
light winna do!'——'Catch me doing that,' cried she, and
bounced into the house again.

" I then laid my lug close to the window, and heard ane asking wha that was she was speaking to ? ' I dinna ken him,' quo' she ; ' but I trow I hae gi'en him a mark to ken him by ; I hae gi'en him a balsam o' boiling water.'

" ' I wish ye may hae peeled a' the hide aff his shins,' quo' the Foumart, and he mudged and leugh ; ' haste ye, dame, rin awa out and lay a plaster o' lime and lin-seed-oil to the lad's trams,' continued he.

" ' I can tell ye wha it is,' said ane o' the hamlet wooers ; ' it will be Jock the Jewel comed down frae the moors ; for I saw him waiting about the chop and the smiddy till the darkness came on. If ye hae disabled him, lady Seabird, the wind will blaw nae mair out o' the west.'

" I durstna trust them wi' my character and me in hearing ; sae, without mair ado, I gangs bauldly ben.—— ' Gude e'en to ye, kimmers a' in a ring,' says I.

" ' Gude-e'en t'ye, honest lad,' quo' the Eagle. ' How does your cauld constitution and our potatoe-broo sort ?'

" ' Thanks t'ye, bonny lass,' says I. ' I hae gotten a right sair skelloch ; but I wish I warna woundit nae deeper somewhere else than i' the shinbanes ; I might shoot a flying herne for a' that's come and gane yet.'

" ' That's weel answered, lad,' quo' the Tod. ' Keep her down, for she's unco glib o' the gab,——especially to stran-gers.'

" ' You will never touch a feather o' her wing, lad,' quo she. ' But if ye could——I'll say nae mair.'

" ' Na, na, Mistress Eagle, ye soar ower high for me, says I. ' I'll bring down nae sky-cleaving harpies to pick the een out o' my sheep, and my ain into the bargain, maybe. I see a bit bonny norland bird in the nook here, that I would rather woo to my little hamely nest. The Eagle maun to her eyry ; or, as the auld ballant says——

> ' Gasp and speel to her yermit riven,
> Amid the mists and the rains of heaven.

It is the innocent, thrifty little Snaw-fleck that will suit me, wi' the white wings and the blue body. She's pleased wi' the hardest and hameliest fare; a picking o' the seeds o' the pipe-bent is a feast to her.' "

" Now, by the faith o' my body, Jewel, that wasna fair. Was that preparing the way for your friend's success ?"

" Naething but sheer banter, man; like friends, ye ken. But ye sall hear. ' The Snaw-fleck's a braw beast,' said I, ' but the Eagle's a waster and a destroyer.'

" ' She's true to her mate, though,' said the dame; ' but the tither is a bird o' passage, and mate to the haill flock.'

" I was a wee startled at this observe, when I thought of the number of wooers that were rinning after the bonny Snaw-fleck. However, I didna like to yield to the haughty Eagle; and I added, that I wad take my chance o' the wee Snaw-bird, for though she war ane of a flock, that flock was an honest ane. This pleased them a'; and the auld slee Tod, he spake up and said, he hadna the pleasure o' being acquaint wi' me, but he hoped he shouldna hae it in his power to say sae again. Only there was ae thing he beggit to remind me o', before I went any farther, and that was, that the law of Padan-aram was established in his family, and he could by no means give a younger daughter in marriage before one that was elder.

" ' I think you will maybe keep them for a gay while, then,' said the Foumart. ' But if the Sea-gull wad stay at hame, I carena if the rest were at Bamph. She's the only usefu' body I see about the house.'

" ' Haud the tongue o' thee, thou illfa'red, cat-witted serf,' said the auld wife. ' I'm sure ony o' them's worth a faggald o' thee! And that lad, gin I dinna forecast aglee, wad do credit to ony kin.'

" ' He's rather ower weel giftit o' the gab,' quo' the menseless thing. This remark threw a damp on my spirits a' the night after, and I rather lost ground than gained ony mair. The ill-hued weazel-blawn thing of a brother, never missed an opportunity of gieing me a yerk wi' his ill-scrapit tongue, and the Eagle was aye gieing

hints about the virtues o' potatoe-broo.   The auld Tod
chewed tobacco and threw his mouth, lookit whiles at ane
and whiles at anither, and seemed to enjoy the joke as
muckle as ony o' them.   As for the bonny Snaw-bird,
she never leugh aboon her breath, but sat as mim and
as sleek as a moudie.   There were some very pretty
smiles and dimples gaun, but nae gaffawing.   She is
really a fine lass."

"There it goes now! I tauld you how it would be! I
tell you, Jewel, the deil a bit o' this is fair play."

"Ane may tell what he thinks—like a friend, ye ken.
Weel—to make a lang tale short—I couldna help seeing
a' the forenight that she had an ee to me.   I couldna
help *that*, ye ken.   Gat mony a sweet blink and smile
thrawn o'er the fire to me—couldna help that either, ye
ken—never lost that a friend gets.   But at length a'
the douce wooers drew off ane by ane—saw it was needless to dispute the point wi' me that night.   Ane had to
gang home to supper his horses, another to fodder the
kye, and another had to be hame afore his master took
the book, else he had to gang supperless to bed.   I sat
still—needless to lose a good boon for lack o' asking.
The potatoes were poured and champit—naebody bade
me bide to supper; but I sat still; and the auld wife she
slippit away to the awmrie, and brought a knoll o' butter
like ane's nieve, and slippit that into the potatoe-pot
hidling ways, but the fine flavour that filled the house
soon outed the secret.   I drew in my seat wi' the rest,
resolved to hae my share.   I saw that I had a hearty
welcome frae them a' but the Foumart, and I loot him
girn as muckle as he likit.   Weel, I saw it was turning
late, and there was a necessity for proceeding to business, else the prayers wad be on.   Sae I draws to my
plaid and staff, and I looks round to the lasses; but in
the mean time I dropt half a wink to the Snaw-fleck, and
I says, 'Weel, wha o' you bonny lasses sets me the
length o' the townhead yett the night?'

"'The feint a ane o' them,' quo' the Foumart wi' a
girn.

" ' The townhead yett the night, honest lad?' quo' the wife. ' Be my certe, thou's no gaun nae siccan a gaet. Dis thou think thou can gang to the muirs the night? Nay, nay, thou shalt take share of a bed wi' our son till it be day, for the night's dark and the road's eiry."

" ' He needna stay unless he likes,' quo' the Foumart.

" ' Haud thy tongue,' said the wife. So I sat down again, and we grew a' unco silent. At length the Eagle rose and flew to the door. It wadna do—I wadna follow; sat aye still, and threw another straight wink to the bonny Snaw-fleck, but the shy shirling sat snug in her corner, and wadna move. At length the Eagle comes gliding in, and in a moment, or ever I kenn'd what I was doing, claps down a wee table at my left hand, and the big Bible and psalm-book on't. I never got sic a stound, and really thought I wad sink down through the floor; and when I saw the lasses shading their faces wi' their hands, I grew waur.

" ' What ails thee, honest lad, that thou looks sae baugh?' said the auld wife. ' Sure thou's no ashamed to praise thy Maker? for an thou be, I shall be ashamed o' thee. It is an auld family custom we hae, aye to gie a stranger the honour o' being our leader in this duty; and gin he refuse that, we dinna countenance him nae mair.'

" That was a yerker! I now fand I was fairly in the mire. For the saul o' me I durstna take the book; for though I had a good deal o' good words by heart, I didna ken how I might gar them compluther. And as I took this to be a sort o' test to try a wooer's abilities, I could easily see that my hough was fairly i' the sheep-crook, and that what wi' sticking the psalm, bungling the prayer, potatoe-broo and a' thegither, I was like to come badly off. Sae I says, ' Gudewife, I'm obliged t'ye for the honour ye hae offered me; and sae far frae being ashamed o' my Maker's service, I rejoice in it; but I hae mony reasons for declining the honour. In the first place, war I to take the task out o' the gudeman's hand, it wad be like the youngest scholar o' the school pretending to teach his master; and were I to stay here a' night; it wad be principally for the purpose of hearing family worship frae his ain lips. But the truth is, and that's my great reason, I *can not* stay a' night. I want just ae single word o' this bonny lass, and then I maun take the road, for I'm far ower late already.'

" 'I bide by my text, young man,' says the Tod; 'the law of Padanaram is the law of this house.'

" 'And, by the troth o' me, thou'lt find it nae bad law for thee, honest lad,' said the wife; 'our eldest will meak the *best* wife for thee—teak thou my word for that.'

" 'Maybe she wad,' said I, 'but I want just a single word wi' this dink chicken; but it isna on my ain account—it is a word frae a friend, and I'm bound in honour to deliver it.'

" 'That is spoken sae like an honest man, and a disinterested ane,' quo' the Tod, 'that I winna refuse the boon. Gae your ways ben to our ben-end, and say what ye hae to say; for I dinna suffer my bairns to gang out i' the dark wi' strangers.'

" 'Come away, then, hinny,' says I. She rose wi' slow and ill will, for I saw she wad rather I had been to speak for mysell; and as I perceived this, as soon as I got her ben the house, and the door fairly steekit, I says till her, says I, 'Now, bonny lassie, I never saw your face afore but aince, and that day I gaed mony fit to see't. I came here the night aince errand to speak a word for a friend, but really'—Here she interrupted me as soon as she heard *but really*.

" 'Could your friend no speak his word himsell?' said she.

" 'As you say,' says I; 'that is good sense—I ca' that good, sound common sense; for a man does always his own turn best; and therefore I maun tell you, that I am fairly fa'en in love wi' you mysell, and am determined to hae you for my ain, cost what it will.' "

At this part of the story, Wat sprung to his feet— " Did you say sae?" said he. " If ye did, ye are a fause

loun, and a villain, and I am determined to hae penny-
worths o' *you*, cost what it will.

" Hout, fych, fie, Wat, man! dinna be a fool. Sit
down, and let us listen to reason, like friends, ye ken.
Ye sall hear, man——ye sall hear."

" I winna hear another word, Jewel. Up to your feet;
either single stick or dry nieves, ony o' them ye like.
Ye gat the lass ben the house on the credit o' my name,
and that was the use you made o't! Ye dinna ken how
near my heart, and how near my life, ye war edging then,
and I'll break every bane in your bouk for it; only ye
shall hae fair play, to smash mine, gin ye can. Up, I
say; for yon was a deed I winna brook."

" Perhaps I was wrang; but I'll speak the truth. Sit
down, and ye shall hear——and then, gin we maun fight,
there's time enough for it after. If I had thought I
acted wrang, I wadna hae tauld it sae plain out; but
when twa folk think the saame gate, it isna a good sign.
' I'm in love wi' you, and am determined to hae you,'
says I.

" ' I winna hear a single word frae ane that's betraying
his friend,' said she;——'not one word, after your avowal
to my father. If he hae ony private word, say it——and
if no, good night.'

" Did she say that, the dear creature? Heaven bless
her bonny face!"

" ' I did promise to a particular friend o' mine to speak
a kind word for him,' said I. ' He is unco blate and
modest, but there's no a better lad; and I never saw ane
as deeply and as distractedly in love; for though I feel
I *do* love, it is with reason and moderation.' "

" There again!" cried Wat, who had begun to hold
out his hand——" There again! Do you ca' that acting
like a faithfu' friend?"

" ' Not a word of yourself,' said she. ' Who is this
friend of yours! And has he any more to say by
you? Not one word more of yourself——at least not
to-night.' "

" At least not to-night!" repeated Wat, again and

again—"Did she say that? I dinna like the addition ava."

"That was what she said; and naething could be plainer than that she was inviting me back; but as I was tied down, I was obliged to say something about you. 'Ye ken Window Wat?' says I. 'He is o'er sight and 'udgment in love wi' you, and he comes here aince or twice every week, just for the pleasure o' seeing you through the window. He's a gay queer compost— for though he is a' soul, yet he wants spirit.' "

"Did ye ca' me a compost? That was rather a queer term, begging your pardon," observed Wat.

" 'I hae seen the lad sometimes,' says she. 'If he came here to see me, he certainly need not be sae muckle ashamed of his errand as not to show his face. I think him a main saft ane.'

" 'Ye're quite i' the wrang, lass,' says I. 'Wat's a great dab. He's an arithmeticker, a 'stronomer, a historian, and a grand poeter, and has made braw sangs about yoursell. What think ye o' being made a wife to sic a hero as him? Od help ye, it will raise ye as high as the moon.' "

" I'll tell ye what it is, Jock the Jewel—the neist time ye gang to court, court for yoursell; for a' that ye hae said about me is downright mockery, and it strikes me that you are baith a selfish knave and a gommeril. Sae good e'en t'ye for the present. I owe you a good turn for your kind offices down by. I'll speak for mysell in future, and do ye the same—*like friends ye ken,*—that's a' I say."

" If I speak for mysell, I ken wha will hae but a poor chance," cried Jock after him.

The next time our two shepherds met, it was in the identical smithy adjoining to Lowrie's Lodge, and that at six o'clock on a December evening. The smith looked exceedingly wise, and when he heard the two swains begin to cut and sneer at one another, it was delicate food for Vulcan. He puffed and blew at the bellows, and thumped at the stithy, and always between put in a disjointed

word or two.—" Mae hunters! mae hunters for the Tod's
bairns—hem, phoogh, phoogh—will be worried now !—
phoogh "—thump, thump—" will be run down now—
hem !"

" Are ye gaun far this way the night, Jewel, an ane
may spier ? "

" Far enough for you, Wat, I'm thinking. How has
the praying been coming on this while bygane ? "

" What d'ye mean, Mr Jewel ? If ye will speak, let
it no be in riddles. Rather speak nonsense, as ye used
to do."

" I am speaking in nae riddles, lad. I wat weel a'
the country-side kens that ye hae been gaun learning
prayers aff Hervey's Meditations, and crooning them o'er
to yoursell in every cleuch o' the glen, a' to tame a young
she-fox wi'."

" And that ye hae been lying under the hands o' the
moor doctor a month, and submitting to an operation,
frae the effects o' somebody's potatoe-broo—isna that as
weel kent ? "

" Till't, lads, till't ! " cried the smith— " that's the right
way o' ganging to wark—phoogh ! "—clink, clink—" pep-
per away ! "—clink, clink—" soon be baith as het as
nailstrings—phoogh ! "

The mention of the potatoe-broo somewhat abated
Jock's sarcastic humour, for he had suffered much incon-
venience from the effects of it, and the circumstance had
turned the laugh against him among his companions. Ere
long he glided from the smithy, and after that Wat sat
in the fidgets for fear his rival had effected a previous
engagement with the Snaw-fleck. The smith perceiving
it, seized him in good-humour, and turned him out at
the door. " Nae time to stay now, lad—nae time to
wait here now. The hunt will be up and the young Tod
holed, if ye dinna make a' the better speed." Then, as
Wat vanished down the way, the smith imitated the
sound of the fox-hounds and the cries of the huntsmen.
" Will be run down now, thae young Tods—heavy metal
laid on now—we'll have a walding heat some night, an

the track keep warm," said the smith, as he fell to the big bellows with both hands.

When Wat arrived at Lowrie's Lodge, he first came in contact with one wooer, and then another, hanging about the corners of the house; but finding that none of them was his neighbour and avowed rival, he hasted to his old quiet station at the back window, not the window where the Jewel stood when he met with his mischance, but one right opposite to it. There he saw the three bonniest birds of the air surrounded with admirers, and the Jewel sitting cheek by cheek with the lovely Snaw-bird. The unbidden tears sprung to Wat's eyes, but it was not from jealousy, but from the most tender affection, as well as intense admiration, that they had their source. The other wooers that were lingering without, joined him at the window; and Wat feeling this an incumbrance, and eager to mar his rival's success, actually plucked up courage, and strode in amongst them all.

———

" How came the twa moorland chiels on at the court-ing the other night ? "

" It's hard to say; there are various accounts about the matter."

" What does the smith say ?—for though his sentences are but short, he says them loud enough, and often enough ower, and folks reckon there's aye some truth in the foundation."

" I can tell ye what he says, for I heard him on the subject aftener than aince, and his information was pre-cisely as follows :—' The Tod's bairns maun gang now, lads—I'm saying, the Tod's bairns maun gang now—eh, Menye ?—fairly run down. Half-a-dozen tykes ower sair for ae young Tod—eh ? Fairly holed the young ane, it seems—I'm saying, the young ane's holed. Nought but a pick and shool wantit to hook her, Jewel has gi'en mouth there—I'm saying, auld Jewel has gi'en mouth there. Poor Wat has been obliged to turn to 'the auld ane——he's on the full track o' her——I'm saying, he's after her, full trot. But some thinks she'll turn her tail to a craig, and wear him up. It was Wat that got the honour o' the beuk, though——I'm saying, it was him that took the beuk——wan gloriously through, too. The saxteenth o' the Romans, without a hamp, hinny. Was that true, think ye?——I'm saying, think ye that was true? Cam to the holy kiss; a' the wooers' teeth watered——eh? ——Think ye that was true, hinny? The Jewel was amaist comed to grips at that verse about the kiss——eh?——I'm saying, the Jewel closed wi' the beauty there, I'm saying ——Ha! ha!——I think that wadna be true.'——This is the length the smith's information gangs."

"I'm sure, gin the Snaw-fleck take the Jewel, in preference to Wat, it will show a strange perversion of taste."

"O, there's naebody can answer for the fancies of a woman. But they're a geyan auld-farrant set the Tods, and winna be easily outwitted. Did ye no hear ought of a moonlight-match that was to be there?"

"Not a word; and if I had, I wadna hae believed it."

"The Jewel has been whispering something to that effect; he's sae uplifted, he canna haud his tongue; and I dinna wonder at it. But, for a' the offers the bonny lass had, that she should fix on him, is a miracle. Time tries a'; and Jock may be cheated yet."

Yes, time is the great trier of human events. Let any man review his correspondences for ten years back, and he will then see how widely different his own prospects of the future have been from the lessons taught him by that hoary monitor Time. But, for the present, matters turned out as the fortunate wooer had insinuated; for, in a short month after this confabulation had taken place, the auld Tod's helpmate arose early one morning, and began a-bustling about the house in her usual busy way, and always now and then kept giving hints to her bonny lasses to rise and begin to their daily tasks.—— "Come, stir ye, stir ye, my bonny bairns. When the sterns o' heaven hae gane to their beds, it is time the

flowers o' the yird war rising—Come, come !—No stir-
ring yet ?—Busk ye, busk ye, like thrifty bairns, and
dinna let the lads say that ye are sleepie dowdies, that
lie in your beds till the sun burns holes in your cover-
lets. Fie, fie !—There has been a reek i' Jean Lowrie's
lum this half-hour. The moor-cock has crawed, the
mawkin cowered, and the whaup yammered abune the
flower. Streek your young limbs—open your young
een—a foot on the cauld floor, and sleep will soon be
aboon the cluds.—Up, up, my winsome bairns !'

The white Lady-Seabird was soon afoot, for she slept
by herself; but the old dame still kept speaking away to
the other two, at one time gibing, at another coaxing
them to rise, but still there was no answer. " Peace be
here, Helen, but this is an unco sleep-sleeping !" said she
—" What has been asteer owernight? I wish your twa
titties haena been out wi' the men ?"

" Ay, I wish they binna out wi' them still ; for I heard
them steal out yestreen, but I never heard them steal in
again."

The old wife ran to the bed, and in a moment was
heard exclaiming,—" The sorrow be i' my een gin ever
I saw the like o' that ! I declare the bed's as cauld as a
curling-stane !—Ay, the nest's cauld, and the birds are
flown. Oh, wae be to the day ! wae be to the day !
Gudeman, gudeman, get up and raise the parishen, for
our bairns are baith stown away !"

" Stown away !" cried the father—" What does the
woman mean ?"

" Ay, let them gang," cried the son; "they're weel
away, gin they bide."

" Tewhoo ! hoo-hoo !" cried the daughter, weeping,
—" That comes o' your laws o' Padanaram ! What had
ye ado with auld Laban's rules ? Ye might hae letten us
gang aff as we could win.—There, I am left to spin tow,
wha might hae been married the first, had it no been for
your daft laws o' Padanaram."

The girl cried, the son laughed, the old woman raved
and danced through very despair, but the gudeman took

the matter quite calmly, as if determined to wait the issue with resignation, for better or worse.

"Haud your tongues, ilk ane o' ye," said he—"What's a' the fy-gae-to about? I hae that muckle to trust to my lasses, that I can lippen them as weel out o' my sight as in my sight, and as weel wi' young men as wi' auld women. Bairns that are brought up in the fear, nurture, and admonition o' their Maker, will aye swee to the right side, and sae will mine. Gin they thought they had a right to choose for themselves, they war right in exercising that right; and I'm little feared that their choices be bad anes, or yet that they be contrary to my wishes. Sae I rede you to haud a' your tongues, and tak nae mair notice o' ought that has happened, than if it hadna been. We're a' in gude hands to guide us; and though we whiles pu' the reins out o' His hand to tak a' gallop our ain gate, yet He winna leave us lang to our ain direction."

With these sagacious words, the auld sly Tod settled the clamour and outcry in his family that morning; and the country has never doubted to this day, that he plowed with his own heifers.

On the evening previous to this colloquy, the family of the Tods went to rest at an early hour. There had been no wooers admitted that night; and no sooner had the two old people begun to breathe deep, than the eldest and youngest girls, who slept in an apartment by themselves, and had every thing in readiness, eloped from their father's cot, the Eagle with a lightsome heart and willing mind, but the younger with many fears and misgivings. For thus the matter stood:—Wat sighed and pined in love for the Snaw-fleck, but he was young and modest, and could not tell his mind; but he was such a youth as a maiden would love,—handsome, respectable, and virtuous; and a match with him was so likely, that no one ever supposed the girl would make objections to it. Jock, on the other hand, was nearly twice her age, talkative, forward, and self-conceited; and, it was thought, rather wanted to win the girl for a brag, than for any

great love he bore her.    But Jock was rich; and when
one has told that, he has told enough.    In short, the
admired, the young, the modest, and reserved Snaw-
fleck, in order to get quit of her father's laws of Padanaram, agreed to make a run-away marriage with Jock
the Jewel.    But what was far more extraordinary, her
youthful lover agreed to accompany her as bridesman,
and, on that account, it may possibly be supposed, her
eldest sister never objected to accompany her as
maid.

The shepherds had each of them provided himself
with a good horse, saddle, and pillion; and, as the custom is, the intended bride was committed to the care of
the best-man, and the Eagle was mounted behind her
brother-in-law that was to be.    It was agreed, before
mounting, that in case of their being parted in the dark
by a pursuit, or any other accident, their place of rendezvous was to be at the Golden Harrow, in the Candle-
maker-Row, towards which they were to make with all
speed.

They had a wild moorland path to traverse for some
space, on which there were a multiplicity of tracks, but
no definitive road.    The night was dark and chill, and,
on such ground, the bride was obliged to ride constantly
with her right hand round Wat's waist, and Wat was
obliged to press that hand to his bosom, for fear of its
being cold; and in the excess of his politeness he mag-
nified the intemperance of the night at least sevenfold.
When pressing that fair hand to his bosom, Wat sometimes thought to himself, what a hard matter it was that
it should so soon be given away to another; and then
he wiped a tear from his eye, and did not speak again
for a good while.    Now the night, as was said, being
very dark, and the bride having made a pleasant remark,
Wat spontaneously lifted that dear hand from his bosom,
in order to attempt passing it to his lips, but (as he told
me himself) without the smallest hope of being permit-
ted.    But behold, the gentle ravishment was never resis-
ted? On the contrary, as Wat replaced the insulted hand

in his bosom, he felt the pressure of his hand gently returned.

Wat was confounded, electrified ! and felt as the scalp of his head had been contracting to a point. He felt, in one moment, as if there had been a new existence sprung up within him, a new motive for life, and for every great and good action ; and, without any express aim, he felt a disposition to push onward. His horse soon began to partake of his rider's buoyancy of spirits, (which a horse always does,) so he cocked up his ears, mended his pace, and, in a short time, was far ahead of the heavy, stagnant-blooded beast on which the Jewel bridegroom and his buxom Eagle rode. She had *her* right arm round *his* waist too, of course ; but her hand lacked the exhilarating qualities of her lovely sister's ; and yet one would have thought that the Eagle's looks were superior to those of most young girls outgone thirty.

" I wish thae young fools wad take time and ride at leisure ; we'll lose them on this black moor a'thegither, and then it is a question how we may foregather again," said the bridegroom ; at the same time making his hazel sapling play yerk on the hind-quarters of his nag. " Gin the gowk let aught happen to that bit lassie o' mine under cloud o' night, it wad be a' ower wi' me—I could never get aboon that. There are some things, ye ken, Mrs Eagle, for a' your sneering, that a man can never get aboon."

" No very-mony o' them, gin a chield hae ony spirit," returned the Eagle. " Take ye time, and take a little care o' your ain neck and mine. Let them gang their gates. Gin Wat binna tired o' her, and glad to get quat o' her, or they win to the Ports o' Edinburgh, I hae tint my computation."

" Na, if he takes care o' *her*, that's a' my dread," rejoined he, and at the same time kicked viciously with both heels, and applied the sapling with great vigour. But " the mair haste the waur speed" is a true proverb ; for the horse, instead of mending his pace, slackened it, and absolutely grew so frightened for the gutters on the

moor, that he would hardly be persuaded to take one of
them, even though the sapling sounded loud and thick
on his far loin.   He tried this ford, and the other ford,
and smelled and smelled with long-drawn breathings.
" Ay, ye may snuff!" cried Jock, losing all patience ;
" the deil that ye had ever been foaled !—Hilloa ! Wat
Scott, where are ye ?"

" Hush, hush, for gudesake," cried the Eagle ; " ye'll
raise the country, and put a' out thegither."

They listened for Wat's answer, and at length heard a
far-away whistle.   The Jewel grew like a man half distracted, and in spite of the Eagle's remonstrances, thrashed on his horse, cursed him, and bellowed out still the
more ; for he suspected what was the case, that, owing
to the turnings and windings of his horse among the
haggs, he had lost his aim altogether, and knew not
which way he went.   Heavens ! what a stentorian voice
he sent through the moor before him ! but he was only
answered by the distant whistle, that still went farther
and farther away.

When the bride heard these loud cries of desperation
so far behind, and in a wrong direction, she was mightily
tickled, and laughed so much that she could hardly keep
her seat on the horse ; at the same time, she continued
urging Wat to ride, and he, seeing her so much amused
and delighted at the embarrassment of her betrothed and
sister, humoured her with equal good-will, rode off, and
soon lost all hearing of the unfortunate bridegroom.
They came to the high-road at Middleton, cantered on
and reached Edinburgh by break of day, laughing all the
way at their unfortunate companions.   Instead, however,
of putting up at the Golden Harrow, in order to render
the bridegroom's embarrassment still more complete, at
the bride's suggestion, they went to a different corner of
the city, namely, to the White Horse, Canongate.
There the two spent the morning, Wat as much embarrassed as any man could be, but his lovely companion
quite delighted at the thoughts of *what* Jock and her
sister *would do.*   Wat could not understand her for his

life, and he conceived that she did not understand herself; but perhaps Wat Scott was mistaken. They
breakfasted together; but for all their long and fatiguing
journey, neither of them seemed disposed to eat. At
length Wat ventured to say, "We'll be obliged to gang
to the Harrow, and see what's become o' our friends."

"O no, no! by no means!" cried she fervently; "I
would not, for all the world, relieve them from such a
delightful scrape. What the two *will do* is beyond my
comprehension."

"If ye want just to bamboozle them a'thegither, the
best way to do that is for you and me to marry," said
Wat, "and leave them twa to shift for themselves."

"O that wad be so grand!" said she.

Though this was the thing nearest to honest Wat's
heart of all things in the world, he only made the proposal by way of joke, and as such he supposed himself
answered. Nevertheless, the answer made the hairs of
his head creep once more. "My truly, but that wad gar
our friend Jock loup twa gates at aince!" rejoined Wat.

"It wad be the grandest trick that ever was played
upon man," said she.

"It wad mak an awfu' sound in the country," said Wat.

"It wad gang through the twa shires like a hand-bell,"
said she.

"Od, I really think it is worth our while to try't,"
said he.

"O by a' manner o' means!" cried she, clasping her
hands together for joy.

Wat's breath cut short, and his visage began to alter.
He was likely to acquire the blessing of a wife rather
more suddenly than he anticipated, and he began to wish
that the girl might be in her perfect senses. "My dear
M——," said he, "are you serious? would you really
consent to marry me?"

"Would I consent to marry you!" reiterated she.
"That is siccan a question to speer!"

"It *is* a question," said Wat, "and I think a very
natural ane."

"Ay, it is a question, to be sure," said she; "but it is ane that ye ken ye needna hae put to me to answer, at least till ye had tauld me whether ye wad marry me or no."

"Yes, faith, I will—there's my hand on it," eagerly exclaimed Wat. "Now, what say ye?"

"No," said she;—"that is, I mean—yes."

"I wonder ye war sae lang o' thinking about that," said Wat. "Ye ought surely to hae tauld me sooner."

"Sae I wad, if ever ye had speered the question,' said she.

"What a stupid idiot I was!" exclaimed Wat, and rapped on the floor with his stick for the landlord. "An it be your will, sir, we want a minister," says Wat.

"There's one in the house, sir," said the landlord, chuckling with joy at the prospect of some fun. "Keep a daily chaplain here—Thirlstane's motto, 'Aye ready.' Could ye no contrive to do without him?"

"Na, na, sir, we're folk frae the country," said Wat; "we hae comed far and foul gate for a preevat but honest hand-fasting."

"Quite right, quite right," said my landlord. "Never saw a more comely country couple. Your business is done for you at once;" at the same time he tapped on the hollow of his hand, as much as to say, some reward must be forthcoming. In a few minutes he returned, and setting the one cheek in at the side of the door, said, with great rapidity, "Could not contrive to do without the minister, then? Better?—no getting off again. Better?—what?—Can't do without him?"

"O no, sir," said Wat, who was beginning a long explanatory speech, but my landlord cut him short, by introducing a right reverend divine, more than half-seas over. He was a neat, well-powdered, cheerful little old gentleman, but one who never asked any farther warrant for the marrying of a couple, than the full consent of parties. About this he was very particular, and advised them, in strong set phrases, to beware of entering rashly into that state ordained for the happiness of mankind.

Wat thought he was advising him against the match, but told him he was very particularly situated. Parties soon came to a right understanding, the match was made, the minister had his fee, and afterwards he and the landlord invited themselves to the honour and very particular pleasure of dining with the young couple at two.

What has become of Jock the Jewel and his partner all this while? We left them stabled in a mossy moor, surrounded with haggs, and bogs, and mires, every one of which would have taken a horse over the back; at least so Jock's great strong plough-horse supposed, for he became so terrified that he absolutely refused to take one of them. Now, Jock's horse happened to be wrong, for I know the moor very well, and there is not a bog on it all that will hold a horse still. But it was the same thing in effect to Jock and the Eagle—the horse would have gone eastward or westward along and along and along the sides of these little dark stripes, which he mistook for tremendous quagmires; or if Jock would have suffered him to turn his head homeward, he would, as Jock said, have galloped for joy; but northwards towards Edinburgh, never a step would he proceed. Jock thrashed him at one time, stroked his mane at another, at one time coaxed, at another cursed him, till, ultimately, on the horse trying to force his head homeward in spite of Jock, the latter, in high wrath, struck him a blow on the far ear with all his might. This had the effect of making the animal take the motion of a horizontal wheel, or millstone. The weight of the riders fell naturally to the outer side of the circle—Jock held by the saddle, and the Eagle held by Jock—till down came the whole concern with a thump on the moss. "I daresay that beast's gane mad the night," said Jock; and, rising, he made a spring at the bridle, for the horse continued still to reel; but, in the dark, our hero missed his hold—off went the horse, like an arrow out of a bow, and left our hapless couple in the midst of a black moor.

"What shall we do now?—shall we turn back?" said Jock."

"Turn back!" said the Eagle; "certainly not, unless you hae ta'en the rue."

"I wasna thinking o' that ava," said he; "but, O, it is an unfortunate-like business—I dinna like their leaving o' us, nor can I ken what's their meaning."

"They war fear'd for being catched, owing to the noise that you were making," said she.

"And wha wad hae been the loser gin we had been catched? I think the loss then wad hae faun on me," said Jock.

"We'll come better speed wanting the beast," said she; "I wadna wonder that we are in Edinburgh afore them yet."

Wearied and splashed with mud, the two arrived at the sign of the Harrow, a little after noon, and instantly made inquiries for the bride and best-man. A description of one man answers well enough for another to people quite indifferent. Such a country gentleman as the one described, the landlady said, had called twice in the course of the day, and looked into several rooms, without leaving his name. They were both *sure* it was Wat, and rested content. The gentleman came *not* back, so Jock and the Eagle sat and looked at one another. "They will be looking at the grand things o' this grand town," said she.

"Ay, maybe," said Jock, in manifest discontent. "I couldna say what they may be looking at, or what they may be doing. When folks gang ower the march to be married, they should gang by themselves twa. But some wadna be tauld sae."

"I canna comprehend where he has ta'en my sister to, or what he's doing wi' her a' this time," said the Eagle.

"I couldna say," said Jock, his chagrin still increasing, a disposition which his companion took care to cherish, by throwing out hints and insinuations that kept him constantly in the fidgets; and he seemed to be repenting heartily of the step he had taken. A late hour arrived, and the two, having had a sleepless night and a toilsome day, ordered supper, and apartments for the night. They had not yet sat down to supper, when the landlord requested permission for two gentlemen, acquaintances of his, to take a glass together in the same room with our two friends, which being readily granted, who should enter but the identical landlord and parson who had so opportunely buckled the other couple! They had dined with Wat and his bride, and the whisky-toddy had elicited the whole secret from the happy bridegroom. The old gentlemen were highly tickled with the oddity of the adventure, and particularly with the whimsical situation of the pair at the Harrow; and away they went at length on a reconnoitring expedition, having previously settled the measures to be pursued.

My landlord of the White Horse soon introduced himself to the good graces of the hapless couple by his affability, jokes, quips, and quibbles, and Jock and he were soon as intimate as brothers, and the maid and he as sweethearts, or old intimate acquaintance. He commended her as the most beautiful, handsome, courteous, and accomplished country lady he ever had seen in his life, and at length asked Jock if the lady was his sister. No, she was not. Some near relation, perhaps, that he had the charge of.—No.—"Oh! Beg pardon—perceive very well—plain—evident—wonder at my blindness," said my landlord of the White Horse—"sweetheart— sweetheart? Hope 'tis to be a match? Not take back such a flower to the wilderness—unappropriated—to blush unseen—waste sweetness on the desert air? What? Hope so? Eh? More sense than that, I hope?"

"You mistak, sir; you mistak. My case is a very particular ane;" said Jock.

"I wish it were mine, though," said he of the White Horse.

'Pray, sir, are you a married man?" said the Eagle.

"Married? Oh yes, mim, married and settled in life, with a White Horse," returned he

"A grey mare, you mean," said the Eagle.

" Excellent ! superlative !" exclaimed my landlord. " Minister, what think you of that ? I'm snubbed—cut down—shorn to the quick ! Delightful girl ! something favoured like the young country bride we dined with to-day. What say you, minister ? Prettier, though—decidedly prettier. More animation, too. Girls from the same country-side have always a resemblance."

" Sir, did you say you dined with a bride from our country-side ?" said Jock.

" Did so—did so."

" What was the bridegroom like ?"

" A soft-soles—milk-and-water."

" And his name ? You will not tell, maybe,—a W and an S ?"

" The same—the same—mum !—W.S., writer to the signet. The same. An M and a T, too. You understand ? Mum !"

" Sir, I'll be muckle obliged to you, gin ye'll tak me to where they are. I hae something to say to them," said Jock, with great emphasis.

" Oh ! you are the father, are you ? Minister, I'll take you a bet this is the bride's father and sister. You are too late, sir ; far too late. They are bedded long ago !"

" Bedded !" cried Jock, in a shrill and desperate tone of voice.

" The case is past redemption now," began mine host ; " a father is to be pitied ! but—"

" Sir, you mistak—I'm not her father."

About this stage of the conversation, a letter was handed in "to Miss Tod, at the Golden Harrow ;" but the bearer went off, and waited no answer. The contents were as follows :—

" DEAR SISTER,

THIS cometh to let you know that I have married Walter, thinking you and John had turned on the height, and that he had taken the rue ; so I thought, after leaving the country to be married, I could never set up my face in it again, without a husband; for you know a woman leaving home with a man, as we both have done, can never be received into a church or family again, unless she be married on him; and you must consider of this; for if you are comed to Edinburg with a man, you need never go home again. John hath used me very bad, and made me do the thing I may rue; but I could not help it. I hope he will die an old bachelor, as he is, and never taste the joys of the married state. We will remain here another night, for some refreshment, and then I go home to his mother. This business will make a terrible noise in the country. I would not have gone home, and me not married, for all the whole world."

When the Eagle read this, she assumed symptoms of great distress, and after much beseeching and great attention from the two strangers, she handed the letter to Jock, showing him that she could never go home again after what had happened. He scratched his head often, and acknowledged that "Maggy's was a ticklish case," and then observed that he would see what was to be done about it to-morrow. My landlord called for a huge bowl of punch, which he handed liberally round. The matter was discussed in all its bearings. The minister made it clearly out, that the thing had been foreordained, and it was out of their power to counteract it. My landlord gave the preference to the Eagle in every accomplishment. Jock's heart grew mellow, while the maid blushed and wept; and, in short, they went to bed that night a married couple, to the great joy of the Eagle's heart; for it was never once doubted that the whole scheme was a contrivance of her own—a bold stroke to get hold of the man with the money. She knew Wat would marry her sister at a word or hint, and then the Jewel had scarcely an alternative. He took the disappointment and affront so much to heart, that he removed with his Eagle to America, at the Whitsunday following, where their success was beyond anticipation, and where they were both living at an advanced age about twelve years ago, without any surviving family.

---

## CHAP. XIII.

### A STRANGE SECRET.

SOME years ago, a poor man named Thomas Henderson came to me, and presented me with a letter from a valued friend. I showed some little kindness to the man ; and as an acknowledgment, he gave me an account of himself, in that plain, simple, and drawling style, which removed all doubts of its authenticity. His story, as a whole, was one of very deep interest to himself, no doubt, but of very little to me, as it would be to the world at large if it were repeated ; but as one will rarely listen to even the most common-place individual without hearing something to reward the attention bestowed upon him, so there was one incident in this man Henderson's life which excited my curiosity very much. I shall give it nearly in his own words :——

I was nine years a servant to the Earl of——, (said he,) and when I left him, he made me a handsome present ; but it was on condition that I should never again come within a hundred miles of his house. The truth is, that I would have been there to this day, had I not chanced to come at the knowledge of something relating to the family that I ought not to have known, and which I never would have known, had I gotten my own will. When the auld Earl died, there was an unco confusion, and at length the young Lord came hame frae abroad, and tuke the command. He hadna been master about twa years when he rings the bell ae morning, and sends for me. I was merely a groom, and no used to gang up stairs to my Lord ; but he often spoke to me in the stables, for I had the charge o' his favourites Cleopatra and

Venus, and I thought he wanted to gie me some directions about them. Weel, up the stair I rins, wanting the
jacket and bonnet, and I opens the door, and I says,
"What is't, my Lord?"—"Shut the door, and come in,"
says he. Hech! what in the world is in the wind now!
thinks I. Am I gaun to be made some grand secreter?

"Tom, has the Lady Julia ordered the coach to-day?"
says he.

"I believe she has, my Lord, I think Hector was saying so."

"And is it still to the old spot again, in the forest?"

"That winna be kenn'd till Hector is on the seat. But
there is little doubt that it is to the same place. She
never drives to ony other."

"Tom, I was long absent from home, but you have
been in the family all the while, and must know all its
secrets—What is it supposed my sister Julia has always
ado with the forester's wife at the shieling of Aberduchra?"

"That has never been kenn'd to ane o' us, my Lord.
But it is supposed there is some secret business connected
wi' her visits there."

"That is a great strength of supposition, indeed, Tom!
Of that there can be no doubt. But what do the servants suppose the secret relates to? Or what do *you*
suppose concerning it? Come, tell me honestly and
freely."

"Ou, naebody kens that, my Lord; for Lady Julia
just lights at a certain point o' the road, and orders the
coach to be there again at a certain hour at night; and
that's a' that has ever been kenn'd about it. But we a'
notice that Lady Julia is sair altered. And folks they
say—but as to that I am ignorant—they say, ye ken, that
auld Eppie Cowan's a witch."

"And that it is on some business of enchantment or
divination that my sister goes to her?"

"Na, na, I dinna say that, my Lord; for a' that I say
is just this, that I believe naebody in this world, except-
ing Lady Julia and auld Eppie themsells twa, kens what

their business is thegither, or how they came to be connected."

" Well, well, Tom, that is what I want particularly to
know. Do you set out just now; go over the shoulder
of Beinny-Veol, and through Glen-Ellich, by the straight
route; get to Aberduchra before my sister; conceal
yourself somewhere, in the house or out of the house, in
a thicket or in a tree; note all that you see Lady Julia
engaged in—who meets her there—what they do, and
what they say, and bring me a true report of every
thing; and your reward shall be according to your success."

Weel, aff I rins, and ower the hills at the nearest, and
sair wark had I afore I got mysell concealed, for auld
Eppie was running out and in, and in and out again, in
an unco fyke, weel kenning wha was to be her visitor that
day; for every time she cam to the door she gae a lang
look down the glen, and then a' round about her, as if
feared for being catched in a fault.

I had by this time got up to the top of a great elm-tree
that almost overlooked the door o' the shieling, but when
I saw the auld roudess looking about her sae sternly, I
grew frighted; for I thought, if she be a witch, I shall
soon be discovered; and then, should she cast ony cantrips that may dumfounder me, or should I see ought to
put me beside mysell, what a fa' I will get! I wad now
hae gien a' the claes on my back to have been safe down
again, and had begun to study a quick descent, when I
perceived Lady Julia coming rapidly up the glen, with
manifest trepidation in her manner. My heart began now
to quake like an aspen leaf, for I suspected that some
awesome scene was gaun to be transacted, that could
bring the accomplished Lady Julia to that wild retired
spot. And yet when she drew near, her modest mien
and fading beauty were sae unlike ony thing wicked or
hellish, that—in short I didna ken what to think or what
to fear, but I had a considerable allowance o' baith.

With many kind and obsequious courtesies did old
Eppie receive the lady on the green, and after exchanging

a few words, they both vanished into the cottage, and shut the door. Now, thinks I, the infernal wark will begin; but goodness be thankit, I'll see nane o't frae here.—I changed my place on the tree, however, and came as near to the top of the lum as the branches would carry me. From thence I heard the voices of the twa, but knew not what they were saying. The Lady Julia's voice was seldom heard, but when it was, it had the sounds of agony; and I certainly thought she was imploring the old hag to desist from something which the other persisted in. The voice of the latter never ceased; it went on with one continued mumble, like the sound of a distant waterfall. The sounds still increased, and I sometimes made myself believe that I heard the voice of a third person. I cannot tell what I would then have given to have heard what was going on, but though I strained my hearing to the uttermost, I could not attain it.

At length, all at once, I heard a piercing shriek, which was followed by low stifled moanings. "They are murdering a bairn, and what *will* I do!" said I to myself, sobbing till my heart was like to burst. And finding that I was just upon the point of losing my senses, as well as my hold, and falling from the tree, I descended with all expedition, and straightway ran and hid mysell under the bank of the burn behind the house, that thereby I might avoid hearing the cries of the suffering innocent, and secure myself from a fall.

Now, here shall be my watch, thinks I; for here I can see every ane that passes out frae or into the house: and as for what is gaun on in the inside, that's mair than I'll meddle wi'.

I had got a nice situation now, and a safe ane, for there was a thick natural hedge of briers, broom, and brambles, down the back o' the kail-yard. These overhung the burn-brae, so that I could hide mysell frae every human ee in case of great danger; and there was an opening in the hedge, through which I could see all that passed, and there I cowered down on my knees, and lay wi' my een stelled on that shieling o' sin and iniquity.

I hadna lain lang in this position till out comes the twasome, cheek for chowe, and the auld ane had a coffin under her arm; and straight on they comes for the very opening o' the hedge where I was lying.   Now, thinks I, I'm a gone man; for in below this very bank where I am sitting, are they coming to hide the corpse o' the poor bairn, and here ten might lie till they consumed, unkenn'd to the haill warld.   Ay, here they are coming, indeed, for there is not another bit in the whole thicket where they can win through; and in half a minute I will have the witch and the murderess baith hinging at my throat like twa wullcats!—I was aince just setting a' my joints to make a clean splash down the middle of the burn like an otter; but the power was denied me, and a' that I could do, was to draw mysell close into my cove, like a hare into her form; and there I sat and heard the following dialogue, and I think I remember it every word.

"Now, my good Eppie, are you certain that no person will come upon us, or within view of us, before we have done?"   (*Good* Eppie! thinks I, Heaven preserve us a' frae sic goodness!)

"Ay, ay, weel am I sure o' that, Leddy July, for my ain goodman is on the watch, and he has a signal that I ken, which will warn us in good time if ony body leave the high-way."

"Then open the lid, and let me look into it once more; for the poor inanimate remains that are in that chest have a hold of this disconsolate and broken heart, which nothing else in this world can ever have again.   O my dear boy! My comely, my beautiful, my murdered boy!"

Here Lady Julia burst into the most violent and passionate grief, shrieking and weeping like one in distraction.   I was terrified out o' a' bounds; but I couldna help thinking to mysell what a strange inconsistent creature a woman was, first to take away a dear little boy's life, and then rair and scraugh over what she had done, like a madwoman.   Her passion was sae violent and sae loud that I couldna take up what the auld crone was saying,

although her tongue never lay for a moment; but I
thought a' the time that she was trying to pacify and
comfort Lady Julia; and I thought I heard her saying
that the boy wasna murdered. Now, thinks I, that dings
a' that ever I heard! If a man aince understands a
woman, he needna be feared to try ought in nature.

"Now here they are, my Leddy July, just as your
own fair hands laid them. There's no ane o' them out
o' its place yet. There they a' lie, little and muckle,
frae the crown o' the head to the soles o' the feet."

"Gude forgie the woman!" says I to mysell—"Can
these be the banes o' bairns that she is speaking about?
It is a question how mony has been put into that black
kist afore this time, and there their banes will be lying,
tier aboon tier, like the contents of a candlemaker's box!"

"Look, here is the first, my Leddy. This is the first
year's anes. Then, below that sheet o' silver paper, is
the second year's, and on sae to the third and the fourth."

I didna think there had been as muckle wickedness in
human nature, thought I; but if thae twa escape out o'
this world without some veesible judgment, I'm unco sair
mistaen!

"Come now, Leddy July, and let us gae through them
a' regularly; and gie ower greeting. See, as I said, this
contains the first year's suits of a' kinds, and here, amang
others, is the frock he was bapteezed in, far, far, frae here.
Ay, weel I mind that day, and sae may ye, Leddy July;
when the Bishop flung the water on your boy's face, how
the little chub looked at him! Ech—ech—ech—I'll
never forget it! He didna whimper and whine, like ither
bairns, but his little arms gae a quiver wi' anger, and sic
a look as he gae the priest! Ay, it was as plain as he
had said it in gude Scots, 'Billy, I'll be about wi' you for
this yet!' He—he—he—my brave boy! Ay, there
needed nae confessions, nor parish registers, to declare
wha was his father! 'Faith, billy, I'll be about wi' you
for this insult!' He—he—he! That was what he
thought plainly enough, and he looked *very* angry at the
Bishop the haill night.—O fie, Leddy July, dinna stain

the bonny frock wi' your tears. Troth, they are sae warm and sae saut, that they will never wash out again. There now, there now. We will hing them a' out to the sun ane by ane."

Shame fa' my stupidity! thought I to mysell. Is the haill terrible affair endit in a bichel o' baby-clouts?—I then heard that they were moving farther away from me, and ventured to peep through the boughs, and saw the coffin standing open, about three feet from my nose. It was a small low trunk, covered with green velvet, lined with white satin, and filled with clothes that had belonged to a princely boy, who, it appeared from what I over-heard, had either been privately murdered, or stolen away, or had somehow unaccountably disappeared. This I gathered from the parts of the dialogue that reached me, for always when they came near to the trunk, they were close beside me, and I heard every word; but as they went farther away, hanging out the bairn's claes to air, I lost the parts between. Auld Eppie spake without intermission, but Lady Julia did little else save cry, and weet the different parts of the dress with tears. It was excessively affecting to see the bonny young lady, wha was the flower o' the haill country, bending ower a wheen claes, pressing them to her bosom, and greeting till the very heart within her was like to melt, and aye crying, between every fit o' sobbing, " O my boy, my dear boy ! my noble, my beautiful boy ! How my soul yearns after thee! Oh, Eppie, may you never know what it is to have but one only son, and to be bereaved of him in such a way as I have been."

At one time I heard the old wife say, " See, here is the silk corslet that he wore next his breast that very day;" on which the Lady Julia seized the little tucker, and kissed it an hundred times, and then said, " Since it once was warmed in his dear little bosom, it shall never cool again as long as his mother's is warm." So saying, she placed the relic in her breast, weeping bitterly.

Eppie's anecdotes of the boy were without end; the bereaved and beautiful mother often rebuking her, but all the while manifestly indulging in a painful pleasure. She showed her a pair of trews that were discoloured, and added, "Ah, I ken brawly what made them sae dim. His foster-brother, Ranald, and he were after a fine painted butterfly one day. The creature took across a mire, a perfect stank. Ranald stopped short, but Lewie made a bauld spring to clear it. He hardly wan by the middle, where he stuck up to the waist in mire. Afore my goodman reached him, there was naething aboon but the blue bonnet and the feather. ' You little imp, how gat you in there?' said my husband. ' That's not your concern, sir, but how I shall get out again,' said the little pestilence. Ah, he was the bairn that had the kind heart when kindness was shown to him; but no ae thing in this 'versal world wad he do by compulsion. We could never make him comprehend the power of death; he always bit his lip, and scowled wi' his eebrows, as if determined to resist it. At first he held him at defiance, threatening to shoot or run him through the body; but when checked so that he durst not openly defy him, his resolution was evidently unchanged. Ha! he was the gallant boy; and if he lives to be a man, he winna have his match in the three kingdoms."

"Alack, alack, my dear boy," exclaimed Lady Julia; "his beauty is long ago defaced, his princely form decayed, and his little unripe bones lie mouldering in some pit or concealed grave. Perhaps he was flung from these rocks, and his fair and mangled form became the prey of the raven or the eagle."

The lady's vehemence some way affected my heart, and raised siccan a disposition in me to join her in crying, that, in spite o' my heart, I fell a-fuffing like a goose as I was, in below the burn-brae. I was overheard; and then all was silence and consternation for about the space of a mmute, till I hears Eppie say, " Did you hear that Leddy July? What say ye? What in the world was that? I wish there may be nae concealed spies. I hope nae unhallowed ee has seen our wark the day, or unblest ear heard our words! Eh?

>Seek butt, seek ben,
>I find the smell o' quick men;
>But be he living or be he dead,
>I'll grind his bones to mix my bread."

So saying, the old hag in one moment rushed through the thin part of the brake, by a retrograde motion, and drapping down from the hanging bank, she lighted precisely with a foot on each side of my neck. I tried to withdraw my head quietly and peaceably, but she held me as if my head had been in a vice, and, with the most unearthly yells, called out for a knife! a knife! I had now no other resource left but to make a tremendous bolt forward, by which I easily overturned the old dame, and off I ran plash for plash down the burn, till I came to an opening, by which I reached the only path down the glen. I had lost my bonnet, but got off with my head, which was more than the roudess intended.

Such screaming and howling as the two carried on behind me, I never heard. Their grand secret was now out; and I suppose they looked upon the discovery as utter ruin, for both of them knew me perfectly well, and guessed by whom I had been sent. I made the best of my way home, where I arrived before dark, and gave my master, the Earl, a full and faithful account of all that I had seen and all that I had heard. He said not a word until I had ended, but his face grew dark, and his eyes as red as a coal, and I easily perceived that he repented having sent me. When I had concluded my narrative, he bit his lip for some time, and then said, in a low smothered voice,—" I see how it has been—I see how it has been; I understand it all perfectly well." Then, after a short pause, he continued, " I believe, Tom, it will be unsafe for you to stay longer here; for, if you do, you will not be alive till to-morrow at midnight. Therefore haste to the south, and never for your life come north of the Tweed again, or you are a dead man, depend on that. If you promise me this, I will make you a present of L.10, over and above your wages; but if you refuse, I will take my chance of having your motions watched, and you may take yours."

As I had often heard hints that certain officious people had vanished from my Lord's mansion before this time, I was glad to make my escape; and taking him at his offer, I was conveyed on shipboard that same night, and have never again looked towards the north.

"It is a great pity, Thomas," said I, when he had finished this recital, "that you can give me no account of the boy—whose son he was, or what became of him. Was Lady Julia ever married?"

I couldna say, sir. I never heard it said either that she was married, or that she was not married. I never had the slightest suspicion that she was married till that day; but I certainly believe sinsyne, that she aince *had* been married at ony rate. Last year I met with one John Ferguson from that country, who told me the Earl was dead, and that there was some dispute about the heirship, and that some strange secrets had come out; and he added, " For you know very weel, Thomas, that that family never could do any thing like other people."

" Think you there is no person in that country to whom I could apply," said I, " for a development of these mysterious circumstances?"

" There is only one person," said Henderson, " and I am sure he knows every thing about it, and that is the Bishop; for he was almost constantly in the family, was sent for on every emergency, and was often away on long jaunts with Lady Julia alone. I am sure he can inform you of every circumstance; but then it is almost certain either that he will not dare, or that he will not choose, to disclose them."

———

This story of Henderson's made so strong an impression upon me that I could not refrain from addressing a letter to the Bishop, requesting, in as polite terms as I could, an explanation of the events to which it referred. I was not aware that the reverend prelate had been in any way personally connected with the events referred

to, nor did his answer expressly admit that he was ; but
I could gather from it, that he had a very intimate share
in them, and was highly offended at the liberty I had
taken, upon an acquaintance that was certainly slight, of
addressing him on the subject.   I was sorry that I should
have inadvertently disturbed his reverence's equanimity,
for his reply betrayed a good deal of angry feeling ; and
as in it he took the trouble of entering at some length
into a defence of the Roman Catholic religion, against
which I had made no insinuation, nor even once referred
to it, I suspected that there had been something wrong,
and, more and more resolved to get to the bottom of the
affair, I next wrote to the Protestant clergyman of the
place.   His reply informed me that it was altogether out
of his power to furnish the information desired, inasmuch
as he had come to the pastoral charge of his parish many
years subsequently to the period alluded to ; and the
Earl of ———'s family being Catholic, he had no intercourse with them.   It was considered unsafe to meddle
with them, he said ; they had the reputation of being a
dangerous race, and, interfering with no man's affairs,
allowed no interference with theirs.   In conclusion, however, my reverend correspondent referred me to a Mr
MacTavish, tenant of Innismore, as one who possessed
more knowledge concerning the Earl's family than any
one out of it.   This person, he farther stated, was seventy
years of age, and had lived in the district all his
life, though the late Earl tried every means to remove
him.

Availing myself of this clew, I made it my business to
address Mr MacTavish in such a way as was most likely
to ensure compliance with my wishes.   I was at some
pains to procure introductions, and establish a sort of
acquaintance with him, and at last succeeded in gaining
a detail of the circumstances, in so far as he knew them,
connected with the adventure of Henderson at the shieling of Aberduchra.   This detail was given me in a series
of letters of different dates, and many of them at long
intervals from each other, which I shall take the liberty

of throwing into a continuous narrative, retaining, however, the old gentleman's own way of telling the story.

———

About the time when the French were all to be killed
in Lochaber (Mr MacTavish's narrative commences), I
was employed in raising the militia soldiers, and so had
often to make excursions through the country, both by
night and day. One morning, before dawn, as I was
riding up the Clunie side of the river, I was alarmed by
perceiving a huge black body moving along the road
before me. I knew very well that it was the Bogle of
Glastulochan, and kept at a respectful distance behind
it. After I had ridden a considerable way in great
terror, but yet not daring to turn and fly, the light became more and more clear, and the size of the apparition
decreased, and, from a huge undefined mass, assumed
sundry shapes, which made it evident that it meditated
an attack on me, or, as I had some faint hopes, to evan-
ish altogether. To attempt to fly from a spirit I knew
to be needless, so I held on my way, in great perturbation. At last, as the apparition mounted an eminence
over which the road winded, and so came more distinctly
between me and the light, I discovered that it was two
persons on horseback, travelling the same way as myself.
On coming up, I recognised the Popish Bishop accompanied by the most beautiful young lady I had ever
seen.

" Good morrow to you, pretty lady, and to you, reverend sir," said I; but not one of them answered a word.
The lady, however, gazed intently at me, as if she expected I had been some other, while the Bishop seemed
greatly incensed, and never once turned round his head.
I cannot tell how it was, but I became all at once greatly in love with the lady, and resolved not to part till I
discovered who she was. So when we came to the house
of Robert Macnab, I said, " Madam, do you cross the
corrie to-day?"

K 2

"No," said she.

"Then I shall stay on this side too," said I.

"Young soldier, we desire to be alone," said the Bishop, (and this was the first time he had spoken,) "therefore be pleased to take your own way, and to free us of your company."

"By no means," said I; "neither the lady nor your Reverence can be the worse of my protection."

When I said "your Reverence," the Bishop started, and stared me in the face; and after a long pause, once more desired me to leave them. I would not do so, however, although I must acknowledge my behaviour was exceedingly improper; but I was under the influence of a strange fascination at the time, which I am the more convinced of now that I know the events that have followed upon that encounter.

"We travel by the Spean," said he.

"It is the nearest way," I replied, "and I shall go that way too." The Bishop then became very angry, and I, I must confess, more and more impertinent. "I know better," said I, "than to trust a Popish priest with such a lovely and beautiful, and amiable dear lady in such a wild and lonely place. I bear his Majesty's commission, and it is my duty to protect all the ladies that are his true subjects." This was taking a good deal upon me, but I thought I perceived that the Bishop had an abashed look, as if detected in an affair he was ashamed of; and so I determined to see the end of it. We travelled together till we arrived at Fort-William, where we were met by a gallant gentleman, who took the lady from her horse, and kissed her, and made many fine speeches; and she wept, and suffered herself to be led away towards the beach. I went with them, and there being a great stir at the shore, and fearing that they were going to take the lady on board by force, I drew my sword, and advancing to the gentleman, commanded him not to take the lady on board against her will, adding, that she was under my protection.

"Is she indeed, sir?" said he. "And pray may I ask

to whom she is indebted for this kind and gratuitous protection?"

" That is to myself, sir," said I.

He pushed me aside in high disdain, and as I continued to show a disposition to oppose by force his purpose of taking the lady on board, I was surrounded by nine or ten fellows who were in readiness to act upon his orders ; they disarmed me, and persuading the spectators that I was insane or intoxicated, bound me, as the only means of preventing me from annoy- ing their master. The whole party then went on board, and sailed down the frith ; and I saw no more of them, nor discovered any more concerning the lady at that time.

Soon after this adventure, the Bishop returned home, but whenever he saw my face, he looked as if he had seen a serpent ready to spring on him. Many a sore and heavy heart I had about the lady that I saw fallen among the Papists, and carried away by them ; but for a long while I remained in ignorance who she was, being only able to conjecture that she was some young woman about to be made a nun, contrary to her own in- clination.

At length a fearful report began to spread through the country of the loss of Lady Julia, and of her having been last seen in the company of her confessor; but the Bishop frequented the Castle the same as before, and therefore people shook their heads whenever the subject was mentioned, as if much were suspected, though little durst be said. I wondered greatly if that lady with whom I fell so much in love in our passage through the Highlands, could have been this Lady Julia. My fa- ther died that year, so I left the regiment in which I had been an officer, and being in Glasgow about the end of September, I went from thence in a vessel to Fort- William. As we passed the island of Illismore, a lady came on board rather in a secret manner. She had a maid-servant with her, who carried a child. The mo- ment the lady stepped up the ship's side, I perceived it to be the identical beautiful creature with whom I had fallen in the year before, when the Bishop was carrying her away. But what a change had taken place in her appearance! her countenance was pale and emaciated, her looks dejected, and she seemed to be heart-broken. At our first rencounter, she looked me full in the face, and I saw that she recognised me, for she hurried past me into the cabin followed by her maid.

When we came to the fortress, and were paying our fares, I observed some dispute between the lady and the mate or master of the boat and a West-Islander, the one charging her for boat-fare, and the other for board and lodging. "I give you my word of honour," she said, "that you shall be paid double your demands in two weeks; but at present I have no means of satisfying you."

"Words of honour won't pass current here, mistress," said the sailor; "money or value I must have, for I am but a servant."

The West-Islander was less uncivil, and expressing his reluctance to press a gentlewoman in a strait, said, if she would tell him who she was, he would ask no more security.

"You are very good," said she, as she wiped away the tears that were streaming down her cheeks; but she would not tell her name. Her confusion and despair became extreme, so much so, that I could no longer endure to see one who appeared so ingenuous, yet compelled to shroud herself in mystery, suffer so much from so paltry a cause; and interfering, I satisfied the demands of the two men. The look of gratitude which she cast upon me was most expressive; but she said nothing. We travelled in company to Inverness, I supplying her with what money was necessary to meet the expenses of the road, which she took without offering a word of explanation. Before we parted, she called me into an apartment, and assuring me that I should soon hear from her, she thanked me briefly for the assistance I had afforded her. "And this little fellow," continued she, "if he live to be a man, shall thank you too for your kindness to his mother." She then asked if I could know the child again, and I answered that I could not, all infants were so much alike. She said there was a good reason why she wished that I should be able to recognise the child at any future period, and she would show me a private mark by which I should know him as long as I lived. Baring his little bosom accordingly, she displayed the mark of a gold ring, with a ruby, immediately below his left breast. I said it was a very curious mark indeed, and one that I could not mistake. She next asked me if I was a Roman Catholic? but I shook my head, and said, God forbid! and so we parted.

I had learned from the West-Islander that his name was Malcolm M'Leod, a poor and honest Roman Catholic, and that the child was born at his house, one of the most remote places in the world, being on a sequestered and inaccessible peninsula in one of the Western Isles. The infant had been baptized privately by the Bishop of Illismore, by the name of Lewis William. But farther the man either could not or would not give me any information.

Before I left Inverness I learned that the lady was no other than the noble and fair Lady Julia, and shortly after I got home to Innismore, I received a blank letter, enclosing the sum I had expended on her behalf. Not long after, a message came, desiring me to come express to the Bishop's house. This was the whole amount of the message, and although no definite object was held out to me, I undertook the journey. Indeed, throughout the whole transactions connected with this affair, I cannot understand what motives they were that I acted on. It seems rather that I was influenced by a sort of fatality throughout, as well as the other persons with whom I had to deal. What human probability was there, for instance, that I would obey a summons of this nature? and yet I was summoned. There was no inducement held out to procure my compliance with the request;

and yet I did comply with it. Upon what pretext was I to gain admittance to the Bishop's house? I could think of none. And if I am called upon to tell how I did gain admittance, if it were not that subsequent events demonstrate that my proceedings were in accordance with the decrees of a superior destiny, I should say that it was by the mere force of impudence. As I approached the house, I heard there such a loud weeping, and screaming, and lamentation, that I almost thought murder was going on within it. There were many voices, all speaking at once; but the cries were heard above all, and grew more woful and bitter. When I entered the house, which I did without much ceremony, and flung open the door of the apartment from which the noise proceeded, there was Lady Julia screaming in an agony of despair, and holding her child to her bosom, who was crying as bitterly as herself. She was surrounded by the Bishop and three other gentlemen, one of them on his knees, as if imploring her to consent to something, and the other three using gentle force to take the child from her. My entrance seemed to strike them with equal terror and astonishment; they commanded me loudly to retire; but I forced myself forward, while Lady Julia called out and named me, saying I was her friend and protector. She was quite in a state of derangement through agony and despair, and I was much moved when I saw how she pressed her babe to her bosom, bathed him with tears, and kissed him and blessed him a thousand times.

"O Mr MacTavish," cried she, "they are going to take my child from me,—my dear, dear boy! and I would rather part with my life. But they cannot take my child from me if you will protect me. They cannot —they cannot!" And in that way did she rave on, regardless of all their entreaties.

"My dear Lady Julia, what madness has seized you?" said a reverend-looking gentleman. "Are you going to bring ruin on yourself and your whole family, and to disgrace the holy religion which you profess? Did you not

promise that you would give up the child? did you not
come here for that special purpose? and do not we all
engage, in the most solemn manner, to see him bred and
educated as becomes his birth?"

"No, no, no, no!" cried she; "I cannot, I cannot!
I will not part with him! I will go with him to the farthest ends of the world, where our names were never
heard of,—but, oh! do not separate me from my dear
boy!"

The men stared at one another, and held their peace.

"Madam," said I, "I will willingly protect your baby
and you, if there is occasion for it, as long as there is a
drop of blood in my body; but it strikes me that these
gentlemen are in the right, and that you are in the
wrong. It is true, I speak in ignorance of circumstances;
but from all that I can guess, you cannot doubt of your
baby's safety, when all these honourable men stand
security to you for him. But if it is necessary that you
should part with him, and if you will not intrust him to
them, give him to me. I will have him nursed and
educated in my own house, and under mine own eye."

"You are very good—you are very good!" said she,
rather calmly. "Well, let this worthy gentleman take
the charge of him, and I yield to give him up."

"No, no!" exclaimed they all at once, "no heretic
can have the charge of the boy; he must be brought up
under our own auspices; therefore, dearest Lady Julia,
bethink you what you are doing, before you work your
own ruin, and his ruin, and the ruin of us all."

Lady Julia then burst into a long fit of weeping, and
I saw she was going to yield; she, however, requested
permission to speak a few words with me in private.
This was readily granted, and all of them retired. When we
were alone, she said to me softly, "They are going to
take my child from me, and I cannot and dare not resist
them any longer, for fear a worse fate befall him. But
I sent for you to be a witness of our separation. You
will know my poor hapless child as long as he lives, from
the mark that I showed you; and when they force him

from me, O watch where they take him, and to what.
ever quarter that may be, follow, and bring me word,
and high shall be your reward.   Now, farewell; remem.
ber I trust in you,—and God be with you! I do not
wish any one to see my last extremity, save those who
cause it, for I know my heart must break.   Desire them
to come in, and say that you have persuaded me to yield
to their will."

I did so ; but I could see that they only regarded me
with looks of suspicion.

I lingered in the narrow lobby, and it was not two
minutes, till two persons, one of whom I had previously
ascertained by his accent to be an Irish gentleman, hurried by me with the child.   I should have followed, but,
as, in their haste, they left open the door of the apartment where Julia was, my attention was riveted on the
lady ; she was paralyzed with affliction, and clasped the
air, as if trying to embrace something,—but finding her
child was no longer in her bosom, she sprung up to an
amazing height, uttered a terrible shriek, and fell down
strongly convulsed.   Shortly after, she uttered a tremulous moan, and died quite away.   I had no doubt that
her heart was broken, and that she had expired ; and indeed the Bishop, and the other gentleman, who remained
with her, seemed to be of the same opinion, and were
benumbed with astonishment.   I called aloud for assistance, when two women came bustling in with water ; but
the Bishop ordered one of them, in an angry tone, to
retire.   He gave the command in Gaelic, and the poor
creature cowered like a spaniel under the lash, and made
all haste out of his sight.   This circumstance caused me
to take a look at the woman, and I perceived at once
that I knew her,—but the hurry and confusion of the
moment prevented me from thinking of the incident, less
or more, until long afterwards.

Lady Julia at length gave symptoms of returning animation, and then I recollected the neglect of the charge
she had committed to me.   I hurried out ; but all trace
of the child was lost.   The two gentlemen who took

him from his mother, were walking and conversing deliberately in the garden, as if nothing had happened, and all my inquiries of them and of others were unavailing.

After the loss of Lady Julia's child, I searched the whole country, but no child could I either see or hear of; and at length my only hope rested on being able to remember who the old woman was whom the Bishop ordered so abruptly out of his presence that day the child was disposed of. I was sure, from the manner in which she skulked away, as if afraid of being discovered, that she had taken him away, either dead or alive. Of all the sensations I ever experienced I was now subjected to the most teasing: I was sensible that I knew the woman perfectly well,—so well, that at first I believed I could call her to my recollection whenever I chose; but, though I put my memory to the rack a thousand and a thousand times, the name, residence, and connexions of the woman went farther and farther from my grasp, till at last they vanished like clouds that mock us with forms of the long-departed.

And now I am going to tell a very marvellous story: One day, when I was hunting in Correi-beg of Glen-Anam, I shot so well that I wondered at myself. Before my unerring aim, whole coveys of moor game fluttered to the earth; and as for the ptarmigans, they fell like showers of hailstones. At length I began to observe that the wounded birds eyed me with strange, unearthly looks, and recollecting the traditions of the glen, and its name, suspected there was some enchantment in the case. What, thought I, if I am shooting good fairies, or little harmless hill spirits, or mayhap whole flocks of Papists trying feats of witchcraft!—and to think that I am carrying all these on my back! While standing in this perplexity, I heard a voice behind me, which said, " O Sandy MacTavish, Sandy MacTavish, how will you answer for this day's work? What will become of me! what will become of me!"

I turned round in great consternation, my hairs all standing on end—but nothing could I see, save a wounded ptarmigan, hoping among the grey stones. It looked at its feathery legs and its snow-white breast all covered with blood,—and at length the creature said, in Gaelic, as before, for it could not be expected that a ptarmigan should have spoken English, " How would you like to find all your family and friends shot and mangled in this way when you gang hame? Ay, if you do not catch me, you will rue this morning's work as long as you live, —and long, long afterwards. But if you catch me, your fortune is made, and you will gain both great riches and respect."

" Then have with you, creature !" exclaimed I, " for it strikes me that I can never make a fortune so easily ;" and I ran at it, with my bonnet in both hands, to catch it.

" Hee-hee-hee !" laughed the creature ; and away it bounded among the grey stones, jumping like a jackdaw with a clipped wing. I ran and ran, and every time that I tried to clap my bonnet above it, down I came with a rattle among the stones—" Hee-hee-hee !" shouted the bird at every tumble. So provoking was this, and so eager did I become in the pursuit, that I flung away my gun and my load of game, and ran after the bird like a madman, floundering over rugged stones, laying on with my bonnet, and sometimes throwing myself above the little creature, which always eluded me.

I knew all this while that the creature was a witch, or a fairy, or something worse,—but natheless I could not resist chasing it, being resolved to catch it, cost what it would ; and on I ran, by cliff and corrie, till I came to a cottage which I remembered having seen once before. The creature, having involved me in the linns of the glen, had got considerably ahead of me, and took shelter in the cottage. I was all covered with blood as well as the bird, and in that state I ran into the bothy after my prey.

On entering, I heard a great bustle, as if all the inmates were employed in effecting the concealment of something. I took it for a concern of smuggling, and went boldly forward, with a " Hilloa ! who bides here ?"

At the question there appeared one I had good reason

to recollect, at sight of whom my heart thrilled. This was no other than the old woman I had seen at the Bishop's house. I knew her perfectly well, for I had been in the same bothy once before, when out hunting, to get some refreshment. I now wondered much that I should never have been able to recollect who the beldam was, till that moment, when I saw her again in her own house. Her looks betrayed the utmost confusion and dismay, as she addressed me in these words, " Hee-hee, good Mr MacTavish, what will you be seeking so far from home to-day ?"

" I am only seeking a wounded ptarmigan, mistress," said I ; " and if it be not a witch and yourself that I have wounded, I must have it,—for a great deal depends upon my getting hold of the creature."

" Ha, ha ! you are coming pursuing after your fortune the day, Mr MacTavish," said she, " and mayhap you may seize her ; but we have a small piece of an operation to go through before that can take place."

" And pray, what is that, Mrs Elspeth ?" said I ; " for if it be any of your witchcraft doings, I will have no hand in it. Give me my bird ; that is all I ask of you."

" And so you really and positively believe it was a bird you chased in here to-day, Mr MacTavish ?"

" Why, what could I think, mistress ? It had the appearance of a bird."

" Margati Cousland ! come hither," said the old witch ; " what is ordained must be done ;—lay hold of him, Margati."

The two women then laid hold of me, and being under some spell, I had no power to resist ; so they bound my hands and feet, and laid me on a table, laughing immoderately at my terrors. They then begged I would excuse them, for they were under the necessity of going on with the operation, though it might not be quite agreeable to me in the first instance.

" And pray, Mrs Elspeth, what is this same operation ?" said I.

" Why," said she, " you have come here chasing after

a great fortune, and there is no other way of attaining it save by one,—and that is, YOUR HEART'S BLOOD MUST BE LET OUT."

"That is a very uncommon way of attaining a fortune, Mrs Elspeth," said I, as good-humouredly as I could, although my heart was quaking within me.

"It is nevertheless a very excellent plan," said the witch, "and it is very rarely that a fortune can be made without it." So saying, the beldam plunged a skein-ochil into my breast, with a loud and a fiendish laugh. "There goes the heart's blood of black Sandy Mac-Tavish!" cried she; and that instant I heard the sound of it rushing to the floor. It was not like the sound of a cataract of blood, however, but rather like the tinkling of a stream of gold guineas. I forced up my head, and behold, there was a stream of pure and shining gold pieces issuing from my bosom; while a number of de-mons, some in black gowns, and others in white petti-coats, were running off with them, and flinging them about in every direction! I could stand this no longer; to have parted with a little blood I found would have been nothing, but to see my vitals drained of a precious treasure, which I knew not had been there, was more than human nature could bear; so I roared out in a voice that made all the house and all the hills to yell, "Murder! thieves! thieves! robbers!—Murder! Ho! ho! ho!" Thus did I continue loudly to shout, till one of the witches, or infernals, as I thought, dashed a pail of water on my face, a portion of which going into my mouth and windpipe, choked my utterance; but nathe-less the remorseless wretch continued to dash water upon me with an unsparing hand, till at last the spell was broke, and the whole illusion vanished.

In order to establish the credibility of the above rela-tion, I must tell another story, which shall be a very short one.

"Our mhaster slheeps fery lhang this tay, Mrs Roy MacCallum," said my man, Donald, to my old house-keeper.

" Huh aye, and that she does, Tonald ; and Cot pe
plessing her slheep to her, honest shentlemans ! Donald
MacIntosh."

" Huh aye, Mrs Roy MacCallum. But hersell looked just pen te house to see if mhaster was waking and
quite coot in health ; and, would you pelieve it, Mrs
MacCallum ? her is lying staring and struggling as if her
were quite mhad."

" Cot forpit, Tonald MacIntosh !"

" Huh aye, to be sure, Mrs MacCallum, Cot forpit,
to be sure ; but her pe mhad for all tat ; and tere pe one
creat trial, Mrs Roy MacCallum, and we mhust mhake
it, and tat is py water."

" It be te creat and lhast trial ; let us ply te water,"
rejoined the sage housekeeper.

With that, Mrs Roy MacCallum and Donald MacIntosh came into my sleeping-room with pails of water, and
began to fling it upon me in such copious showers that I
was well nigh choked ; and to prevent myself from being
drowned, I sprung up ; but still they continued to dash
water upon me. At length I knew my own man Donald's voice as I heard him calling out, " Clash on, Mrs
MacCallum ! it pe for life or teath."

" Huh aye, ply on te water, Tonald !" cried the other.

" Hold, hold, my good friends," cried I, skipping
round the room all dripping wet—" Hold, hold, I am
wide awake now, and better."

" Huh ! plessit pe Cot, and plessit pe te creat Mac-
Tavish !" cried they both at once.

" But where is the witch of the glen ?" cried I. " And
where is the wounded ptarmigan ?—and where is all the
gold that came out with my heart's blood ?"

" Clash on te water, Mrs MacCallum !" exclaimed
Donald ; and the indefatigable pails of Donald and the
housekeeper were again put in requisition to some purpose. Having skipped about for some time, I at last
escaped into a closet, and locked the door. I had then
leisure to remonstrate with them through the keyhole ;
but still there were many things about which we could

not come to a right understanding, and I began to dread
a tremendous shower-bath from above, as I heard them
carrying water up stairs; and that dread brought me first
to my proper and right senses.

It will now be perceived that the whole of my adventure in the glen, with the ptarmigan and the witches, was
nothing more than a dream. But yet in my opinion it
was more than a dream, for it was the same as reality to
me. I had all the feelings and sensations of a rational
being, and every circumstance was impressed on my mind
the same as if I had transacted it awake. Besides, there
was a most singular and important revelation imparted to
me by the vision: I had discovered who the old woman
was whose identity had before perplexed me so much,
and who I was sure either had Lady Julia's boy, or knew
where he was. About five years previous to this I had
come into the same woman's house, weary and hungry, and
laden with game, and was very kindly treated. Of
course, her face was quite familiar to me; but till I had
this singular dream, all the efforts of my memory could
not recall the woman's name and habitation, nor in what
country or circumstances I had before seen her. From
that morning forth I thought of nothing else save another
visit to the forester's cottage in the glen; and, though my
heart foreboded some evil, I rested not till I had accomplished it.

It was not long till I made a journey to Aberduchra,
in search of the old witch whom I had seen in my dream.
I found her; and apparently she had recently suffered
much from distress of mind; her eyes were red with
weeping, her hairs were hanging in elf-switches, and her
dress in much disorder. She knew me and said, "God
bless you, Mr MacTavish, where are you travelling this
way?"

"In truth, Mrs Cowan," I replied, "I am just come
to see after Lady Julia's little boy, poor Lewis William
you know, who was put under your care by the Bishop
on the first of November last year."

She held up her hands and stared, and then fell a-crying most bitterly, striking her breast, and wringing her hands, like one distracted, but still without answering me one word.

" Ochon, ochon !" said I ; " then it is all as I suspected, and the dear child is indeed murdered !"

On this she sprung to her feet, and uttered an appalling scream, and then yelled out, " Murdered ! murdered ! Is the dear boy murdered ? Is he—is he murdered ?"

This vehemence of feeling on her part at the idea of the boy's being cut off, convinced me that she had not murdered the child herself; and being greatly relieved in my heart, I sat still as in astonishment, until she again put the question if her dear foster-child was murdered.

" Why, Mrs Cowan, not to my knowledge," I replied. " I did not see him murdered ; but if he has not been foully dealt with, what has become of him ?—for well I know he was put under your charge; and before the world, and before the judges of the land, I shall make you render an account of him."

" Was the boy yours, Mr MacTavish," said she, " that you are so deeply interested in him ? For the love of Heaven, tell me who was his father, and then I shall confess to you every thing that I know concerning him."

I then told the woman the whole story as I have here related it, and requested her to inform me what had become of the boy.

" He was delivered to me after the most solemn injunctions of concealment," said she ; "and these were accompanied with threatenings, in case of disobedience, of no ordinary nature. He was to be brought up in this inaccessible wild with us as our grandson ; and farther than that, no being was to know. Our reward was to be very high—too high, I am afraid, which may have caused his abstraction. But O he was a dear delightful boy ! and I loved him better than my own grandson. He was so playful, so bold, and, at the same time, so forgiving and generous !"

" Well, he lived on with us, and grew, and no one acknowledged or noticed him until a little while ago, that one Bill Nicol came into the forest as foxhunter, and came here to board, to be near the foxes, having, as he pretended, the factor's orders for doing so; and every day he would sport with the two boys, who were both alike fond of him,—and every day would he be giving them rides on his pony, which put them half crazy about the man. And then one day, when he was giving them a ride time about, the knave mounted behind little Lewie, and rode off with him altogether into the forest, and there was an end of him. Ranald ran crying after them till he could run no farther, and then, losing sight of them, he sat down and wept. I was busy at work, and thought always that my two little fellows were playing not far off, until I began to wonder where they could be, and ran out to the top of the little birky knowe-head there, and called, and louder called them; but nothing answered me, save the echoes of my own voice from the rocks and trees; so I grew very greatly distracted, and ran up Glen-Caolas, shouting as I went, and always praying between whiles to the Holy Virgin and to the good saints to restore me my boys. But they did not do it—Oh no, they never did! I then began to suspect that this pretended foxhunter might have been the Wicked One come in disguise to take away my children; and the more so, as I knew not if Lewie had been blessed in holy church. But what could I do but run on, calling and crying, and raving all the way, until I came to the pass of Bally-keurach, and then I saw that no pony's foot had passed on that path, and turned and ran home; but it was growing dark, and there was nobody there, so I took to the woods again. How I spent that night I do not know, but I think I had fallen into a trance through sorrow and fatigue.

" Next morning, when I came to my senses, the first thing I saw was a man who came by me, chasing a wounded bird, like a white moorfowl, and he was always trying to catch it with his bonnet, and many a hard fall he got

among the stones. I called after him, for I was glad to
see a human being in that place, and I made all the speed
I could to follow; but he regarded me not, but ran after
the wounded bird. He went down the linns, which
retarded him a good deal, and I got quite near him.
Then from that he went into a small hollow straight before me, to which I ran, for I wanted to tell him my tale,
and beg his assistance in raising the country in the strath
below. When I came into the little hollow, he had
vanished, although a hare could not have left it without
my seeing it. I was greatly astonished, assured that I
had seen a vision. But how much more was I astonished
to find, on the very spot where he had disappeared, my
grandson, Ranald, lying sound asleep, and quite motionless, through hunger and fatigue! At first I thought he
was dead, and lost all recollection of the wonderful way
in which I had been led to him; but when I found he
was alive and breathing, I took him up in my arms, and
carried him home, and there found the same man, or rather the same apparition, busily employed hunting the
wounded bird within this same cottage, and he declared
that have it he must. I was terrified almost out of my
wits, but tried to thank the mysterious being for leading
me to my perishing child. His answer—which I shall
never forget—was, ' Yes, I have found one, and I will
find the other too, if the Almighty spare me in life.' And
when the apparition said so, it gave me such a look in the
face—Oh! ah! What is this! what is this!''

Here the old woman began to shriek like one distracted, and appeared in an agony of terror; and, to tell the
truth, I was not much better myself, when I heard the
story of the wounded ptarmigan. But I tried to support
the old woman, and asked what ailed her.

" Well you may ask what ails me!'' said she. " Oh
Mr MacTavish, what did I see just now but the very
same look that the apparition gave that morning! The
same look, and from the very same features; for indeed
it was the apparition of yourself, in every lineament, and
in every article of dress:—your very self. And it is the

most strange vision that ever happened to me in all my visionary life!"

"I will tell you what it is, Mrs Elspeth Cowan," said I, "you do not know one half of its strangeness yet; but tell me the day of the week and the day of the month when you beheld this same vision of myself."

"Ay, that day I never shall forget," answered Elspeth; "for of all the days of the year it was the one after I lost my dear foster-son, and that was the seventh of Averile. I have always thought my boy was stolen to be murdered, or put out of the way most unfairly, till this very day; but now, when I see the same man in flesh and blood, whom I saw that day chasing the wounded bird, I am sure poor Lewie will be found; for with that very look which you gave me but a minute ago, and in that very place where you stand, your apparition of yourself said to me, 'Yes, I have found the one, and I will find the other, if the Almighty spare me in life.' "

"I do not recollect of saying these words, Mrs Cowan," said I.

"Recollect?" said she; "what is it you mean? Sure you were not here your ownself that morning?"

"Why, to tell you the solemn truth," replied I, "I was in the glen that very morning chasing a wounded ptarmigan, and I now have some faint recollection of seeing a red-haired boy lying asleep in a little green hollow beside a grey stone,—and I think I did say these words to some one too. But was not there something more? Was not there something about letting out somebody's heart's blood?"

"Yes; but then that was only a dream I had," said she, "while the other was no dream, but a sad reality. But how, in the name of the blessed saints, do you happen to know of that dream?"

"It is not easy, now-a-days," answered I, "to say what is a dream and what is a reality. For my part, from this moment I renounce all certainty of the distinction. It is a fact, that on that very morning, and at that hour, I was in this glen and in this cottage,—and yet I was neither in this glen nor in this cottage. So, if you can unriddle that, you are welcome."

"I knew you were not here in flesh and blood. I knew it was your wraith, or *anam*, as we call it; for, first, you vanished in the hollow before my eyes; then you appeared here again, and when you went away in haste, I followed you to beg your assistance; and all that I could hear was your spirit howling under a waterfall of the linn."

This confounded me more than ever, and it was some time before I recovered my self-possession so far as to inquire if what she had related to me was all she knew about the boy.

"Nothing more," she said, "save that you are destined to discover him again, either dead or alive—for I can assure you, from the words that I heard out of your own spirit's mouth, that if you do not find him, and restore him to his birthright, he never will be discovered by mortal man. I went, poor, sachless, and helpless being as I was, to the Bishop, and told him my woful story; for I durst do nothing till I asked counsel of him. He was, or rather pretended to be, very angry, and said I deserved to be burnt for my negligence, for there was no doubt the boy had fallen over some precipice. It was in vain that I told him how my own grandson had seen him carried off on the pony by the pretended foxhunter; he persisted in his own belief, and would not suffer me to mention the circumstances to a single individual. So, knowing that the counsel of the Lord was with his servant, I could do nothing but weep in secret, and hold my peace."

Thus ended my interview with Elspeth of the glen.

After my visit to the old sibyl, my mind ran much on the extraordinary vision I had had, and on the old witch's having actually seen a being in my shape at the very instant of time that I myself weened and felt that I was there.

I have forgot whether I went to Lady Julia that very night or some time after, but I did carry her the tidings,

which threw her into an agony of the deepest distress.
She continued for a long space to repeat that her child
was murdered,—her dear, her innocent child.    But
before I left her, she said her situation was a very pecu-
liar one, and therefore she entreated me to be secret, and
to tell no one of the circumstance, yet by all means to
lose no time in endeavouring to trace the foxhunter, and
to find out, if possible, whether the boy was dead or alive.
She concluded by saying, " Exert yourself like a man and
a true friend, as you have always been to me.    Spare no
expense in attaining your object, and my whole fortune
is at your disposal."    I was so completely involved in the
business, that I saw no alternative but that of proceeding,—and not to proceed with vigour was contrary to my
nature.

Lady Julia had all this time been kept in profound
ignorance where the child had been concealed, and the
very next day after our interview, she paid a visit to old
Elspeth Cowan at the remote, cottage of Aberduchra, and
there I again met with her as I set out on the pursuit.
Long and serious was our consultation, and I wrote down
all the marks of the man, and the horse from Elspeth's
mouth ; and the child Ranald also gave me some very
nice marks of the pony.

The only new thing that had come out, was that the
boy Ranald had persisted in saying, that the foxhunter
took his brother Lewie *down* the glen, in place of up,
which every other circumstance seemed to indicate.    Elspeth had seen them go all three up the glen, the two
boys riding on the pony, and the foxhunter leading it,
and Ranald himself was found far up the glen ; but yet
when we took him to the spot, and pointed up the glen ;
he said, No, they did not go that way, but the other.
Elspeth said it was not possible, but I thought otherwise,
for when I asked at Ranald where he thought Nicol the
foxhunter was going with his brother, he said he thought
he was taking him home, and that he would come back
for him.'    Elspeth wanted me to take the route through
the hills towards the south ; but as soon as I heard the

boy's tale, I suspected the Bishop had had some share in the abstraction of the missing child, and set out on my search in the direction of his mansion. I asked at every house and at every person, for such a man and such a pony as I described, making no mention of a boy; but no such man had been seen. At length I chanced to be asking at a shieling, within a mile of the Bishop's house, if, on such a day, they had seen such a man ride by on a black pony. They had not seen him; but there was a poor vagrant boy chanced to be present, who heard my inquiry, and he said he saw a man like that ride by on a black pony one day, but it could not be the man I wanted, for he had a bonny boy on the horse before him.

"Indeed?" said I. "O, then, it could not be the man I want. Had the pony any mark by which you could remember it?"

"*Cheas gear*" said the boy. This was the very mark that little Ranald had given me of the pony. Oho! I have my man now! thought I; so I said no more, but shook my head and went away. Every thing was kept so close about the Bishop's house, I could get no intelligence there, nor even entrance——and in truth, I durst hardly be seen about the premises.

In this dilemma, I recollected the words of the sibyl of the glen, as I had heard them in my strange vision, namely, that my only sure way of making a fortune was by letting out my heart's blood; and also, that when my heart's blood was let out, it proved to be a flood of guineas. Now, thought I to myself, what does making a fortune mean but carrying out successfully any enterprise one may have in hand? and though to part with money is a very hard matter, especially in an affair in which I have no concern, yet I will try the efficacy of it here, and so learn whether the experiment is worth making in other cases where I am more closely interested.—The truth is, I found that I *was* deeply interested in the affair, although, not being able to satisfy my own mind with reasons why I should be so, I affected to

consider myself mightily indifferent about it. In pur-
suance, therefore, of the plan suggested in my dream,
and on a proper opportunity, by means of a present ad-
ministered to one of the bishop's servants, I learnt, that
about the time when the boy had been carried off by the
foxhunter, a priest of the name of O'Callaghan had made
his appearance at the Bishop's house; that he was dressed
in a dark grey jacket and trowsers, and rode a black
pony with cropped ears; that he was believed to have
some secret business with the Bishop, and had frequent
consultations with him; and my informant, becoming
more and more free in his communications, as the facts,
one after another, were drawn from him, confessed to me
that he had one night overheard quarrelling between
O'Callaghan and his master, and having stolen to the
door of the apartment, listened for some time, but was
unable to make out more of the angry whisperings within than a threat from O'Callaghan, that if the Bishop
would not give him more, "he (O'Callaghan) would
throw him overboard into the first salt dub he came to."
On interrogating my informant if he knew whom O'Callaghan meant, when he said he would "throw him overboard," he replied that he could not guess. I had, however, no doubt, that it was the boy I was in search of,
and I had as little doubt that the fellow knew to whom
the threat referred; but I have often known people have
no scruple in telling all about a secret, so as to give any
one a key to the complete knowledge of it, who would
yet, upon no consideration, give utterance to the secret
itself; and judging this to be the case in the present instance, I contented myself with learning farther, that
when the priest left the Bishop's, he went directly to
Ireland, of which country he was a native, and would,
in all probability, ere long revisit Scotland.

Possessed of this clew, I was nevertheless much at a
loss to determine what was the most advisable way of
following it out. My inclination led me to wait the fellow's return, and to have him seized and examined. But
then I bethought me, if I could be instrumental in saving

the boy's life, or of discovering where he was placed, or how circumstanced, it would avail me more, and give Lady Julia more satisfaction than any punishment that might be inflicted on the perpetrators of this deed afterwards. So after a troubled night and day, which I spent in preparation, I armed myself with a pair of pistols and a pair of Highland dirks, a long and a short one, and set out in my arduous undertaking, either to recover the boy or perish in the attempt. And it is needless for me to deny to you, sir, that the vision, and the weird wife of the glen's prophecy, had no small part in urging me to this adventure.

I got no trace of the priest till I went to Abertarf, where I found out that he had lodged in the house of a Catholic, and that he had shown a good deal of kindness and attention to the boy, while the boy seemed also attached to him, but still more to the pony. I went to the house of this man, whose name was Angus Roy MacDonald; but he was close as death, suspicious, and sullen, and would tell me nothing of O'Callaghan's motions. I succeeded, however, in tracing him till he went on board of a Liverpool sloop at Arisaig. I was much at a loss how to proceed. when, in the evening, perceiving a vessel in the offing, bearing against the tide, and hoping that the persons I sought might be aboard of her, I hired a boat to take me out; but we lost sight of her in the dusk of the evening, and I was obliged to bribe the boatmen to take me all the way to Tobermory, having been assured that the Liverpool vessel would be obliged to put in there, in order to clear at the custom-house. We did not reach Tobermory till the next day at noon; and as we entered the narrow passage that leads into the harbour, a sloop came full sail by us right before the wind, and I saw a pretty boy standing on the poop. I called out " Lewis" to him, but he only looked over his shoulder as for some one else, and did not answer me. The ship going on, as she turned her stern right towards us, I saw " The Blake of Boston" in golden letters, and thought no more of the encounter till I went on shore, and there

I learned on the quay that she was the identical Liverpool vessel of which I was in pursuit, and the boy I had seen, the very one I was in search of. I learnt that he was crying much when ashore, and refused to go on ship board again till taken by force; and that he told the people boldly, that that man, Nicol the foxhunter, had taken him from his mother and father, and his brother Ranald, having enticed him out to give him a ride, and never taken him home again. But the fellow telling them a plausible story, they durst not meddle in the matter. It was known, however, that the vessel had to go round by the Shannon, as she had some valuable loading on board for Limerick.

This was heavy news, as how to get a passage thither I wist not. But the thoughts of the poor boy crying for his home hung about my heart, and so, going to Greenock I took a passage for Belfast, and travelled on foot or on horseback as I could, all the way to Limerick. When I got there, matters looked still worse. The Blake had not come up to Limerick, but discharged her bales at the mouth of the river, and again sailed; and here was I in a strange country with no one perhaps to believe my tale. The Irish, however, showed no signs of apathy or indifference to my case, as my own countrymen did. They manifested the utmost sympathy for me, and the utmost indignation against O'Callaghan; and the man being known in the country, he was soon found out by the natives. Yet, strange to say! though found out by twenty men all eagerly bent on the discovery, as soon as he gave them a hint respecting the person by whom he was employed, off they went, and never so much as came back to tell either the Mayor or myself that their search had been successful or not.

But two or three officers, who were Protestants, being dispatched in search of him, they soon brought him to Limerick, where he and I were both examined, and he was committed to jail till the next court day. He denied all knowledge of the boy, and all concern whatever in the crime he was charged with; and the ship being gone I could procure no evidence against him. There was nothing but the allegations of parties, upon which no judgment could be given; I had to pay the expenses of process, and he gave securities for his appearance at the court of Inverness, if he should be cited. I spent nine days more in searching for the boy on the Clare side of the river; but all my efforts were fruitless. I found that my accusation of their vagrant priest rendered me very unpopular among the natives, and was obliged to relinquish the investigation.

O'Callaghan was in Scotland before me, and on my arrival I caused him to be instantly seized, secure now of enough of witnesses to prove the fact of his having taken off the boy. Old Elspeth of the glen and her husband were summoned, as were Lady Julia and Angus Roy MacDonald. When the day of trial came, O'Callaghan's indictment was read in court, charging him with having abstracted a boy from the sheiling of Aberduchra. The Bishop being present, and a great number of adherents, the panel boldly denied every circumstance; and what was my astonishment to find, on the witnesses' names being called, not one of them was there! The officers were called and examined, who declared that they could not find one of the witnesses in the whole country. The forester and his wife, they said, had left Aberduchra, and gone nobody knew whither; Lady Julia had gone to France, and Angus MacDonald to the Lowlands, it was supposed, with cows. The court remarked it was a singular and rather suspicious circumstance, that the witnesses should all be absent. O'Callaghan said something in his own defence, and having made a reference to the Bishop for his character, his reverence made a long speech in his praise. The consequence was, that as not one witness was produced in support of the accusation, O'Callaghan was once more liberated.

I would never have learned what became of the boy, had not a young soldier, a cousin's son of mine, come to Innismore the other year. He was a fine lad, and I soon became a good deal attached to him; and he being one of a company stationed in the neighbourhood to guard the passes for the prevention of smuggling, he lived a good deal at my house, while his officer remained nightly at the old mansion-house, the guest of Lady Julia and the young Lord.

It is perhaps proper here to mention that Lady Julia was now the only remaining member of the late Earl's family, and the heir of entail, being the son of a distant relation, had been sent from Ireland to be brought up by Lady Julia. He was a perverse and wicked boy, and grieved her heart every day.

The young man, my relation, was one day called out to follow his captain on a private expedition against some smugglers. The next day one of his comrades came and told me that they had had a set battle with a great band of smugglers, in which several were killed and wounded. "Among the rest," said he, "our gallant commander, Captain MacKenzie, is killed, and your nephew is lying mortally wounded at the still-house."

I lost no time in getting ready, and mounting one horse, and causing the soldier to take another, I bade him lead the way, and I followed. It may well be supposed that I was much astonished on finding that the lad was leading me straight to the cottage of Aberduchra! Ever since the old forester and his wife had been removed, the cottage had stood uninhabited; and it seems that, from its inaccessible situation, it had been pitched upon as a still-house, and occupied as such, for several years, by a strong band of smugglers from the Deveron. They were all bold, resolute fellows, and when surprised by MacKenzie and his party, and commanded to yield, they soon showed that there was nothing farther from their intention. In one moment every one had a weapon in his hand; they rushed upon the military with such fury that in a few minutes they beat them back, after having run their captain and another man through the body, and wounded several besides. Captain MacKenzie had slain one of the smugglers at the first onset; but the next instant he fell, and his party retired. The smugglers then

staved their casks, and fled, leaving the military in possession of the field of battle, and of the sheiling, in which
nothing was found save a great rubbish of smashed uten-
sils and the killed and wounded of both sides.

In this state I found the cottage of Aberduchra. There
were a smuggler and a soldier quite dead, and a number
badly wounded; and among the latter was the young
man, my relative, who was sorely wounded in the left
shoulder. My whole attention was instantly turned towards him. He was very faint, but the bleeding was
stanched, and I had hopes of his recovery. I gave him
some brandy and water, which revived him a great deal ;
and as soon as he could speak, he said, in a low voice,
" For God's sake, attend to our gallant captain's wound.
Mine is nothing, but, if he is still living, his, I fear, is
dangerous ; and a nobler youth never breathed."

I found him lying on a bed of rushes, one soldier supporting his head, and another sitting beside him with a
dish of cold water. I asked the captain how he did ; but
he only shook his head, and pointed to the wound in his
side. I mixed a good strong cup of brandy and water,
and gave it him. He swallowed it greedily, and I had
then no doubt that the young man was near his last. " I
am a great deal the better of that," said he. I requested
him not to speak, and then asked the soldiers if the
wound had bled freely, but they said no, it had scarcely
bled any. I was quite ignorant of surgery, but it struck
me that if possible the wound should be made to bleed, to
prevent it from bleeding inwardly. Accordingly, the men
having kindled a good fire in the cottage, I got some warm
water, and began to foment the wound. As the stripes of
crusted blood began to disappear, judge of my astonishment when I perceived the mark of a ruby ring below his
left breast! There was no mistaking the token. I knew
that moment that I was administering to Lady Julia's
son, for whom I had travelled so far in vain, and over
whom my soul had yearned as over a lost child of my
own. The basin fell from my hands, my hair stood on
end, and my whole frame grew rigid, so that the soldiers

stared at me, thinking I was bewitched, or seized with some strange malady. The captain, however, made signs for them to proceed with the fomentation, which they did, until the wound bled considerably; and I began to have some hopes that there might be a possibility of saving his life. I then sent off a soldier on one of my horses for the nearest surgeon, and I myself rode straight to the Castle to Lady Julia, and informed her of the captain's wound, and the miserable state in which he was lying at the sheiling of Aberduchra. She held up her hands, and had nearly fainted, and made a lamentation so grievous, that I was convinced she already knew who the young man was. She instantly ordered the carriage to be got ready, and a bed put into it, in order to have the captain conveyed straight to the Castle. I expected she would have gone in the carriage herself, but when she only gave charges to the servants and me, I then knew that the quality and propinquity of her guest were not known to her.

My reflections on the scenes that had happened at that cottage, made a deep impression on me that night, as well they might, considering how singular they were. At that cottage, I had once been in spirit, though certainly not in the body, yet there my bodily form was seen speaking and acting as I would have done, and as at the same moment I believed I was doing. By that vision I discovered where the lost boy was to be found, and there I found him; and when he was lost again, on that very same spot was I told that I should find him, else he never would be discovered by man. And now, after a lapse of fifteen years, and a thousand wanderings on his part overgone, on that very same spot did I again discover him.

Captain MacKenzie was removed to the Castle, and his recovery watched by Lady Julia and myself with the utmost solicitude—a solicitude on her part which seemed to arise from some mysterious impulse of the tie that connected her with the sufferer; for had she known that she was his mother, her care and anxiety about him could scarcely have been greater. When his wound was so far recovered, that no danger was to be apprehended from the agitating discovery, the secret of his birth was communicated to himself and Lady Julia. It is needless for me to trace farther the details of their eventful history. That history, the evidence adduced before the courts of law for the rights of heritage, and before the Peers for the titles, have now been divulged and laid quite open, so that the deeds done in darkness have been brought to light, and that which was meant to have been concealed from the knowledge of all mankind, has been published to the whole world, even in its most minute and intricate windings. It is therefore needless for me to recapitulate all the events that preceded the time when this narrative begins. Let it suffice, that Lady Julia's son has been fully proved legitimate, and we have now a Protestant Earl, in spite of all that the Bishop did to prevent it. And it having been, in a great measure, owing to my evidence that the identity of the heir was established, I have now the prospect of being, if not the richest, at least, the most independent man of either Buchan or Mar.

## CHAP. XIV.

### THE MARVELLOUS DOCTOR.

WHEN my parents lived in the old Manse of Ettrick, which they did for a number of years, an old grey-headed man came one summer and lived with them nearly a whole half year, paying my mother at the rate of ten shillings a-month for bed, board, and washing. He was a mysterious being, and no one knew who he was, or what he was; but all the neighbourhood reckoned him "uncanny;" which in that part of the country means, a warlock, or one some way conversant with beings of another nature.

I remember him well; he was a tall ungainly figure, dressed in a long black coat, the longest and the narrowest coat I ever saw; his vest was something like blue velvet, and his breeches of leather, buckled with silver knee-buckles. He wore always white thread stockings, and as his breeches came exactly to the knap of the knee, his legs appeared so long and thin that it was a marvel to me how they carried him. Take in black spats, and a very narrow-brimmed hat, and you have the figure complete; any painter might take his likeness, provided he did not make him too straight in the back, which would never answer, as his formed the segment of a great circle. He was a doctor; but whether of law, medicine, or divinity, I never learned; perhaps of them all, for a doctor he certainly was——we called him so, and never knew him by any other name; some, indeed, called him the Lying Doctor, some the Herb Doctor, and some the Warlock Doctor; but my mother, behind his back, called him always THE MARVELLOUS DOCTOR, which I have chosen to retain, as the one about whose accuracy there can be no dispute.

His whole occupation was in gathering flowers and herbs, and arranging them; and, as he picked a number of these out of the churchyard, the old wives in the vicinity grew terribly jealous of him. He seemed, by his own account, to have been over the whole world, on what business or in what capacity he never mentioned; but from his stories of himself, and of his wonderful feats, one might have concluded that he had been every thing. I remember a number of these stories quite distinctly, for at that time I believed them all for perfect truth, though I have been since led to suspect that it was scarcely consistent with nature or reason they could be so. One or two of these tales I shall here relate, but with this great disadvantage, that I have, in many instances, forgot the names of the places where they happened. I knew nothing about geography then, or where the places were; and the faint recollection I have of them will only, I fear, tend to confuse my narrative the more.

One day, while he was very busy arranging his flowers and herbs, and constantly speaking to himself, my mother said to him, " Doctor, you that kens sae weel about the nature of a' kinds o' plants and yirbs, will ye tell me gin there be sic a yirb existing as that, if ye pit it either on beast or body, it will gar that beast or body follow you ?"

" No, Margaret, there is not an herb existing which has that power by itself ; but there is a decoction from certain rare herbs, of which I have had the honour, or rather the misfortune, to be the sole discoverer, which has that effect infallibly."

" Dear Doctor, there was sic a kind of charm i' the warld hunders o' years afore ye were born."

" So it has been said, Margaret, so it has been said ; but falsely, I assure you. It cost me seven years' hard study and hard labour, both by night and by day, and some thousands of miles' travelling ; but at last I effected it, and then I thought my fortune was made. But—would you believe it, Margaret ?—my fortune was lost, my time was lost, and I myself was twenty times on the point of being lost too."

" Dear Doctor, tell us some o' your ploys wi' that drog ; for they surely must be very curious, especially if you used it as a love-charm to gar the lasses follow you."—The Doctor, be it observed, was one of the most unlikely persons in the world to be the object of a tender passion.

" I did use it as a love-charm," replied the sage, smiling grimly ; " and sometimes got those to follow me that I did not want, as you shall hear by and by. But before I proceed, I may inform you, that I was offered a hundred thousand pounds by the College of Physicians in Spain, and twice the sum by the Queen of that country, if I would impart my discovery to them in full ; and I refused it ! Yes, for the sake of human nature I refused it. I durst not take the offer, for my life"

" What for, Doctor ?"

" What for, woman ? Do you say, what for ? Don't

you see that it would have turned the world upside down, and inverted the whole order of nature? The lowest miscreant in the country might have taken away the first lady—might have taken her from her parents, or her husband, and kept her a slave to him for life; and no opiate in nature to counteract the power of the charm. The secret shall go to the grave with me; for were it once to be made public in any country, that country would be ruined; and for the sake of good order among mankind, I have slighted all the grandeur that this world could have bestowed. The first great trial of my skill was a public one;"—and the Doctor went on to relate that it occurred as follows:

## The Spanish Professor.

HAVING brought my valued charm to full perfection abroad, I returned to Britain to enjoy the fruit of my labours, convinced that I would ensure a patent, and carry all the world before me. But on my arrival in London, I was told that a great Spanish professor had made the discovery five years before, and had arrived at great riches and preferment on that account, under the patronage of the Queen. Convinced that no man alive was thoroughly master of the charm but myself, I went straight to Spain, and waited on this eminent Professor, whose name was Don Felix de Valdez. This man lived in a style superior to the great nobility and grandees of his country. He had a palace that was not exceeded in splendour by any in the city, and a suite of lacqueys, young gentlemen, and physicians, attending him, as if he had been the greatest man in the world. It cost me much trouble, and three days' attendance, before I could be admitted to his presence; and even then he received me so cavalierly that my British blood boiled with indignation.

" What is it you want with me, fellow?" said he.

" Sir, I would have you know," said I, " that I am an English Doctor, and Master of Arts, and *your* fellow in any respect. So far good. I was told in my own country, sir, that you are a pretender to the profound art of attachment; or, in other words, that you have made a discovery of that divine elixir, which attaches every living creature touched with it to your person. Do you pretend to such a discovery? Or do you not, sir?"

"And What if I do, most sublime Doctor and Master of Arts? In what way does that concern your great sapience?"

"Only thus far, Professor Don Felix de Valdez," says I, "that the discovery is my own, wholly my own, and solely my own; and after travelling over half the world in my researches for the proper ingredients, and making myself master of the all-powerful nostrum, is it reasonable, do you think, that I should be deprived of my honour and emolument without an effort? I am come from Britain, sir, for the sole purpose of challenging you to a trial of skill before your sovereign and all his people, as well as the learned world in general. I throw down the gauntlet, sir. Dare you enter the lists with me?"

"Desire my lacqueys to take away this mad foreigner," said he to an attendant. "Beat him well with staves, for his impertinence, and give him up to the officers of police, to be put in the House of Correction; and say to Signior Philippo that I ordered it."

"You ordered it!" said I. "And who are you, to order such a thing? I am a free-born British subject, a Doctor, and Master of Arts and Sciences, and I have a pass from your government to come to Madrid to exercise my calling; and I dare any of you to touch a hair of my head."

"Let him be taken away," said he, nodding disdainfully, "and see that you deal with him as I have commanded."

The students then conducted me gently forth, pretending to pay me great deference; but when I was put into the hands of the vulgar lacqueys, they made sport of me, and having their master's orders, used me with great rudeness, beating me, and pricking me with needle-pointed stilettos, till I was in great fear for my life, and was glad when put into the hands of the police.

Being liberated immediately on making known my country and erudition, I set myself with all my might to bring this haughty and insolent Professor to the test. A number of his students having heard the challenge, it soon made a great noise in Madrid; for the young King, Charles the Third, and particularly his Queen, were half mad about the possession of such a nostrum at that period. In order, therefore, to add fuel to the flame now kindled, I published challenges in every one of the Spanish journals, and causing three thousand copies to be printed, I posted them up in every corner of the city, distributing them to all the colleges of the kingdom, and to the college of Toledo in particular, of which Don Felix was the principal—I sent a sealed copy to every one of its twenty-four professors, and caused some hundreds to be distributed amongst the students.

This challenge made a great noise in the city, and soon reached the ears of the Queen, who became quite impatient to witness a trial of our skill in this her favourite art. She harassed his Majesty with such effect, that he was obliged to join her in a request to Professor Don Felix de Valdez, that he would vouchsafe a public trial of skill with this ostentatious foreigner.

The Professor besought that he might be spared the indignity of a public exhibition along with the crazy half-witted foreigner, especially as his was a secret art, and ought only to be practised in secret. But the voices of the court and the colleges were loud for the trial, and the Professor was compelled to consent and name a day. We both waited on their Majesties to settle the order and manner of trial; and on drawing lots who was to exhibit first, the Professor got the preference. The Prado was the place appointed for the exhibition, and Good Friday the day. The Professor engaged to enter the lists precisely at half past twelve o'clock; but he begged that he might be suffered to come in disguise, in order to do away all suspicions of a private understanding with others; and assured their Majesties that he would soon be known to them by his works.

When the appointed day arrived, I verily believed that all Spain had assembled to witness the trial. I was placed next to the royal stage, in company with many learned doctors, the Queen being anxious to witness the effect that the display of her wonderful Professor's skill produced on me, and to hear my remarks. The anxiety that prevailed for almost a whole hour was wonderful; for no one knew in what guise the Professor would appear, or how attended, or who were the persons on whom the effect of the unguent was to be tried. Whenever a throng or bustle was perceived in any part of the parade, then the buzz began, " Yonder he is now ! Yon must be he, our great Professor, Don Felix de Valdez, the wonder of Spain and of the world !"

The Queen was the first to perceive him, perhaps from some private hint given her in what disguise he would appear; on which she motioned to me, pointing out a mendicant Friar as my opponent, and added, that she thought it but just and right that I should witness all his motions, his feats, and the power of his art. I did so, and thought very meanly of the whole exhibition, it being, in fact, nothing else than a farce got up among a great number of associates, all of whom were combined to carry on the deception, and share in the profits accruing therefrom. The Friar did nothing till he came opposite to the royal stage, when, beckoning slightly to her Majesty, he began to look out for his game, and perceiving an elegant lady sitting on a stage with her back towards him, he took a phial from his bosom, and letting the liquid touch the top of his finger, he reached up that finger and touched the hem of the lady's robe. She uttered a scream, as if pierced to the heart sprung to her feet, and held her breast as if wounded ; then, after looking round and round, as if in great agitation, she descended from the stage, followed the Friar, kneeled at his feet, and entreated to be allowed to follow and serve him. He requested her to depart, as he could not be served by woman ; but she wept and followed on. He came to a thick-lipped African, who was standing grin-hing at the scene.  The Professor touched him with his unguent, and immediately blackie fell a-striving with the lady, who should walk next the wonderful sage, and the two actually went to blows, to the great amusement of the spectators, who applauded these two feats prodigiously, and hailed their Professor as the greatest man in the world.  He walked twice the length of the promenade, and certainly every one whom he touched with his ointment followed him; so that if he had been a stranger in the community as I was, there could scarcely have been a doubt of the efficacy of his unguent of attraction. When he came last before the royal stage, and ours, he was encumbered by a crowd of persons following and kneeling to him; apparently they were of all ranks, from the highest to the lowest.   He then caused proclamation to be made from a stage, that if any doubted the power of his elixir, he might have it proved on himself without danger or disgrace; a dowager lady defied him, but he soon brought her to her knee with the rest, and no one of the whole begged to be released.

The King and Queen, and all the judges, then declaring themselves satisfied, the Professor withdrew, with his motley followers, to undo the charm in secret; after that, he returned in most brilliant and gorgeous array, and was received on the royal stage, amid deafening shouts of applause.  The King then asked me, if I deemed myself still able to compete with his liege kinsman, Professor Don Felix de Valdez? or if I joined the rest in approval, and yielded the palm to his merits in good fellowship.

I addressed his Majesty with all humility, acknowledged the extent of the Professor's powers, as very wonderful, provided they were all real; but of that there was no proof to me   " If he had been a foreigner, and a stranger as I am, in this place, and if prejudices had been excited against him," added I, " then I would have viewed this exhibition of his art as highly wonderful ; but, as it is, I only look on it as a well contrived farce."

The Professor reddened, and bit his lip in the height

of scorn and indignation; and indeed their Majesties and all the nobility seemed offended at my freedom; on which I added, " My exhibition, my liege, shall be a very short one; and I shall at least convince your Majesty, that there is no deceit nor collusion in it." And with that I took a small syringe from my bosom, which I had concealed there for the purpose, as the liquor, to have due effect, must be always warm with the heat of the body of him that sprinkles it; and with that small instrument, I squirted a spray of my elixir on Professor Don Felix's fine head of hair, that hung in wavy locks almost to his waist.

At that moment there were thousands all standing agape, eager to witness the effect of this bold appeal. The Professor stood up, and looked at me, while the tears stood in his eyes. That was the proudest moment of my life! For about the space of three minutes, his pride seemed warring with his feelings; but the energy and impulse of the latter prevailed, and he came and kneeled at my feet.

" Felix, you dog! what is the meaning of this?' cried I. " How dare you go and dress yourself like a grandee of the kingdom, and then come forth and mount the stage in the presence of royalty, knowing, as you do, that you were born to be my slave? Go this instant! doff that gorgeous apparel, and put on my livery, and come and wait here at my heel. And, do you hear, bring my horse properly caparisoned, and one to yourself; for I ride into the country to dinner. Take note of what I order, and attend to it, else I'll beat you to a jelly, and have you distilled into the elixir of attraction. Presumption indeed, to come into my presence in a dress like that!"

He ran to obey my orders, and then the admiration so lately expressed was turned into contempt. All the people were struck with awe and astonishment. They could not applaud, for they were struck dumb, and eyed me with terror, as if I had been a divinity. " This exceeds all comprehension," said the judges. "If he had told me that he could have upheaved the Pyrenean mountains from their foundations, I could as well have believed it," said the King.   But the Queen was the most perverse of all, for she would not believe it, though she witnessed it ; and she declared she never would believe it to be a reality, for I had only thrown glamour in their eyes.   " Is it possible," said she, " that the most famous man in Spain , or perhaps in the world, who has hundreds to serve him, and run at his bidding, should all at once, by his own choice, submit to become a slave to an opponent whom he despised, and be buffeted like a dog, without resenting it ?   No ; I'll never believe it is any thing but an illusion.

" There is no denying of your victory," said King Charles to me ; " for you have humbled your opponent in the dust.——You must dine with me to-night, as we have a great entertainment to the learned of our kingdom, over all of whom you shall be preferred to the highest place.   But as Don Felix de Valdez is likewise an invited guest, let me entreat you to disenchant him, that he may be again restored to his place in society."

" I shall do myself the distinguished honour of dining with your exalted and most Catholic Majesty," I replied. " But will it be no degradation to your high dignity, for the man who has worn my livery in public, to appear the same day at the table of royalty ?"

" This is no common occurrence," answered the King. " Although, by one great effort of art, nature has been overpowered, it would be hard that a great man should remain degraded for ever."

" Well, then, I shall not only permit him to leave my service, but I shall order him from it, and beat him from it.   I can do no more to oblige your Majesty at present."

" What ! can you not then remove the charm ?" said he.   " You saw the Professor could do that at once."

" A mere trick," said I.   " If the Professor Don Felix, had been in the least conscious of the power of his liquor, he would at once have attacked and degraded me. It is quite evident.   I expected a trial at least, as I am sure all the company did ; but I stood secure, and held him and his art at defiance. He is a sheer impostor, and his boasted discovery a cheat."

" Nay, but I have tried the power of his unguent again and again, and proved it," said the Queen. " But indeed, its effect is of very short duration; therefore, all I request is, that you will give the Professor his liberty; and take my word for it, it will soon be accepted."

I again promised that I would; but at the same time I shook my head, as much as to signify to the Queen, she was not aware of the power of my elixir; and I de- termined to punish the Professor for his insolence to me, and the sound beating I got in the court of his hotel. While we were speaking, Don Felix approached us, dressed in my plain yellow livery, leading my horse, and mounted on a grand one of his own, that cost two hun- dred gold ducats, while mine was only a hack, and no very fine animal either.

" How dare you have the impudence to mount my horse, sir?" exclaimed I, taking his gold-headed whip from him, and lashing him with it. "Get off instantly, you blundering booby, take your own spavined jade, and ride off where I may never see your face again."

" I beg your pardon, honoured master," said he, hum- bly; " I will take any horse you please; but I thought this had been mine."

" You thought, sirrah! What right have you to think?" I demanded. " I desire no more of your attendance," I continued. " Here, before their Majesties, and all their court and people, I discharge you my service, and dare you, on the penalty of your life, ever to approach my presence."

" Pardon me this time," said he; " I'll sooner die than leave you."

" But you shall leave me or do worse," said I, " and therefore disappear instantly;" and I pushed him through the throng away from me, and lashed him with the whip till he screamed and wept like a lubberly boy.

" You must have some one to ride with you and be

your guide," he said ; "and why will you not suffer me
to do so ? You know I cannot leave you."

His Majesty, taking pity on the helpless Professor,
sent a liveryman to take his place, and attend me on my
little jaunt, at the same time entreating him to desist,
and remember who he was. It was all in vain. He
fought with the King's servant for the privilege, mounted
my hack, and followed me to the villa, about six miles
from the city, where I had been engaged to dine. The
news had not arrived of my victory when I got there.
The lord of the manor was at the exhibition, and he not
having returned, the ladies were all impatience to learn
the result.

" It becomes not me, noble ladies," said I, " to bring
the news of my own triumph, which you might very reasonably expect to be untrue, or overcharged ; but you
shall witness my power yourselves.

Then they set up eldrich screams in frolic, and begged,
for the sake of the Virgin, that I would not put my skill
to the test on any of them, for they had no desire to follow to England even a master of the arts and sciences ;
and every one assured me personally that she would be
a horrid plague to me, and that I had better pause before I made the experiment.

" My dear and noble dames," said I, "there is nothing farther from my intention than to make any of you
the objects of fascination. But come all hither," and I
threw up the sash of the window—" Come all hither, and
behold a proof; and if more is required, it shall not
be lacking. See ; do you all know that gentleman
there ?"

" What gentleman ? Where is he ? I see no gentleman,"
was the general rejoinder.

" That gentleman who is holding my horse—he on
the sorry hack there, with yellow livery. You all know
him assuredly. That is your great Professor, Don Felix
de Valdez, accounted the most wonderful man in Spain,
and by many of you the greatest in the world."

They would not believe it, until I called him close up

to the door of the chateau, and showed him to them like any wild beast or natural curiosity, and called him by his name. Then they grew frightened, or pretended to be so, at being in the presence of a man of so much power, for they all knew the Professor personally; and if one could have believed them, they were like to go into hysterics for fear of fascination. Yet, for all that, I perceived they were dying for a specimen of my art, and that any of them would rather the experiment should be made on herself than not witness it.

Accordingly, there was a very handsome and engaging brunette of the party, named Donna Rashelli, on whom I could not help sometimes casting an eye, being a little fascinated myself. This was soon perceived by the lively group, and they all gathered round me, and teased me to try the power of my philtre on Rashelli. I asked the lady's consent, on which she answered rather disdainfully, that "she *would* be fascinated *indeed* if she followed *me!* and therefore she held me at defiance, provided I did not *touch* her, which she would *not* allow."

Without more ado, I took my tube from my bosom, and squirted a little of the philtre on her left-foot shoe —at least I meant it so, though I afterwards perceived that some of it had touched her stocking.

" And now, Donna Rashelli," said I, " you are in for your part in this drama, and you little know what you have authorized." She turned from me in disdain; but it was not long till I beheld the tears gathering in her eyes; she retired hastily to a recess in a window, covered her face with her hands, and wept bitterly. The others tried to comfort her, and laugh her out of her frenzy, but that was of no avail; she broke from them, and, drowned in tears, embraced my knees, requesting in the most fervent terms to be allowed the liberty of following me over the world.

The ladies were all thrown by this into the utmost consternation, and besought me to undo the charm, both for the sake of the young lady herself and her honourable

kin; but I had taken my measures, and paid no regard
to their entreaties.   On the contrary, I made my apo-
logy for not being able to dine there, owing to the King's
commanding my attendance at the palace, took a hasty
leave, mounted my horse, and, with Don Felix at my
back, rode away.

I knew all their power could not detain Donna Rashelli, and, riding slowly, I heard the screams of madness
and despair as they tried to hold her.   She tore their
head-dresses and robes in pieces, and fought like a fury,
till they were glad to suffer her to go; but they all followed in a group, to overtake and entreat me to restore
their friend to liberty.

I forded the stream that swept round the grounds, and
waited on the other bank, well knowing what would occur,
as a Spanish maiden never crosses even a rivulet without
taking off her shoes and stockings.   Accordingly she
came running to the side of the stream, followed by all
the ladies of the chateau, calling to me, and adjuring me
to have pity on them.   I laughed aloud at their tribula-
tion, saying, I had done nothing but at their joint request, and they must now abide by the consequences.
Rashelli threw off her shoes and stockings in a moment,
and rushed into the stream, for fear of being detained;
but before taking two steps, the charm being removed
with her left-foot shoe, she stood still, abashed; and so
fine a model of blushing and repentant beauty I never
beheld, with her raven hair hanging dishevelled far over
her waist, her feet and half her limbs of alabaster bathing
in the stream, and her cheek overspread with the blush
of shame.

"What am I about?" cried she.   "Am I mad? or
bewitched? or possessed of a demon, to run after a
mountebank, that I would order the menials to drive
from my door!"

"So you are gone, then, dear Donna Rashelli?" cried
I.   "Farewell, then, and peace be with you.   Shall I
not see you again before leaving this country?" but she
looked not up, nor deigned to reply.   Away she tripped,

led by one lady on each hand, barefooted as she was, till they came to the gravel walk, and then she slipped on her morocco shoes. The moment her left-foot shoe was on, she sprung towards me again, and all the dames after her full cry. It was precisely like a hare-hunt, and so comic, that even the degraded Don Felix laughed amain at the scene. Again she plunged into the stream, and again she returned, weeping for shame; and this self-same scene was acted seven times over. At length I took compassion on the humbled beauty, and called to her aunt to seize her left-foot shoe, and wash it in the river. She did so; and I, thinking all was then over and safe, rode on my way. But I had not gone three furlongs till the chase again commenced as loud and as violently as ever, and in a short time the lady was again in the stream. I was vexed at this, not knowing what was the matter, and terrified that I might have attached her to me for life; but I besought her friends to keep her from putting on her stocking likewise, till it was washed and fomented as well as her shoe. This they went about with great eagerness, an old dame seizing the stocking, and hiding it in her bosom; and when I saw this I rode quickly away, afraid I should be too late for my engagement with the King.

We had turned the corner of a wood, when again the screams and yells of females reached our ears.

"What, in the name of St Nicholas, is this now?" said I.

"I suppose the hunt is up again, sir; but surely our best plan is to ride off and leave them," replied Don Felix.

"That will never do," returned I; "I cannot have a lady of rank attending me at the palace; and no power on earth, save iron and chains, can detain her, if one-thousandth part of a drop of my elixir remain about her person."

We turned back, and behold there was the old dowager coming waddling along, with a haste and agitation not to be described, and all her daughters, nieces, and maidens,

after her.    She had taken the river at the broadest, shoes
and all, and had got so far ahead of her pursuers that
she reached me first, and seizing me by the leg, embraced
and kissed it, begging and praying all the while for my
favour, in the most breathless and grotesque manner
imaginable.    I knew not what to do; not in the least
aware how she became affected, till Donna Rashelli called
out, " O, the stocking, sir, the stocking !" on which I
caused them to take it from her altogether, and give it
to me, and then they went home in peace.

I dined that night with their Majesties, not indeed at
the same table, but at the head of the table in the ante-
room, from whence I had a full view of them.    I was
a great and proud man that night, and neither threats nor
persuasions could drive the great Professor from waiting
at the back of my chair, and frequently serving me kneeling.    After dinner I had an audience of the Queen, who
offered me a galleon laden with gold for the receipt of my
divine elixir of love.    But I withstood it, representing
to her Majesty the great danger of imparting such a secret,
because, after it had escaped from my lips, I could no
more recall it, and knew not what use might be made of
it; I accounted myself answerable, I said, to my Maker
for the abuse of talents bestowed on me, and, therefore,
was determined that the secret should go to the grave
with me.    I was, however, reduced to the necessity of
giving her Majesty a part of the pure and sublime elixir
ready prepared, taking her solemn promise, however, not
to communicate any portion of it to another.    She had
found a ready use for it, for in a few days she requested
more, and more, and more, till I began to think it was
high time for me to leave the country.

Having now got as much money as I wanted, and a
great deal more than I knew what to do with, I prepared
for leaving Spain ; for I was afraid that I should be made
accountable for the effects produced by the charm in the
hands of a capricious woman.    Had I yielded to the re-
quests of the young nobles for supplies, I might almost
have exhausted the riches of Spain ; but as it was, I had

got more than my own weight in gold; part of which I forwarded to London, and put the remainder out to interest in Spain, and left Madrid not without fear of being seized and sent to the Inquisition as a necromancer. In place of that, however, the highest honours were bestowed on me, and I was accompanied to the port by numbers of the first people of the realm, and by all the friends of the Professor Don Felix de Valdez. These people had laid a plot to assassinate me, which they would have executed but for the fear that the charm would never leave their friend; and as Felix himself discovered it to me, I kept him in bondage till the very day I was about to sail; then I caused his head to be shaved, and washed with a preparation of vinegar, alum, and cinnamon; and he returned to his senses and right feelings once more. But he never could show his face again in the land wherein he had been so much caressed and admired, but changed his name and retired to Peru, where he acquired both fame and respectability.

## The Countess.

WHEN a man gains great wealth too suddenly and with much ease, it is not unusual for him to throw it away with as little concern as he had anxiety in the gathering of it. This I was aware of, and determined to avoid. I began therefore, without loss of time, to look about me for a respectable settlement in life; and having, after much inquiry, obtained a list of the unmarried ladies possessing the greatest fortunes in England, I fixed on a young Countess, who was a widow, had a large fortune, and suited my wishes in every respect. Possessing as I did the divine cordial of love, I had no fears of her ready compliance; so, after providing myself with a suitable equipage, I set off to her residence to court and win her without any loss of time.

On arriving at her mansion about noon, I was rather coldly received, which was not surprising, for I had no introduction, but trusted to my own powers alone.

Though shy and reserved at first, she, however, at length invited me to an early dinner, letting me know at the same time that no visitor remained there overnight when her brother was not present.   This was so much gained; so I made my acknowledgments, and accepted the invitation,—thinking to myself, My pretty Countess, before you and I part, your haughtiness shall be wonderfully abated!—I waited my opportunity, and as she was leaving the apartment, aimed a small sprinkling of my cordial at her bushy locks; but owing to a sudden cast of her head, as ladies will affect pretty airs of disdain, the spray of my powerful elixir of love fell on an embroidered scarf that hung gracefully on her shoulder.

I was now sure of the effect, provided she did not throw the scarf aside before I got her properly sprinkled anew, but I had hopes its operation would be too instant and potent to permit that.   I judged right; in three minutes she returned to the drawing-room, and proposed that we two should take a walk in her park before dinner, as she had some curiosities to show me.   I acquiesced with pleasure, as may well be supposed.—I have you now, my pretty Countess, thought I; if it be in your power to escape me, I shall account you more than woman.

This park of hers was an immense field enclosed with a high wall, with a rail on the top.   She had some roes in it, one couple of fallow deer, and a herd of kine.   This last was what she pretended that she wished to show me; they were all milk-white, nay, as white as snow.   They were not of the wild bison breed, but as gentle and tame as lambs—came to her when called by their names, and seemed so fond of being caressed, that several were following and teasing her at the same time.   One favourite in particular was so fond, that she became troublesome; and the lady wished to be quit of her.   But the beast would not go away.   She followed on humming, and rubbing on her mistress with her cheek, till at last the latter, to rid herself of the annoyance, took her scarf, and struck the cow sharply across the face with it!   The tassels of the scarf fastened on the far horn of the cow, and the animal being a little hurt by the stroke, as well as blinded, it sprung away; and in one moment the lady lost hold of her scarf. This was death and destruction to me; for the lady was thus bereaved of all her attachment to me in an instant, and what the Countess had lost was transferred to the cow. I therefore pursued the animal with my whole speed, calling her many kind and affectionate names, to make her stop. These she did not seem to understand, for stop she would not; but perceiving that she was a little blindfolded with the scarf, I slid quietly forward, and making a great spring, seized the embroidered scarf by the corner. The cow galloped, and I ran and held, determined to have the scarf, though I should tear it all to pieces,—for I knew well that my divine elixir had the effect of rousing animals into boundless rage and madness,—and held with a desperate grasp. I could not obtain it! All that I effected was to fasten the other horn in it likewise, and away went the cow flaunting through the park, like a fine madam in her gold embroidery.

I fled to the Countess as fast as my feet could carry me, and begged her, for Heaven's sake, to fly with me, for that our lives were at stake. She could not understand this; and moreover, she, that a minute or two before had been clinging to me with as much confidence as if our acquaintance had been of many years' standing, and of the most intimate kind, appeared to have conceived a sort of horror of me, and would not allow me to approach her. There was no time to parley; so I left her to shift for herself, and fled with all my might towards the gate at which we entered, knowing of no other point of egress. Time was it; for the creature instantly became furious, and came after me at full speed, bellowing like some agonized fiend escaped from the infernal regions. The herd was roused by the outrageous sounds, and followed in the same direction, every one galloping faster and roaring louder than another, apparently for company's sake; but, far ahead of them all, the cow came with the embroidered scarf flying over her shoulders, hanging out her

tongue and bellowing, and gaining every minute on me.
Next her in order came a stately milk-white bull, tall as
a hunting steed, and shapely as a deer. My heart became chill with horror; for of all things on this earth, I
stood in the most mortal terror of a bull. I saw, however, that I would gain the wicket before I was overtaken; and, in the brightness of hope, I looked back to see
what had become of the Countess. She had fallen down
on a rising ground in a convulsion of laughter! This
nettled me exceedingly; however, I gained the gate;
but, O misery and despair! it was fast locked, the Countess having the pass-key. To clear the wall was out of
my power in such a dilemma as I then was, so I had
nothing left for it but swiftness of foot. Often had I
valued myself on that qualification, but little expected
ever to have so much need of it. So I ran and ran, pursued by twenty milk-white kine and a bull, all bellowing
like as many infernal creatures. Never was there such
another chase! I tried to reach the place where the
Countess was, thinking she might be able by her voice,
to stay them, or, at all events, that she would tell me
how I could escape from their fury. But the drove having
all got between her and me, I could not effect it, and was
obliged to run at random, which I continued to do, strain-
ing with all my might, but now found that my breath
was nearly gone, and the terrible race drawing to a crisis.

What was to be done? Life was sweet, but expedients there were none. There were no trees in the park
save young ones, dropped down, as it were, here and
there, with palings round them, to prevent the cattle
from destroying them. The only one that I could perceive was a tall fir, I suppose of the larch species, which
seemed calculated to afford a little shelter in a desperate
case; so I made towards it with a last effort. There was
a triangular paling around it, setting my foot on which,
I darted among the branches, clomb like a cat, and soon
vanished among the foliage.

Then did I call aloud to the Countess for assistance,
imploring her to raise the country for my rescue; but all

that she did, was to come towards me herself, slowly and with lagging pace, for she was feeble with laughing; and when she did come, the cattle were all so infuriated that they would not once regard her.

" What is the matter with my cattle, sir?' cried she. "They are surely bewitched."

" I think they are bedeviled, and that is worse, madam," returned I. " But, for Heaven's sake, try to regain the scarf. It is the scarf which is the cause of all this uproar."

" What is in the scarf?" said she. " It can have no effect in raising this deadly enmity against you, if all is as it should be, which I now begin to suspect, from some strange diversity of feelings I have experienced."

" It is merely on account of the gold that is on it, madam," said I. " You cannot imagine how mad the sight of gold, that pest of the earth, makes some animals; and it was the effort I made to get it from the animal that has excited in her so much fury against me."

" That is most strange indeed!" exclaimed the lady. " Then the animal shall keep it for me, for I would not for half my fortune that these favourites should be driven to become my persecutors."

She now called the cattle by their names, and some of them left me; for it was evident that, save the charmed animal, the rest of the herd were only running for company or diversion's sake. Still their looks were exceedingly wild and unstable, and the one that wore the anointed shawl, named Fair Margaret, continued foaming mad, and would do nothing but stand and bellow, toss her adorned head, and look up to the tree. I would have given ten thousand pounds to have got hold of that vile embroidered scarf, but to effect it, and retain my life, at that time was impracticable.

And now a scene ensued, which, for horror to me could not be equalled, although to any unconcerned beholder, it must have appeared ludicrous in the extreme. The bull, perceiving one of his favourite mates thus distempered, showed a great deal of anxiety; he went round her, and round her, and perceiving the flaunting thing on her head and shoulders, he seemed to entertain some kind of idea that it was the cause of this unwonted and obstreperous noise. He tried to fling it off with his horns, I know not how oft; but so awkward were his efforts that they all failed. Enraged at being thus baffled, he then had recourse to a most unexpected expedient—he actually seized the scarf with his great mouth, tore it off, and in a few seconds swallowed it every thread!

What was I to do now? Here was a new enemy, and one ten times more formidable than the other, who had swallowed up the elixir, and whom, therefore, it was impossible ever to discharm; who, I knew, would pursue me to the death, even though at the distance of fifty miles. I was in the most dreadful agony of terror imaginable, as well I might, for the cow went away shaking her ears, as if happily quit of a tormenter, and the bull instantly began to tear up the earth with hoof and horn, while the late bellowings of the cow were, to his, like the howl of a beagle to the roar of a lion. They made the very earth to quake; while distant woods, and walls, and the very skies, returned the astounding echoes. He went round and round the tree, digging graves on each side of it; and his fury still increasing, he broke through the paling as if it had been a spider's web, and setting his head to the trunk, pushed with all his mighty force, doubled by supernatural rage. The tree yielded like a bulrush, until I hung dangling from it as if suspended from a cross-beam; still I durst not quit my hold, having no other resource. While in this situation, I observed the Countess speeding away. It seemed to me as if she were Hope flying from me and abandoning me to my fate, and I uttered some piercing cries of desperation. The tree, however, was young and elastic, and always as the infuriated animal withdrew his force for a new attack, it sprung up to its original slender and stately form, and then down it went again; so that there was I swinging between heaven and earth, expecting every moment to be my last; and if the bull had not, in his mad efforts, wheeled round to the contrary side, I might have been swinging to this day. When he changed sides, the fibres of the tree weakened, and at last I came down to the earth, and he made at me with full force; it was in vain that I called to him to keep off, and bullied him, and pretended to hunt dogs on him; on he came, and plunged his horns into the foliage; the cows did the same for company's sake, and, I'm sure, never was there a poor soul so completely mobbed by a vulgar herd. Still the tree had as much strength left as to heave me gently above their reach, and no more, and I now began to lose all power through terror and despair, and merely kept my hold instinctively, as a drowning man would hold by a rush. The next push the tree got it was again laid prostrate, and again the bull dashed his horns into the foliage, and through that into the earth. I now saw there was no longer any hope of safety if I remained where I was, and therefore quitted hold of the tree. How I escaped I scarce can tell, but I did escape through amongst the feet of the cows.

At first I stole away like a hare from a cover, and could not help admiring the absurdity of the cows, that continued tossing and tearing the tree with their horns, as if determined not to leave a stiver of it; whilst the bull continued grovelling with his horns, down through the branches and into the ground. Heavens! with what velocity I clove the wind! I have fled from battle—I have fled from the face of the lions of Asia, the dragons of Africa, and the snakes of America—I have fled before the Indians with their scalping knives; but never in my life was I enabled to run with such speed as I did from this infuriated monster.

He was now coming full speed after me, as I knew he would, the moment he disengaged himself; but I had got a good way ahead, and, I assure you, was losing no time, and as I was following a small beaten track, I came to a stile over the wall. I never was so thankful for any thing since I was born! It was a crooked stone stair, with angles to hinder animals from passing, and a locked. door on the top, about the height of an ordinary man. I easily surmounted this, by getting hold of the iron spikes on the top; and now, being clear of my adversary, I set my head over the door and looked him in the face, mocking and provoking him all that I could, for I had no other means of retaliation, and felt exceedingly indignant at having been put in danger of my life by so ignoble an enemy. I never beheld a more hideous picture of rage ! He was foaming at the mouth, and rather belching than bellowing; his tail was writhing in the air like a serpent, and his eyes burning like small globes of bright flame. He grew so enraged at length, that he rushed up the stone stair, and the frame-work at the angles began to crash before him. Thinks I to myself, Friend, I do not covet such a close vicinity with you : so, with your leave, I'll keep a due distance; and then descending to the high road, I again began to speed away, though rather leisurely, knowing that he could not possibly get over the iron-railed wall.

There was now a close hedge on every side of me, about eight or ten feet high, and as a man who has been in great jeopardy naturally looks about him for some safe retreat in case of an emergency, so I continued jogging on and looking for such, but perceived none; when, hearing a great noise far behind me, I looked back, and saw the irresistible monster coming tumbling from the wall, bringing gates, bars, and railing, all before him. He fell with a tremendous crash, and I had great hopes his neck was broken, for at first he tried to rise, and, stumbling, fell down again ; but, to my dismay, he was soon again on the chase, and making ground on me faster than ever. He came close on me at last, and I had no other shift than to throw off my fine coat, turn round to await him and fling it over his horns and eyes.

This not only marred him, but detained him long wreaking his vengeance on the coat, which he tore all to pieces with his feet and horns, taking it for a part of me. By this time I had reached a willow-tree in the hedge, the twigs of which hung down within reach. I seized on two or three of these, wrung them together like a rope, and by the assistance of that, swung myself over the hedge. Still I slackened not my pace, knowing that the devil was in the beast, and that nothing but blood would allay his fury. Accordingly, it was not long till I saw him plunging in the hedge ; and through it he came.

I now perceived a fine sheet of water on my left, about a mile broad, I knew not whether a lake or river, never having been in those bounds before. I made towards it with all my remaining energy, which was not great. I cleared many common stone-walls in my course, but these proved no obstacles to my pursuer, and before I reached the lake, he came so close upon me, that I was obliged to fling my hat in his face, and as he fortunately took that for my head, it served him a good while to crush it in pieces, so that I made to the lake and plunged in. At the very first, I dived and swam under water as long as I could keep my breath, assured that my enemy would lose all traces of me then ; but, when I came to the surface, I found him puffing within two yards of me. I was in such horror, that I knew not what to do, for I found he could swim twice as fast as I could ; so I dived again, but my breath being gone, I could not remain below, and whenever I came to the surface, there was he.

If I had had the smallest reasoning faculty left, or had once entertained a thought of resistance, I might easily have known that I was now perfectly safe. The beast could not harm me. Whenever he made a push at me, his head went below the water, which confounded him. My perturbation was so extreme, that I was on the point of perishing from exhaustion, before I perceived this to be the case. When, however, I did observe it, I took courage, seized him by the tail, clomb upon his back, and then rode in perfect safety.

I never got a more complete and satisfactory revenge of an enemy, not even over the Spanish Professor, and that was complete enough ; but here I had nothing to do but to sit exulting on the monster's back, while he kept wallowing and struggling in the waves. I then took my penknife, and stabbed him deliberately over the whole body, letting out his heart's blood. He took this very much amiss, but he had now got enough of blood around him, and began to calm himself. I kept my seat nevertheless, to make all sure, till his head sunk below the water, while his huge hinder parts turned straight upmost, and I left him floating away like a huge buoy that had lost its anchor.

———

" Now, Doctor, gin a' tales be true, yours is nae lee, that is certain," said my mother, at the conclusion of this narration; "but I want some explanations—it's a grand story, but I want to tak the consequences alang wi' me. What did the Queen o' Spain wi' a' the oint-ment you left wi' her? I'm thinking there wad be some strange scenes about that Court for a while."

" Why, Margaret, to say the truth, the elixir was not used in such a way as might have been expected. The truth appeared afterwards to have been this: The King had at that time resolved on that ruinous, and then very unpopular war, about what was called the Family Compact; and finding that the clergy, and a part of the principal nobility, were in opposition to it, and that, without their concurrence, the war could not be prosecuted with any effect, the Queen took this very politic method of purchasing plenty of my divine elixir of attachment, and giving them all a touch of it every one. The effect was, of course, instant, potent, and notorious; and it is a curious and incontestable fact, that the effects of that sprinkling have continued the mania of attachment among that class of Spain to this day."

" And how came you on wi' your grand Countess? Ye wad be a bonny figure gaun hame again to her place, half-naked, and like a droukit craw, wi' the life of her favourite animal to answer for!"

" That is rather a painful subject, Margaret—rather a painful subject. I never saw her again! I had lost my coat and hat. I had lost all my money, which was in notes, in swimming and diving. I had lost my carriage and horses, and I had lost my good name, which was worst of all; for from that day forth, I was branded and shunned as a necromancer. The abrupt and extraordinary changes in the lady's sentiments had not escaped her own notice, while the distraction of the animals on the transference of the enchanted scarf to them, confirmed her worst suspicions, that I was a dealer in unlawful arts, and come to gain possession of herself and fortune, by the most infamous measures; and as I did not choose to come to an explanation with her on that subject, I escaped as quietly from the district as possible.

"It surely can be no sin to dive into the hidden mysteries of nature, particularly those of plants and flowers. Why, then, have I been punished as never pharmacopolist was punished before; can you tell me that, Margaret?"

" Indeed, can I—weel enough—Doctor. Other men have studied the qualities o' yirbs to assist nature; but ye have done it only to pervert nature,—and I hope you hae read your sin in your punishment."

" The very sentiment that my heart has whispered to me a thousand times! It indeed occurred to me, whilst skulking about on my escape after the adventure with the Countess; but it was not until farther and still more bitter experience of the dangerous effects of my secret, that I could bring myself to destroy the maddening liquid. It had taken years of anxiety and labour to perfect a mixture, from which I anticipated the most beneficial results. The consequences which it drew upon me, although, at first, they promised to be all I could wish, proved in the end every way annoying, and often well nigh fatal, and I carefully consumed with fire every drop of the potion, and every scrap of writing, in which the progress of the discovery had been noted. I cannot myself forget the painful and tedious steps by which it was obtained. And

even after all the disasters to which it has subjected me
—after the miserable wreck of all my high-pitched am-
bition, I cannot but feel a pride in the consciousness
that I carry with me the knowledge of a secret never
before possessed by mortal man, which no one shall
learn from me, and which it is all but certain that none
after me will have perseverance enough, or genius, to
arrive at ?"

The learned Doctor usually wound up the history of
an adventure with a sonorous conclusion like the above,
the high-wrought theatrical tone of which, as it was incomprehensible to his hearers, for the most part produced
a wonderful effect. Looking upon the gaunt form of the
sage, I was penetrated with immeasurable reverence, and
though the fascination of his marvellous stories kept me
listening with eager curiosity while they lasted, I always
retired shortly after he ceased speaking, not being able
to endure the august presence of so wise a personage as
he appeared to me to be.

Many of his relations were still more marvellous than
those I have preserved ; but these are sufficient for a
specimen, and it would be idle to pursue the Doctor's
hallucinations farther. All I can say about these adventures of his is, that when I heard them first, I received
them as strictly true ; my mother believed them most
implicitly, and the Doctor related them as if he had
believed in the truth of them himself. But there were
disputes every day between my mother and him about
the invention of the charm, the former always maintaining that it was known to the chiefs of the gipsy tribes for
centuries bygone ; and as proofs of her position, she
cited Johnie Faa's seduction of the Earl of Cassillis's
lady, so well known in Lowland song, and Hector Ken-
nedy's seduction of three brides, all of high quality, by
merely touching the palms of their hands, after which no
power could prevent any of them from following him.
She likewise told a very affecting story of an exceedingly
beautiful girl, named Sophy Sloan, who left Kirkhope,
and eloped after the gipsies, though she had never ex-

changed a word with one of them. Her father and uncle followed, and found her with them in an old kiln on the water of Milk. Her head was wounded, bloody, and tied up with a napkin. They had pawned all her good clothes, and covered her with rags, and though weeping with grief and despair, yet she refused to leave them. The man to whom she was attached had never asked her to go with him; he even threatened her with death if she would not return with her father, but she continued obstinate, and was not suffered long to outlive her infatuation and disgrace. This story *was* a fact; yet the Doctor held all these instances in utter contempt, and maintained his prerogative, as the sole and original inventor of THE ELIXIR OF LOVE.

There was not a doubt that the Doctor was skulking, and in terror of being apprehended for some misdemeanour, all the time he was at Ettrick Manse; and never one of us had a doubt that it was on account of some enchantment. But I had reason to conclude, long afterwards, that his seclusion then, and all the latter part of his life, was owing to an unfortunate and fatal experiment in pharmacy, which deprived society of a number of valuable lives. The circumstances are related in a note to the third volume of Eustace's *Pharmacopœia*, and it will there be seen that the description of the delinquent suits exactly with that of THE MARVELLOUS DOCTOR.

---

# CHAP. XV.

### THE WITCHES OF TRAQUAIR.

THERE was once a young man, a native of Traquair, in the county of Peebles, whose name was Colin Hyslop, and who suffered more by witchcraft, and the intervention of supernatural beings, than any man I ever heard of.

Traquair was a terrible place then! There was a witch almost in every hamlet, and a warlock here and there besides. There were no fewer than twelve witches in one straggling hamlet, called Taniel Burn, and five in Kirk Row. What a desperate place Traquair had been in those days! But there is no person who is so apt to overshoot his mark as the Devil. He must be a great fool in the main; for, with all his supposed acuteness, he often runs himself into the most confounded blunders that ever the leader of an opposition got into the midst of. Throughout all the annals of the human race, it is manifest, that whenever he was aiming to do the most evil, he was uniformly employed in such a way as to bring about the most good; and it seems to have been so, in a particular manner, in the case with which my tale shall make the reader acquainted.

The truth is that Popery was then on its last legs, and the Devil, finding it (as then exercised) a very convenient and profitable sort of religion, exerted himself beyond measure to give its motley hues a little more variety; and the making witches and warlocks, and holding nocturnal revels with them, where every sort of devilry was exercised, was at that time with him a favourite plan. It was also favourably received by the meaner sort of the populace. Witches gloried in their power, and warlocks in their foreknowledge of events, and the energies of their master. Women, beyond a certain age, when the pleasures and hopes of youth delighted no more, flew to an intercourse with the unseen powers, as affording an excitement of a higher and more terrible nature; and men, whose tempers had been soured by disappointment and ill usage, betook themselves to the Prince of the Power of the Air, enlisting under his banner, in hopes of obtaining revenge on their oppressors, or those against whom they had conceived displeasure. However extravagant this may appear, there is no doubt of the fact, that, in those days, the hopes of attaining some energies beyond the reach of mere human capability, inflamed the ignorant and wicked to attempts and acts of the most diabolical nature; for hundreds acknowledged their principles, and gloried in them, before the tribunals that adjudged them to the stake,

"I am now fairly under the power of witchcraft," said Colin Hyslop, as he sat on the side of the Feathen Hill, with his plaid drawn over his head, the tears running down his brown manly cheek, and a paper marked with uncouth lines and figures in his hand,—"I am now fairly under the power of witchcraft, and must submit to my fate; I am entangled, enchained, enslaved; and the fault is all my own, for I have committed that degree of sin which my sainted and dying father assured me would subject me to the snares of my hellish neighbours and sworn adversaries. My pickle sheep have a' been bewitched, and a great part o' them have died dancing hornpipes and French cotillions. I have been changed, and ower again changed, into shapes and forms that I darena think of, far less name; and a' through account of my ain sin. Hech! but it is a queer thing that sin! It has sae mony inroads to the heart, and outlets by the senses, that we seem to live and breathe in it. And I canna trow that the Deil is the wyte of a' our sins neither. Na, na; black as he is, he canna be the cause and the mover of a' our transgressions, for I find them often engendering and breeding in my heart as fast as maggots on tainted carrion; and then it is out o' the power of man to keep them down. My father tauld me, that if aince I let the Deil get his little finger into *ane* o' my transactions, he wad soon hae his haill hand into them a'. Now I hae found it in effect, but not in belief; for, from all that I can borrow frae Rob Kirkwood, the warlock, and my aunty Nans, the wickedest witch in Christendye, the Deil appears to me to be a geyan obliging chap. That he is wayward and fond o' sin, I hae nae doubt; but in that he has mony neighbours. And then his great power over the senses and conditions of men, over the winds, the waters, and the element of flame, is to me incomprehensible, and would make him appear rather a sort of vicegerent over the outskirts and unruly parts of nature, than an opponent to its lawful lord.——What then shall I do with this?" looking at the scroll; "shall I subscribe to the conditions, and enlist under his banner, or shall I not? O love, love! were it not for thee, all the torments that Old Mahoun and his followers could inflict, should not induce me to quit the plain path of Christianity. But that disdainful, cruel, and lovely Barbara! I must and will have her, though my repentance should be without measure and without end. So then it is settled! Here I will draw blood from my arm—blot out the sign of the cross with it, and form that of the crescent, and these other things, the meaning of which I do not know.——Halloo! What's that? Two beautiful deers, as I am a sinner, and one of them lame. What a prey for poor ruined Colin! and fairly off the royal bounds, too. Now for it, Bawty, my fine dog! now for a clean chase! A' the links o' the Feathen Wood winna hide them from your infallible nose, billy Bawty. Halloo! off you go! and now for the bow and the broad arrow at the head slap!—What! ye winna hunt a foot-length after them, will ye no? Then, Bawty, there's some mair mischief in the wind for me! I see what your frighted looks tell me. That they dinna leave the scent of other deers in their track, but ane that terrifies you, and makes your blood creep. It is hardly possible, ane wad think, that witches could assume the shapes of these bonny harmless creatures; but their power has come to sic a height hereabouts, that nae man alive can tell what they can do. There's my aunt Nans has already turned me into a gait, then to a gainder, and last of a' into a three-legged stool!

"I am a ruined man, Bawty! your master is a ruined man, and a lost man, that's far waur. He has sold himself for love to one beautiful creature, the comeliest of all the human race. And yet that beautiful creature must be a witch, else how could a' the witches o' Traquair gie me possession o' her?

"Let me consider and calculate. Now, supposing they are deceiving me—for that's their character; and supposing they can never put me in possession of her, then I hae brought myself into a fine scrape. How terrible a thought this is! Let me see; is all over? Is this scroll signed and sealed; and am I wholly given up to this unknown and untried destiny?" (Opens his scroll with trembling agitation, and looks over it.) No, thanks to the Lord of the universe, I am yet a Christian. The cross stands uncancelled, and there is neither sign nor superscription in my blood. How did this happen? I had the blood drawn—the pen filled—and the scroll laid out. Let me consider what was it that prevented me? The deers? It was, indeed, the two comely deers. What a strange intervention this is! Ah! these were no witches! but some good angels, or happy fays, or guardian spirits of the wild, sent to snatch an abused youth from destruction. Now, thanks be to Heaven, though poor and reduced to the last extremity, I am yet a free man, and in my Maker's hand. My resolution is changed—my promise is broken, and here I give this mystic scroll to the winds of the glen.

"Alas, alas! to what a state sin has reduced me! Now shall I be tortured by night, and persecuted by day; changed into monstrous shapes, torn by cats, pricked by invisible bodkins, my heart racked by insufferable pangs of love, until I either lose my reason, and yield to the dreadful conditions held out to me, or abandon all hope of earthly happiness, and yield up my life. Oh, that I were as free of sin as that day my father gave me his last blessing! then might I withstand all their charms and enchantments. But that I will never be. So as I have brewed so must I drink. These were his last words to me, which I may weel remember:—' You will have many enemies of your soul to contend with, my son; for your nearest relations are in compact with the devil; and as they have hated and persecuted me, so will they hate and persecute you; and it will only be by repeating your prayers evening and morning, and keeping a conscience void of all offence towards God and towards man, that you can hope to escape the snares that will be laid for you. But the good angels from the presence of the Almighty will, perhaps, guard my poor orphan boy, and protect him from the counsels of the wicked.'

" Now, in the first place, I have never prayed at all ; and, in the second place, I have sinned so much, that I have long ago subjected myself to their snares, and given myself up for lost. What will become of me ? flight is in vain, for they can fly through the air, and follow me wherever I go. And then, Barbara,—O that lovely and bewitching creature ! in leaving her I would leave life and saul behind !"

After this long and troubled soliloquy, poor Colin burst into tears, and wished himself a dove or a sparrow-hawk, or an eagle, to fly away and be seen no more; but, in either case, to have bonny Barbara for his mate. At this instant Bawty began to cock up his ears, and turn his head first to the one side and then to the other ; and, when Colin looked up, he beheld two hares cowering away from a bush behind him. There was nothing that Colin was so fond of as a chase. He sprung up, pursued the hares, and shouted to his dog, Halloo, hallop ! No, Bawty would not pursue them a foot, but whenever he came to the place where he had seen them, and put his nose to the ground, ran back, hanging his tail, and uttering short barks, as he was wont to do when attacked by witches in the night. Colin's hair rose up on his head, for he instantly suspected that the two hares were Robin Kirkwood and his aunt Nans, watching his motions, and the fulfilment of his promise to them. Colin was horrified, and knew not what to do. He did not try to pray, for he could not ; but he wished in his heart that his father's dying prayer for him had been heard.

He rose, and hastened away in the direction contrary to that the hares had taken, as may well be supposed ; and as he jogged along, in melancholy mood, he was aware of two damsels who approached him slowly and cautiously. They were clothed in white, with garlands on their heads ; and, on their near approach, Colin perceived that one of them was lame, and the other supported her by the hand.

The two comely hinds that had come upon him so suddenly and unexpectedly, and had prevented him, at the very decisive moment, from selling his salvation for sensual enjoyment, instantly came over Colin's awakened recollection, and he was struck with indescribable awe. Bawty was affected somewhat in the same manner with his master.   The dismay he manifested was different from that inspired by the attacks of witches and warlocks ; he crept close to the ground, and turning his face half away from the radiant objects, uttered a sort of stifled murmur, as if moved both by respect and fear.   Colin perceived, from these infallible symptoms, that the beings with whom he was now coming in contact were not the subjects of the Power of Darkness.

He therefore threw his plaid over his shoulder in the true shepherd style, took his staff below his left arm, so that his right hand might be at liberty to lift his bonnet when the fair damsels accosted him, and, not choosing to advance direct upon them, he paused at a respectful distance, straight in their path.   When they came within a few paces of him, they turned gently from the path, as if to pass him on the left side, but all the while kept their bright eyes fixed on him, and whispered to each other. Colin was grieved that so much comeliness should pass by without saluting them, and kept his regretful eyes steadily on them.   At length they paused, and one of them called in a sweet but solemn voice, " Ah, Colin Hyslop, Colin Hyslop ! you are on the braid way for destruction."

" How do you ken that, madam ?" returned Colin. " Do you ca' the road up the Kirk Rigg the braid way to destruction."

" Ay, up the rigg or down the rigg, cross the rigg or round the rigg, all is the same for you, Colin.   You are a lost man ; and it is a great pity.   One single step farther on the path you are now treading, and all is over."

" What wad ye hae me to do, sweet madam ?   Wad ye hae me to stand still and starve here on the crown o' the Kirk Rigg ?"

" Better starve in a dungeon than take the steps you
are about to take.   You were at a witch and warlock
meeting yestreen."

" It looks like as gin you had been there too, madam,
that you ken sae weel."

" Yes, I *was* there, but under concealment, and not
for the purpose of making any such vows and promises as
you made.   O wretched Colin Hyslop, what is to become
of you !"

" I did naething, madam, but what I couldna help ;
and my heart is sair for it the day."

" Can you lay your hand on that heart and say so ?"

" Yes, I can, dear madam, and swear to it too."

" Then follow us down to this little green knowe, and
account to us the circumstances of your life, and I will
inform you of a secret I heard yestreen."

" Aha, madam, but yon is a fairy ring, and I hae gotten sae mony cheats wi' changelings, that I hae muckle
need to be on my guard.   However, things can hardly
be waur wi' me.   Lead on, and I shall e'en follow."

The two female figures walked before him to a fairy
knowe, on the top of the Feathen Hill, and sat down,
with their faces towards him, till he recounted the incidents of his life, the outline of which was this :—His
father was a sincere adherent of the Reformers, and a
good Christian ; but poor Colin was born at Taniel-Burn,
in the midst of Papists and witches ; and the nearest relation he had, a maternal aunt, was the leading witch of
the neighbourhood.   Consequently, Colin was nurtured
in sin, and inured to iniquity, until all the kindly and
humane principles of his nature were erased, or so much
distorted, as to appear like their very opposites ; and
when this was accomplished, his wicked aunt, and her
associate hags, judging him fairly gained, and without
the pale of redemption, began to exercise cantrips, the
most comical, and at the same time, the most refined in
cruelty, at his expense ; and at length, on being assured
of every earthly enjoyment, he engaged to join their hellish community, only craving three days to study their

mysteries, before he should bleed himself, and, with the blood extracted from his veins, extinguish the sign of the cross, and thereby renounce his hope in mercy, and likewise make some hieroglyphics of strange shapes and mysterious efficacy, and finally subscribe his name to the whole.

When the relation was finished, one of the lovely auditors said,—" You are a wicked and abandoned person, Colin Hyslop. But you were reared up in iniquity, and know no better; and the mercy of Heaven is most readily extended to such. You have, besides, some good points in your character still; for you have told us the truth, however much to your own disadvantage."

" Aha, madam! How do you ken sae weel that I hae been telling you a' the truth?"

" I know all concerning you better than you do yourself. There is little, very little, of a redeeming nature in your own history; but you had an upright and devout father, and the seed of the just may not perish for ever. I have been young, and now am old, yet have I never seen the good man forsaken, nor his children cast out as vagabonds in the land of their fathers."

" Ah, na, na, madam! ye canna be auld. It is impossible! But goodness kens! there are sad changelings now-a-days. I have seen an auld wrinkled wife blooming o'ernight like a cherub."

" Colin, you are a fool! And folly in youth leads to misery in old age. But I am your friend, and you have not another on earth this night but myself and my sister here, and one more. Pray, will you keep this little vial, and drink it for my sake?"

" Will it no change me, madam?"

" Yes, it will."

" Then I thank you; but will have nothing to do with it. I have had enow of these kind o' drinks in my life."

" But suppose it change you for the better? Suppose it change you to a new creature?"

" Weel, suppose it should, what will that creature be?

Tell me that first.    Will it no be a fox, nor a gainder, nor a bearded gait, nor—nor—a three-legged stool, which is no a creature ava?"

"Ah, Colin, Colin!" exclaimed she, smiling through tears, "your own wickedness and unbelief gave the agents of perdition power over you.    It is that power which I wish to counteract.    But I will tell you nothing more.    If you will not take this little vial, and drink it, for my sake,—why, then, let it alone, and follow your own course."

"O dear madam! ye ken little thing about me.    I was only joking wi' you, for the sake o' hearing your sweet answers.    For were that bit glass fu' o' rank poison, and were it to turn me intil a taed or a worm, I wad drink it aff at your behest.    I hae been sae little accustomed to hear aught serious or friendly, that my very heart clings to you as it wad do to an angel coming down frae heaven to save me.    Ay, and ye said something kind and respectfu' about my auld father too.    That's what I hae been as little used to.    Ah, but he was a douce man!    Wasna he, mem?—Drink that bit bottle o' liquor for your sake!    Od, I wish it were fu' to the brim, and that's no what it is by twa-thirds."

"Ay, but it has this property, Colin, that drinking will never exhaust it; and the langer you drink it, the sweeter it will become."

"Say you sae?    Then here's till ye.    We'll see whether drinking winna exhaust it or no."

Colin set the vial to his lips, with intent of draining it; but the first portion that he swallowed made him change his countenance, and shudder from head to heel.

"Ah! sweeter did you say, madam?    by the faith of my heart, it has muckle need; for siccan a potion for bitterness never entered the mouth of mortal man.    Oh, I am ruined, poisoned, and undone!"

With that poor Colin drew his plaid over his head, fell flat on his face, and wept bitterly, while his two comely visitants withdrew, smiling at the success of their mission.    As they went down by the side of the Feathen

Wood, the one said to the other, " Did you not perceive two of that infatuated community haunting this poor hap-less youth to destruction? Let us go and hear their schemes, that we may the better counteract them."

They skimmed over the lea fields, and, in a thicket of brambles, briers, and nettles, they found—not two hares, but the identical Rob Kirkwood, the warlock, and Colin's aunt Nans, in close and unholy consultation. This bush has often been pointed out to me as the scene of that memorable meeting. It perhaps still remains at the side of a little hollow, nigh to the east corner of the Feathen arable fields ; and the spots occupied by the witch and warlock, without a green shrub on them, are still as visi-ble as on the day they left them. The two sisters, hav-ing chosen a disguise that, like Jack the Giant-Killer's coat of darkness, completely concealed them, heard the following dialogue, from beginning to end.

" Kimmer, I trow the prize is won. I saw his arm bared ; the red blood streaming ; the scroll in the one hand, and the pen in the other."

" He's ours ! he's ours !"

" He's nae mair yours."

" We'll ower the kirkstyle, and away wi' him !"

" I liked not the appearance of yon two pale hinds at such a moment. I wish the fruit of all our pains be not stolen from us when ready for our lord and master's board. How he will storm and misuse us if this has be-fallen !"

" What of the two hinds? What of them, I say? I like to see blood. It is a beautiful thing blood."

" Thou art as gross as flesh and blood itself, and hast nothing in thee of the true sublimity of a supernatural being. I love to scale the thundercloud ; to ride on the topmost billow of the storm ; to roost by the cataract, or croon the anthem of hell at the gate of heaven. But *thou* delightest to see blood,—rank, reeking, and baleful Christian blood. What pleasure is in that, dotard?"

" Humph ! I like to see Christian blood, howsomever. It bodes luck, kimmer—it bodes luck."

"It bodes that thou art a mere block, Rob Kirkwood! but it is needless to upbraid thee, senseless as thou art. Listen then to me:—It has been our master's charge to us these seven years to gain that goodly stripling, my nephew; and you know that you and I engaged to accomplish it; if we break that engagement, woe unto us! Our master bore a grudge at his father; but he particularly desires the son, because he knows that, could we gain him, all the pretty girls of the parish would flock to our standard.—But Robin Kirkwood, I say, Robin Kirkwood, what two white birds are these always hopping around us? I dinna like their looks unco weel. See, the one of them is lame too; and they seem to have a language of their own to one another. Let us leave this place, Robin; my heart is quaking like an aspen."

"Let them hap on. What ill can wee bits o' birdies do till us? Come, let us try some o' yon cantrips our master learned us. Grand sport yon, Nans!"

"Robin, did not you see that the birds hopped three times round us! I am afraid we are charmed to the spot."

"Never mind, auld fool, it's a very good spot.—Some of our cantrips! some of our cantrips!"

What cantrips they performed is not known; but on that day fortnight, the two were found still sitting in the middle of the bush, the two most miserable and disgusting figures that ever shocked humanity. Their cronies came with a hurdle to take them home; but Nans expired by the way, uttering wild gibberish and blasphemy, and Rob Kirkwood died soon after he got home. The last words he uttered were, "Plenty o' Christian blood soon! It will be running in streams!—in streams!—in streams!"

We now return to Colin, who, freed of his two greatest adversaries, now spent his time in a state bordering on happiness, compared with the life he had formerly led. He wept much, staid on the hill by himself, and pondered deeply on something—nobody knew what, and it was believed he did not know well himself. He was in love

—over head and ears in love; which may account for any thing in man, however ridiculous. He was in love with Barbara Stewart, an angel in loveliness as well as virtue; but she had hitherto shunned a young man so dissolute and unfortunate in his connexions. To her rejection of his suit were attributed Colin's melancholy and retirement from society; and it might be partly the cause, but there were other matters that troubled his inmost soul.

Ever since he had been visited by the two mysterious dames, he had kept the vial close in his bosom, and had drunk of the bitter potion again and again. He felt a change within him, a certain renovation of his nature, and a new train of thoughts, to which he was an utter stranger; yet he cherished them, tasting oftener and oftener his vial of bitterness, and always, as he drank, the liquor increased in quantity.

While in this half-resigned, half-desponding state, he ventured once more to visit Barbara. He thought to himself that he would go and see her, if but to take farewell of her; for he resolved not to harass so dear a creature with a suit which was displeasing to her. But, to his utter surprise, Barbara received him kindly. His humbled look made a deep impression on her; and, on taking leave, he found that she had treated him with as much favour as any virtuous maiden could display.

He therefore went home rather too much uplifted in spirit, which his old adversaries, the witches, perceived, and having laid all their snares open, to entrap him, they in part prevailed, and he returned in the moment of temptation, to his old courses. The day after, as he went out to the hill, he whistled and sung,—for he durst not think,—till, behold, at a distance, he saw his two lovely monitors approaching. He was confounded and afraid, for he found his heart was not right for the encounter; so he ran away with all his might, and hid himself in the Feathen Wood.

As soon as he was alone, he took the phial from his bosom, and, wondering, beheld that the bitter liquid was dried up all to a few drops, although the glass was nearly full when he last deposited it in his bosom.   He set it eagerly to his lips, lest the last remnant should have escaped him ; but never was it so bitter as now ; his very heart and spirit failed him, and, trembling, he lay down and wept.   He tried again to drain out the dregs of his cup of bitterness ; but still, as he drank, it increased in quantity, and became more and more palatable ; and he now continued the task so eagerly, that in a few days it was once more nearly full.

The two lovely strangers coming now often in his mind, he regretted running from them, and longed to see them again.   So, going out, he sat down within the fairy ring, on the top of the Feathen Hill, with a sort of presentiment that they would appear to him.   Accordingly, it was not long till they made their appearance, but still at a distance, as if travelling along the kirk-road.   Colin, perceiving that they were going to pass, without looking his way, thought it his duty to wait on them.   He hasted across the moor, and met them ; nor did they now shun him.   The one that was lame now addressed him, while she who had formerly accosted him, and presented him with the vial, looked shy, and kept a marked distance, which Colin was exceedingly sorry for, as he loved her best.   The other examined him sharply concerning all his transactions since they last met.   He acknowledged every thing candidly—the great folly of which he had been guilty, and likewise the great terror he was in of being changed into some horrible bestial creature, by the bitter drug they had given him.   " For d'ye ken, madam," said he, " I fand the change beginning within, at the very core o' the heart, and spreading aye outward and outward, and I lookit aye every minute when my hands and my feet wad change into clutes ; for I expeckit nae less than to have another turn o' the gait, or some waur thing, kenning how weel I deserved it.   And when I saw that I keepit my right proportions, I grat for my ain wickedness, that had before subjected me to such unhallowed influence."

The two sisters now looked to each other, and a hea-

venly benevolence shone through the smiles with which
that look was accompanied. The lame one said, " Did I
not say, sister, that there was some hope?" She then
asked a sight of his vial, which he took from his bosom,
and put into her hands; and when she had viewed it
carefully, she returned it, without any injunction ; but
taking from her own bosom a medal of pure gold, which
seemed to have been dipped in blood, she fastened it round
his neck with a chain of steel. " As long as you keep that
vial, and use it," said she, "the other will never be taken
from you, and with these two you may defy all the Powers
of Darkness."

As soon as Colin was alone, he surveyed his purple
medal with great earnestness, but could make nothing
of it ; there was a mystery in the characters and figures
which he could not in the least comprehend ; yet he kept
all that had happened closely concealed; and walked
softly.

The witches now found that he was lost to their community, and, enraged beyond measure at being deprived
of such a prize, which they had judged fairly their own,
and of which their master was so desirous, they now laid
a plan to destroy him.

Colin went down to the Castle one night to see Barbara
Stewart, who talked to him much of religion and of the
Bible ; but of these things Colin knew very little. He
engaged, however, to go with her to the house of prayer
—not the Popish chapel, where he had once been a most
irreverent auditor, but to the Reformed church, which
then began to divide the parish, and the pastor of which
was a devout man.

On taking leave of Barbara, and promising to attend
her on the following Sabbath, a burst of eldrich laughter
arose close by, and a voice, with a hoarse and giggling
sound, exclaimed, " No sae fast, canny lad—no sae fast.
There will maybe be a whipping o' cripples afore that
play be played."

Barbara consigned them both to the care of the Almighty with great fervency, wondering how they could

have been watched and overheard in such a place. Colin
trembled from head to foot, for he knew the laugh too
well to be that of Maude Stott, the leading witch of the
Traquair gang, now that his aunt was removed. He had
no sooner crossed the Quair, than, at the junction of a
little streamlet, called to this day the Satyr Sike, he was
set upon by a countless number of cats, which surrounded
him, making the most infernal noises, and putting themselves into the most threatening attitudes. For a good
while they did not touch him, but leaped around him,
often as high as his throat, screaming most furiously;
but at length his faith failed him, and he cried out in
utter despair. At that moment, they all closed upon
him, some round his neck, some round his legs, and
some endeavouring to tear out his heart and bowels. At
length one or two that came in contact with the medal in
his bosom fled away, howling most fearfully, and did not
return. Still he was in great jeopardy of being instantly
torn to pieces; on which he flung himself flat on his
face in the midst of his devouring enemies, and invoked
a sacred name. That moment he felt partial relief, as
if some one were driving them off one by one, and on
raising his head, he beheld his lovely lame visitant of the
mountains, driving these infernals off with a white wand,
and mocking their threatening looks and vain attempts to
return. "Off with you, poor infatuated wretches!"
cried she: "Minions of perdition, off to your abodes of
misery and despair! Where now is your boasted whipping of cripples? See if one poor cripple cannot whip
you all!"

By this time the monsters had all taken their flight,
save one, that had fastened its talons in Colin's left side,
and was making a last and desperate effort to reach his
vitals; but he, being now freed from the rest, lent it a
blow with such good-will, as made it speedily desist, and
fly tumbling and mewing down the brae. He shrewdly
guessed who this inveterate assailant was. Nor was he
mistaken; for next day Maude Stott was lying powerless
on account of a broken limb, and several of her cronies

were in great torment, having been struck by the white rod of the Lady of the Moor.

But the great Master Fiend, seeing now that his emissaries were all baffled and outdone, was enraged beyond bounds, and set himself with all his wit, and with all his power, to be revenged on poor Colin. As to his power, no one disputed it; but his wit and ingenuity always appear to me to be very equivocal. He tried to assault Colin's humble dwelling that same night, in sundry terrific shapes; but many of the villagers perceived a slender form, clothed in white, that kept watch at his door until the morning twilight. The next day, he haunted him on the hill in the form of a great shaggy bloodhound, infected with madness; but finding his utter inability to touch him, he uttered a howl that made all the hills quake, and, like a flash of lightning, darted into Glendean Banks.

He next set himself to procure Colin's punishment by other means, namely, by the hands of Christian men, the only way now left for him. He accordingly engaged his emissaries to inform against him to holy Mother Church, as a warlock and necromancer. The crown and the Church had at that time joined in appointing judges of these difficult and interesting questions. The quorum amounted to seven, consisting of the King's Advocate, and an equal number of priests and laymen, all of them in opposition to the principles of the Reformation, which was at that time obnoxious at court. Colin was seized, arraigned, and lodged in prison at Peebles; and never was there such clamour and discontent in Strathquair. The young women wept, and tore their hair, for the goodliest lad in the valley; their mothers scolded; and the old men scratched their grey polls, bit their lips, and remained quiescent, but were at length compelled to join the combination.

Colin's trial came on; and his accusers being summoned as witnesses against him, it may well be supposed how little chance he had of escaping, especially as the noted David Beatoun sat that day as judge, a severe and bigoted Papist. There were many things proven against poor Colin,—as much as would have been at one time sufficient to bring all the youth of Traquair to the stake.

For instance, three sportsmen swore, that they had started a large he-fox in the Feathen Wood, and, after pursuing him all the way to Glenrath-hope, with horses and hounds, on coming up, they found Colin Hyslop lying panting in the midst of the hounds, and caressing and endeavouring to pacify them. It was farther deponed, that he had been discovered in the shape of a huge gander sitting on eggs ; and in the shape of a three-legged stool, which, on being tossed about and overturned, as three-legged stools are apt to be, had groaned, and given other symptoms of animation, by which its identity with Colin Hyslop was discovered.

But when they came to the story of a he-goat, which had proceeded to attend the service in the chapel of St John the Evangelist, and which said he-goat proved to be the unhappy delinquent, Beatoun growled with rage and indignation, and said, that such a dog deserved to suffer death by a thousand tortures, and to be excluded from the power of repentance by the instant infliction of them. The most of the judges were not, however, satisfied of the authenticity of this monstrous story, and insisted on examining a great number of witnesses, both young and old, many of whom happened to be quite unconnected with the horrid community of the Traquair witches. Among the rest, a girl, named Tibby Frater, was examined about that, as well as the three-legged stool ; and her examination may here be copied verbatim. The querist, who was a cunning man, began as follows :—

" Were you in St John's Chapel, Isabel, on the Sunday after Easter ?"

" Yes."

" Did you there see a man changed into a he-goat ?"

" I saw a gait in the chapel that day."

" Did he, as has been declared, seem intent on disturbing divine worship ?"

" He was playing some pranks. But what else could you expect of a gait?"

" Please to describe what you saw."

" Oo, he was just rampauging about, and dinging folk ower. The clerk and the sacristan ran to attack him, but he soon laid them baith prostrate. Mess John prayed against him, in Latin, they said, and tried to lay him, as if he had been a deil; but he never heedit that, and just rampit on."

" Did he ever come near or molest you in the chapel?"

" Ay, he did that."

" What did he do to you?—describe it all."

" Oo, he didna do that muckle ill, after a'; but if it was the poor young man that was changed, I'll warrant he had nae hand in it, for dearly he paid the kain. Ere long there were fifty staves raised against him, and he was beaten till there was hardly life left in him."

" And what were the people's reasons for believing that this he-goat and the prisoner were the same."

" He was found a' wounded and bruised the next day. But, in truth, I believe he never denied these changes wrought on him, to his intimate friends; but we a' ken weel wha it was that effected them. Od help you! ye little ken how we are plaguit and harassed down yonder-abouts, and what scathe the country suffers, by the emissaries o' Satan! If there be any amang you that ken the true marks o' the beast, you will discern plenty o' them here-about, amang some that hae been witnessing against this poor abused and unfortunate young man."

The members of the community of Satan were now greatly astounded. Their eyes gleamed with the desire of vengeance, and they gnashed their teeth on the maiden. But the buzz ran through the assembly against them, and execrations were poured from every corner of the crowded court. Cries of—" Plenty o' proof o' what Tibby has said!"—" Let the saddle be laid on the right horse!"—" Down wi' the plagues o' the land!" and many such exclamations, were sent forth by the good people of Traquair. They durst not meddle with the witches at home, because, when any thing was done to disoblige them, the sheep and cattle were seized with new and frightful distempers, the corn and barley were shaken, and the honest people themselves quaked under agues, sweatings, and great horrors of mind. But now that they had them all collected in a court of justice, and were all assembled themselves, and holy men present, they hoped to bring the delinquents to due punishment at last. Beatoun, however, seemed absolutely bent on the destruction of Colin, alleging, that the depravity of his heart was manifest in every one of his actions during the periods of his metamorphoses, even although he himself had no share in effecting these metamorphoses; he therefore sought a verdict against the prisoner, as did also the King's Advocate. Sir James Stuart of Traquair, however, rose up, and spoke with great eloquence and energy in favour of his vassal, and insisted on having his accusers tried face to face with him, when, he had no doubt, it would be seen on which side the sorcery had been exercised. " For I appeal to your honourable judgments," continued he, "if any man would transform himself into a fox, for the sake of being hunted to death, and torn into pieces by hounds? Neither, I think, would any any person choose to translate himself into a gander, for the purpose of bringing out a few worthless goslings! But, above all, I am morally certain, that no living man would turn himself into a three-legged stool, for no other purpose but to be kicked into the mire, as the evidence shows this stool to have been. And as for a very handsome youth turning himself into a he-goat, in order to exhibit his prowess in outbraving and beating the men of the whole congregation, that would be a supposition equally absurd. But as we have a thousand instances of honest men being affected and injured by spells and enchantments, I give it as my firm opinion, that this young man has been abused grievously in this manner, and that these his accusers, afraid of exposure through his agency, are trying in this way to put him down."

Sir James's speech was received with murmurs of applause through the whole crowded court : but the principal judge continued obstinate, and made a speech in reply. Being a man of a most austere temperament, and as bloody-minded as obstinate, he made no objections to the seizing of the youth's accusers, and called to the officers to guard the door ; on which the old sacristan of Traquair remarked aloud, "By my faith in the holy Apostle John, my lord governor, you must be quick in your seizures ; for an ye gie but the witches o' Traquair ten minutes, ye will hae naething o' them but moorfowls and paitricks blattering about the rigging o' the kirk ; and a' the offishers ye hae will neither catch nor keep them."

They were, however, seized and incarcerated. The trials lasted for three days, at which the most amazing crowds attended ; for the evidence was of the most extraordinary nature ever elicited, displaying such a system of diablerie, malevolence, and unheard-of wickedness, as never came to light in a Christian land. Seven women and two men were found guilty, and condemned to be burnt at the stake ; and several more would have shared the same fate, had the private marks, which were then thoroughly and perfectly known, coincided with the evidence produced. This not having been the case, they were banished out of the Scottish dominions, any man being at liberty to shoot them, if found there under any shape whatever, after sixty-one hours from that date.

There being wise men who attended the courts in those days, called Searchers or Triers, they were ordered to take Colin into the vestry, (the trials having taken place in a church,) and examine him strictly for the diabolical marks. They could find none ; but in the course of their investigation they found the vial in his bosom, as well as the medal that wore the hue of blood, and which was locked to his neck, so that the hands of man could not remove it. They returned to the judge, bearing the vial in triumph, and saying they had found no private mark, as proof of the master he served, but that here

was an unguent, which they had no doubt was proof
sufficient, and would, if they judged aright, when accompanied by proper incantations, transform a human being
into any beast or monster intended.  It was handed
to the judge, who shook his head, and acquiesced with
the searchers,  It was then handed around, and Mr
Wiseheart, or Wishart, a learned man, deciphered these
words on it, in a sacred language,—" The Vial of Repentance."

The judges looked at one another when they heard
these ominous words so unlooked for ; and Wishart remarked, with a solemn assurance, that neither the term,
nor the cup of bitterness, was likely to be in use among
the slaves of Satan, and the bounden drudges of the land
of perdition.

The searchers now begged the Court to suspend their
judgment for a space, as the prisoner wore a charm of
a bloody hue, which was locked to his body with steel,
so that no hands could loose it, and which they judged
of far more ominous import than all the other proofs put
together.  Colin was then brought into Court once more,
and the medal examined carefully ; and lo ! on the one
side were engraved, in the same character, two words,
the meanings of which were decided to be, " Forgiveness,"
above, and " Acceptance," below.  On the other side was
a representation of the Crucifixion, and these words in
another language, *Cruci, dum spiro, fido ;* which words
struck the judges with great amazement.  They forthwith ordered the bonds to be taken off the prisoner, and
commanded him to speak for himself, and tell, without
fear and dread, how he came by these precious and holy
bequests.

Colin, who was noted for sincerity and simplicity,
began and related the circumstances of his life, his temp-
tations, his follies, and his disregard of all the duties of
religion, which had subjected him in no common degree
to the charms and enchantments of his hellish neighbours,
whose principal efforts and energies seemed to be aimed
at his destruction.  But when he came to the vision of

the fair virgins on the hill, and of their gracious bequests, that had preserved him thenceforward, both from the devil in person, and from the vengeance of all his emissaries combined, so well did this suit the strenuous efforts then making to obtain popularity for a falling system of faith, that the judges instantly claimed the miracle to their own side, and were clamorous with approbation of his modesty, and cravings of forgiveness for the insults and contumely which they had heaped upon this favourite of Heaven. Barbara Stewart was at this time sitting on the bench close behind Colin, weeping for joy at this favourable turn of affairs, having, for several days previous to that, given up all hopes of his life, when Mr David Beatoun, pointing to the image of the Holy Virgin, asked if the fair dame who bestowed these invaluable and heavenly relics bore any resemblance to that divine figure. Colin, with his accustomed blunt honesty, was just about to answer in the negative, when Barbara exclaimed in a whisper behind him, " Ah ! how like !"

" How do you ken, dearest Barbara ?" said he, softly, over his shoulder.

. " Because I saw her watching your door once when surrounded by fiends—Ah ! how like !"

. " Ah, how like !" exclaimed Colin, by way of response to one whose opinion was to him as a thing sacred, and not to be disputed. How much hung on that moment ! A denial might perhaps have still subjected him to obloquy, bonds, and death, but an anxious maiden's ready expedient saved him ; and now it was with difficulty that Mr Wishart could prevent the Catholic part of the throng from falling down and worshipping him, whom they had so lately reviled and accused of the blackest crimes.

Times were now altered with Colin Hyslop. David Beatoun took him to Edinburgh in his chariot, and presented him to the Queen Regent, who put a ring on his right hand, a chain of gold about his neck, and loaded him with her bounty. All the Catholic nobles of the court presented him with valuable gifts, and then he was caused to make the tour of all the rich abbeys of Fife and the Border; so that, without ever having one more question asked him about his tenets, he returned home the richest man of all Traquair, even richer, as men supposed, than Sir James Stuart himself. He married Barbara Stewart, and purchased the Plora from the female heirs of Alexander Murray, where he built a mansion, planted a vineyard, and lived in retirement and happiness till the day of his death.

I have thus recorded the leading events of this tale, although many of the incidents, as handed down by tradition, are of so heinous a nature as not to bear recital. It has always appeared to me to have been moulded on the bones of some ancient religious allegory, and by being thus transformed into a nursery tale, rendered unintelligible. It would be in vain now to endeavour to restore its original structure, in the same way as Mr Blore can delineate an ancient abbey from the smallest remnant; but I should like exceedingly to understand properly what was represented by the two lovely and mysterious sisters, one of whom was lame. It is most probable that they were supposed apparitions of renowned female saints; or perhaps Faith and Charity. This, however, is manifest, that it is a Reformer's tale, founded on a Catholic allegory.

Of the witches of Traquair there are many other traditions extant, as well as many authentic records; and so far the tale accords with the history of the times. That they were tried and suffered there is no doubt; and the Devil lost all his popularity in that district ever after, being despised by his friends for his shallow and rash politics, and hooted and held up to ridicule by his enemies. I still maintain, that there has been no great personage since the world was framed, so apt to commit a manifest blunder, and to overshoot his mark, as he is.

# CHAP. XVI.

## SHEEP.

THE sheep has scarcely any marked character, save that of natural affection, of which it possesses a very great share. It is otherwise a stupid, indifferent animal, having few wants, and fewer expedients. The old black-faced, or Forest breed, have far more powerful capabilities than any of the finer breeds that have been introduced into Scotland ; and therefore the few anecdotes that I have to relate, shall be confined to them.

So strong is the attachment of sheep to the place where they have been bred, that I have heard of their returning from Yorkshire to the Highlands. I was always somewhat inclined to suspect that they might have been lost by the way. But it is certain, however, that when once one, or a few sheep, get away from the rest of their acquaintances, they return homeward with great eagerness and perseverance. I have lived beside a drove-road the better part of my life, and many stragglers have I seen bending their steps northward in the spring of the year. A Shepherd rarely sees these journeyers twice ; if he sees them, and stops them in the morning, they are gone long before night ; and if he sees them at night, they will be gone many miles before morning. This strong attachment to the place of their nativity, is much more predominant in our old aboriginal breed, than in any of the other kinds with which I am acquainted.

The most singular instance that I know of, to be quite well authenticated, is that of a black ewe, that returned with her lamb from a farm in the head of Glen-Lyon, to the farm of Harehope, in Tweeddale, and accomplished the journey in nine days. She was soon missed by her owner, and a shepherd was dispatched in pursuit of her, who followed her all the way to Crieff, where he turned, and gave her up. He got intelligence of her all the

way, and every one told him that she absolutely persisted in travelling on—She would not be turned, regarding
neither sheep nor shepherd by the way.    Her lamb was
often far behind, and she had constantly to urge it on,
by impatient bleating.    She unluckily came to Stirling
on the morning of a great annual fair, about the end of
May, and judging it imprudent to venture through the
crowd with her lamb, she halted on the north side of the
town the whole day, where she was seen by hundreds,
lying close by the road-side.    But next morning, when
all became quiet, a little after the break of day, she was
observed stealing quietly through the town, in apparent
terror of the dogs that were prowling about the streets.
The last time she was seen on the road, was at a toll-bar
near St Ninian's ; the man stopped her, thinking she was a
strayed animal, and that some one would claim her.    She
tried several times to break through by force when he
opened the gate, but he always prevented her, and at
length she turned patiently back.    She had found some
means of eluding him, however, for home she came on
a Sabbath morning, the 4th of June; and she left the
farm of Lochs, in Glen-Lyon, either on the Thursday
afternoon, or Friday morning, a week and two days before.    The farmer of Harehope paid the Highland farmer
the price of her, and she remained on her native farm
till she died of old age, in her seventeenth year.

There is another peculiarity in the nature of sheep, of
which I have witnessed innumerable examples.    But as
they are all alike, and show how much the sheep is a
creature of habit, I shall only relate one :

A shepherd in Blackhouse bought a few sheep from
another in Crawmel, about ten miles distant.    In the
spring following, one of the ewes went back to her native
place, and yeaned on a wild hill, called Crawmel Craig.
One day, about the beginning of July following, the shepherd went and brought home his ewe and lamb—took
the fleece from the ewe, and kept the lamb for one of
his stock.    The lamb lived and throve, became a hog
and a gimmer, and never offered to leave home; but

when three years of age, and about to have her first
lamb, she vanished; and the morning after, the Crawmel
shepherd, in going his rounds, found her with a new-
yeaned lamb on the very gair of the Crawmel Craig,
where she was lambed herself. She remained there till
the first week of July, the time when she was brought a
lamb herself, and then she came home with hers of her
own accord; and this custom she continued annually
with the greatest punctuality as long as she lived. At
length her lambs, when they came of age, began the
same practice, and the shepherd was obliged to dispose
of the whole breed.

With regard to the natural affection of this animal,
stupid and actionless as it is, the instances that might be
mentioned are without number. When one loses its
sight in a flock of short sheep, it is rarely abandoned to
itself in that hapless and helpless state. Some one always attaches itself to it, and by bleating calls it back
from the precipice, the lake, the pool, and all dangers
whatever. There is a disease among sheep, called by
shepherds the Breakshugh, a deadly sort of dysentery,
which is as infectious as fire, in a flock. Whenever a
sheep feels itself seized by this, it instantly withdraws
from all the rest, shunning their society with the greatest
care; it even hides itself, and is often very hard to be
found. Though this propensity can hardly be attributed
to natural instinct, it is, at all events, a provision of nature of the greatest kindness and beneficence.

Another manifest provision of nature with regard to
these animals, is, that the more inhospitable the land is
on which they feed, the greater their kindness and attention to their young. I once herded two years on a
wild and bare farm called Willenslee, on the border of
Mid-Lothian, and of all the sheep I ever saw, these were
the kindest and most affectionate to their young. I was
often deeply affected at scenes which I witnessed. We
had one very hard winter, so that our sheep grew lean
in the spring, and the thwarter-ill (a sort of paralytic affection) came among them, and carried off a number.

Often have I seen these poor victims when fallen down to rise no more, even when unable to lift their heads from the ground, holding up the leg, to invite the starving lamb to the miserable pittance that the udder still could supply.  I had never seen aught more painfully affecting.

It is well known that it is a custom with shepherds, when a lamb dies, if the mother have a sufficiency of milk, to bring her from the hill, and put another lamb to her.  This is done by putting the skin of the dead lamb upon the living one ; the ewe immediately acknowledges the relationship, and after the skin has warmed on it, so as to give it something of the smell of her own progeny, and it has sucked her two or three times, she accepts and nourishes it as her own ever after.  Whether it is from joy at this apparent reanimation of her young one, or because a little doubt remains on her mind which she would fain dispel, I cannot decide ; but, for a number of days, she shows far more fondness, by bleating, and caressing, over this one, than she did formerly over the one that was really her own.

But this is not what I wanted to explain ; it was, that such sheep as thus lose their lambs, must be driven to a house with dogs, so that the lamb may be put to them ; for they will only take it in a dark confined place.  But at Willenslee, I never needed to drive home a sheep by force, with dogs, or in any other way than the following : I found every ewe, of course, standing hanging her head over her dead lamb, and having a piece of twine with me for the purpose, I tied that to the lamb's neck, or foot, and trailing it along, the ewe followed me into any house or fold that I chose to lead her.  Any of them would have followed me in that way for miles, with her nose close on the lamb, which she never quitted for a moment, except to chase my dog, which she would not suffer to walk near me.  I often, out of curiosity, led them in to the side of the kitchen fire by this means, into the midst of servants and dogs ; but the more that dangers multiplied around the ewe, she clung the closer to her dead offspring, and thought of nothing whatever but protecting it.

One of the two years while I remained on this farm, a severe blast of snow came on by night about the latter end of April, which destroyed several scores of our lambs ; and as we had not enow of twins and odd lambs for the mothers that had lost theirs, of course we selected the best ewes, and put lambs to them. As we were making the distribution, I requested of my master to spare me a lamb for a hawked ewe which he knew, and which was standing over a dead lamb in the head of the hope, about four miles from the house. He would not do it, but bid me let her stand over her lamb for a day or two, and perhaps a twin would be forthcoming. I did so, and faithfully she did stand to her charge ; so faithfully, that I think the like never was equalled by any of the woolly race. I visited her every morning and evening, and for the first eight days never found her above two or three yards from the lamb ; and always, as I went my rounds, she eyed me long ere I came near her, and kept tramping with her foot, and whistling through her nose, to frighten away the dog ; he got a regular chase twice a-day as I passed by : but, however excited and fierce a ewe may be, she never offers any resistance to mankind, being perfectly and meekly passive to them. The weather grew fine and warm, and the dead lamb soon decayed, which the body of a dead lamb does particularly soon ; but still this affectionate and desolate creature kept hanging over the poor remains with an attachment that seemed to be nourished by hopelessness. It often drew the tears from my eyes to see her hanging with such fondness over a few bones, mixed with a small portion of wool. For the first fortnight she never quitted the spot, and for another week she visited it every morning and evening, uttering a few kindly and heart-piercing bleats each time ; till at length every remnant of her offspring vanished, mixing with the soil, or wafted away by the winds.

## CHAP. XVII.

### PRAYERS.

THERE is, I believe, no class of men professing the Protestant faith, so truly devout as the shepherds of Scotland. They get all the learning that the parish schools afford ; are thoroughly acquainted with the Scriptures ; deeply read in theological works, and really, I am sorry to say it, generally much better informed on these topics than their masters. Every shepherd is a man of respectability—he must be so, else he must cease to be a shepherd. His master's flock is entirely committed to his care, and if he does not manage it with constant attention, caution, and decision, he cannot be employed. A part of the stock is his own, however, so that his interest in it is the same with that of his master ; and being thus the most independent of men, if he cherishes a good behaviour, and the most insignificant if he loses the esteem of his employers, he has every motive for maintaining an unimpeachable character.

It is almost impossible, also, that he can be other than a religious character, being so much conversant with the Almighty in his works, in all the goings-on of nature, and in his control of the otherwise resistless elements. He feels himself a dependent being, morning and evening, on the great Ruler of the universe ; he holds converse with him in the cloud and the storm—on the misty mountain and the darksome waste—in the whirling drift and the overwhelming thaw—and even in voices and sounds that are only heard by the howling cliff or solitary dell. How can such a man fail to be impressed with the presence of an eternal God, of an omniscient eye, and an almighty arm ?

The position generally holds good ; for, as I have said, the shepherds are a religious and devout set of men, and among them the antiquated but delightful exercise of family worship is never neglected. It is always gone about with decency and decorum ; but formality being a thing despised, there is no composition that I ever heard so truly original as these prayers occasionally are, sometimes for rude eloquence and pathos, at other times for a nondescript sort of pomp, and not unfrequently for a plain and somewhat unbecoming familiarity.

One of the most notable men for this sort of family eloquence was Adam Scott, in Upper Dalgliesh. I had an uncle who herded with him, from whom I heard many quotations from Scott's prayers :—a few of them are as follows.

" We particularly thank thee for thy great goodness to Meg, and that ever it came into your head to take any thought of sic an useless baw-waw as her." (This was a little girl that had been somewhat miraculously saved from drowning.)

" For thy mercy's sake—for the sake of thy poor sinfu' servants that are now addressing thee in their ain shilly-shally way, and for the sake o' mair than we dare weel name to thee, hae mercy on Rob. Ye ken yoursell he is a wild mischievous callant, and thinks nae mair o' committing sin than a dog does o' licking a dish ; but put thy hook in his nose, and thy bridle in his gab, and gar him come back to thee wi' a jerk that he'll no forget the langest day he has to leeve."

" Dinna forget poor Jamie, wha's far away frae amang us the night. Keep thy arm o' power about him, and O, I wish ye wad endow him wi' a like spunk and smeddum to act for himsell. For if ye dinna, he'll be but a bauchle in this world, and a backsitter in the neist."

" We desire to be submissive to thy will and pleasure at a' times ; but our desires are like new-bridled colts, or dogs that are first laid to the brae—they run wild frae under our control. Thou hast added one to our family —so has been thy will ; but it would never hae been mine. If it's of thee, do thou bless and prosper the connexion ; but if the fool hath done it out of carnal desire, against all reason and credit, may the cauld rainy cloud of adversity settle on his habitation, till he shiver in the flame that his folly hath kindled." (I think this was said to be in allusion to the marriage of one of his sons.)

"We're a' like hawks, we're a' like snails, we're a' like slogie riddles; like hawks to do evil, like snails to do good, and like slogie riddles, that let through a' the good, and keep the bad."

"Bring down the tyrant and his lang neb, for he has done muckle ill the year, and gie him a cup o' thy wrath, and gin he winna tak that, gie him kelty." (*Kelty* signifies double, or two cups. This was an occasional petition for one season only, and my uncle never could comprehend what it meant.)

The general character of Scott was one of decision and activity; constant in the duties of religion, but not over strict with regard to some of its moral precepts.

I have heard the following petitions sundry times in the family prayers of an old relation of my own, long since gone to his rest.

"And mairower and aboon, do thou bless us a' wi' thy best warldly blessings—wi' bread for the belly and theeking for the back, a lang stride and a clear ee-sight. Keep us from a' proud prossing and upsetting—from foul flaips, and stray steps, and from all unnecessary trouble."

But, in generalities, these prayers are never half so original as when they come to particular incidents that affect only the petitioners; for some things happen daily, which they deem it their bounden duty to remember before their Maker, either by way of petition, confession, or thanksgiving. The following was told to me as a part of the same worthy old man's prayer occasionally, for some weeks before he left a master, in whose father's service and his own the decayed shepherd had spent the whole of his life.

"Bless my master and his family with thy best blessings in Christ Jesus. Prosper all his worldly concerns, especially that valuable part which is committed to my care. I have worn out my life in the service of him and his fathers, and thou knowest that I have never bowed a knee before thee without remembering them. Thou knowest, also, that I have never studied night's rest, nor

day's comfort, when put in competition with their interest.
The foulest days and the stormiest nights were to me as
the brightest of summer ; and if he has not done weel in
casting out his auld servant, do thou forgive him.   I forgive him with all my heart, and will never cease to pray
for him ; but when the hard storms o' winter come, may
he miss the braid bonnet and the grey head, and say to
himsell, ' I wish to God that my auld herd had been here
yet !'   I ken o' neither house nor habitation this night,
but for the sake o' them amang us that canna do for themsells, I ken thou wilt provide ane ; for though thou hast
tried me with hard and sair adversaries, I have had more
than my share of thy mercies, and thou kens better than
I can tell thee that thou hast never bestowed them on an
unthankful heart."

This is the sentence exactly as it was related to me,
but I am sure it is not correct ; for, though very like his
manner, I never heard him come so near the English
language in one sentence in my life.   I once heard him
say, in allusion to a chapter he had been reading about
David and Goliath, and just at the close of his prayer:
" And when our besetting sins come bragging and blows-
tering upon us, like Gully o'Gath, O enable us to fling
off the airmer and hairnishin o' the law, whilk we haena
proved, and whup up the simple sling o' the gospel, and nail
the smooth stanes o' redeeming grace into their foreheads."

Of all the compositions, for simple pathos, that I ever
saw or heard, his prayer, on the evening of that day on
which he buried his only son, excelled ; but at this distance of time, it is impossible for me to do it justice ; and
I dare not take it on me to garble it.   He began the subject of his sorrows thus :—

" Thou hast seen meet, in thy wise providence, to
remove the staff out of my right hand, at the very time
when, to us poor sand-blind mortals, it appeared that I
stood maist in need o't.   But O it was a sicker ane, and
a sure ane, and a dear ane to my heart ! and how I'll
climb the steep hill o' auld age and sorrow without it,
thou mayst ken, but I dinna."

His singing of the psalms surpassed all exhibitions that ever were witnessed of a sacred nature. He had not the least air of sacred music; there was no attempt at it; it was a sort of recitative of the most grotesque kind; and yet he delighted in it, and sung far more verses every night than is customary. The first time I heard him, I was very young; but I could not stand it, and leaned myself back into a bed, and laughed till my strength could serve me no longer. He had likewise an out-of-the-way custom, in reading a portion of Scripture every night, of always making remarks as he went on. And such remarks! One evening I heard him reading a chapter—I have forgot where it was—but he came to words like these: "And other nations, whom the great and noble Asnapper brought over"——John stopped short, and, considering for a little, says: "Asnapper! whaten a king was he that? I dinna mind o' ever hearing tell o' him afore."—"I dinna ken," said one of the girls; "but he has a queer name."—"It is something like a goolly knife," said a younger one. "Whisht, dame," said John, and then went on with the chapter. I believe it was about the fourth or fifth chapter of Ezra. He seldom, for a single night, missed a few observations of the same sort.

Another night, not long after the time above noticed, he was reading of the feats of one Sanballat, who set himself against the building of the second temple; on closing the Bible John uttered a long hemh! and then I knew there was something forthcoming. "He has been anither nor a gude ane that," added he; "I hae nae brow o' their Sandy-ballet."

Upon another occasion he stopped in the middle of a chapter and uttered his "hemh!" of disapproval, and then added, "If it had been the Lord's will, I think they might hae left out that verse."—"It hasna been his will though," said one of the girls.—"It seems sae," said John. I have entirely forgot what he was reading about, and am often vexed at having forgot the verse that John wanted expunged from the Bible. It was in some of the minor prophets.

There was another time he came to his brother-in-law's house, where I was then living, and John being the oldest man, the Bible was laid down before him to make family worship. He made no objections, but began, as was always his custom, by asking a blessing on their devotions; and when he had done, it being customary for those who make family worship to sing straight through the Psalms from beginning to end, John says, "We'll sing in your ordinary. Where is it?"—"We do not always sing in one place," said the goodman of the house. "Na, I daresay no, or else ye'll make that place threadbare," said John, in a short crabbed style, manifestly suspecting that his friend was not regular in his family devotions. This piece of sharp wit after the worship was begun had to me an effect highly ludicrous.

When he came to give out the chapter, he remarked, that there would be no ordinary there either, he supposed. "We have been reading in Job for a lang time," said the goodman. "How lang?" said John slyly, as he turned over the leaves, thinking to catch his friend at fault. "O, I dinna ken that," said the other; "but there's a mark laid in that will tell you the bit."—"If you hae read *verra* lang in Job," says John, "you will hae made him threadbare too, for the mark is only at the ninth chapter." There was no answer, so he read on. In the course of the chapter he came to these words—"Who commandeth the sun, and it riseth not."—"I never heard of Him doing that," says John. "But Job, honest man, maybe means the darkness that was in the land o' Egypt. It wad be a fearsome thing an the sun warna till rise." A little farther on he came to these words—"Which maketh Arcturus, Orion, and Pleiades, and the chambers of the south."—"I hae often wondered at that verse," says John. "Job has been a grand philosopher! The Pleiades are the Se'en Sterns,—I ken them; and Orion, that's the King's Ellwand; but I'm never sae sure about Arcturus. I fancy he's ane o' the plennits, or maybe him that hauds the Gowden Plough."

On reading the last chapter of the book of Job, when he came to the enumeration of the patriarch's live stock, he

remarked, " He has had an unco sight o' creatures.
Fourteen thousand sheep !   How mony was that ?"—
" He has had seven hundred scores," said one.   " Ay,'
said John, " it was an unco swarm o' creatures.   There
wad be a dreadfu' confusion at his clippings and spain-
ings.   Six thousand camels, a thousand yoke of oxen,
and a thousand she-asses.   What, in the wide warld, did
he do wi' a' thae creatures?   Wad it no hae been mair
purpose-like if he had had them a' milk kye ?"—" Wha
wad he hae gotten to have milked them ?" said one of the
girls.   " It's verra true," said John.

One time, during a long and severe lying storm of
snow, in allusion to some chapter he had been reading,
he prayed as follows : (This is from hearsay.) " Is the
whiteness of desolation to lie still on the mountains of
our land for ever ?  Is the earthly hope o' thy servants to
perish frae the face of the earth ?  The flocks on a thousand hills are thine, and their lives or deaths wad be
naething to thee—thou wad neither be the richer nor the
poorer ; but it is a great matter to us.   Have pity, then,
on the lives o' thy creatures, for beast and body are a'
thy handywark, and send us the little wee cludd out o'
the sea like a man's hand, to spread and darken, and pour
and plash, till the green gladsome face o' nature aince
mair appear."

During the smearing season one year, it was agreed
that each shepherd, young and old, should ask a blessing
aud return thanks at meal-time, in his turn, beginning at
the eldest, and going off at the youngest ; that, as there
was no respect of person with God, so there should be
none shown among neighbours.   John being the eldest,
the graces began with him, and went decently on till they
came to the youngest, who obstinately refused.  Of course
it devolved again on John, who, taking off his broad
bonnet, thus addressed his Maker with great fervency :—

" O our gracious Lord and Redeemer, thou hast said,
in thy blessed word, that those who are ashamed of thee
and thy service, of them thou wilt be ashamed when thou
comest into thy kingdom.   Now, all that we humbly

beg of thee at this time is, that Geordie may not be reckoned amang that unhappy number. Open the poor chield's heart and his een to a sight o' his lost condition; and though he be that prood. that he'll no ask a blessing o' thee, neither for himsell nor us, do thou grant us a' thy blessing ne'ertheless, and him amang the rest for Christ's sake. Amen."

The young man felt the rebuke very severely, his face grew as red as flame, and it was several days before he could assume his usual hilarity. Had I lived with John a few years, I could have picked up his remarks on the greater part of the Scriptures, for to read and not make remarks was out of his power. The story of Ruth was a great favourite with him—he often read it to his family of a Sabbath evening, as " a good lesson on naturality ;" but he never failed making the remark, that " it was nae mair nor decency in her to creep in beside the douss man i' the night-time when he was sleeping."

---

## CHAP. XVIII.

### ODD CHARACTERS.

MANY single anecdotes of country life might be collected—enough, perhaps, to form a volume as amusing as others connected with higher names—but in this place I shall confine myself to a few, of which several relate to the same person, and are thus illustrative of individual character. The first that claim attention are those concerning a man very famous in his own sphere, an ancestor of my own,—the redoubted

### Will o' Phaup.

WILL o' PHAUP, one of the genuine Laidlaws of Craik was born at that place in 1691. He was shepherd in Phaup for fifty-five years. For feats of frolic, strength,

and agility, he had no equal in his day. In the hall of
the laird, at the farmer's ingle, and in the shepherd's cot,
Will was alike a welcome guest; and in whatever company he was, he kept the whole in one roar of merriment.
In Will's days, brandy was the common drink in this
country; as for whisky, it was, like silver in the days of
Solomon, nothing accounted of. Good black French
brandy was the constant beverage; and a heavy neighbour Will was on it. Many a hard bouse he had about
Moffat, and many a race he ran, generally for wagers of
so many pints of brandy; and in all his life he never was
beat. He once ran at Moffat for a wager of five guineas,
which one of the chiefs of the Johnstons betted on his
head. His opponent was a celebrated runner from Crawford-Muir, of the name of Blaikley, on whose head, or
rather on whose feet, a Captain Douglas had wagered.
Will knew nothing of the match till he went to Moffat,
and was very averse to it. " No that he was ony fear'd
for the chap," he said; " but he had on a' his ilka-day
claes, and as mony leddies and gentlemen war to be there
to see the race, he didna like to appear afore them like
an assie whalp."

However, he was urged, and obliged to go out and
strip; and, as he told it, " a poor figure I made beside
the chield wi' his grand ruffled sark. I was sae affrontit
at thinking that Will o' Phaup should hae made sic a
dirty shabby appearance afore sae mony grit folks and
bonny leddies, that not a fit I could rin mair nor I had
been a diker. The race was down on Annan-side, and
jimply a mile, out and in; and, at the very first, the man
wi' the ruffled sark flew off like a hare, and left poor
Will o' Phaup to come waughling up ahint him like a
singit cur, wi' his din sark and his cloutit breeks. I had
neither heart nor power, till a very queer accident befell
me; for, Scots grund! disna the tying o' my cloutit
breeks brek loose, and in a moment they were at my
heels, and there was I standing like a hapshekel'd staig!
' Off wi' them, Phaup! Off wi' them!' cries ane. Od,
sir, I just sprang out o' them; and that instant I fand my

spirits rise to the proper pitch. The chield was clean afore me, but I fand that if he were a yeagle I wad o'ertak him, for I scarcely kenn'd whether I was touching the grund or fleeing in the air, and as I came by Mr Welch, I heard him saying, 'Phaup has him yet;' for he saw Blaikley failing. I got by him, but I had not muckle to brag o', for he keepit the step on me till within a gun-shot o' the starting-post.

"Then there was sic a fraze about me by the winning party, and naething wad serve them but that I should dine wi' them in the public room. 'Na, fiend be there then, Mr Johnston,' says I, 'for though your leddies only leuch at my accident, if I war to dinner wi' them in this state, I kenna how they might tak it.'"

When Will was a young lad, only sixteen years of age, and the very first year he was in Phaup, his master betted the price of his whole drove of Phaup hogs on his head, at a race with an Englishman on Stagshawbank. James Anderson, Esq. of Ettrickhall, was then farmer of Phaup, and he had noted at the shedding, before his young shepherd left home, that whenever a sheep got by wrong, he never did more than run straight after it, lay hold of it by sheer speed, and bring it back in his arms. So the laird having formed high ideas of Will's swiftness, without letting him know of the matter, first got an English gentleman into a heat, by bragging the English runners with Scots ones, and then proffered betting the price of his 300 wedder hogs, that he had a poor starved bare-footed boy who was helping to drive them,—whom he believed to be about the worst runner in Scotland,—who would yet beat the best Englishman that could be found in Stagshawbank-fair.

The Englishman's national pride was touched, as well it might, his countrymen being well known as the superior runners. The bet was taken, and Will won it with the greatest ease for his master, without being made aware of the stake for which he ran. This he never knew till some months afterwards, when his master presented him with a guinea, a pair of new shoes, and a load of oatmeal, for winning him the price of the Phaup hogs. Will was exceedingly proud of the feat he had performed, as well as of the present, which, he remarked, was as much to him as the price of the hogs was to his master. From that day forth he was never beat at a fair race.

He never went to Moffat, that the farmers did not get him into their company, and then never did he get home to Phaup sober. The mad feats which he then perform-ed, were, for an age, the standing jokes of the country, and many of his sayings settled into regular proverbs or by-words. His great oath was " Scots grund !" And " Scots grund, quo' Will o' Phaup," is a standing excla-mation to this day—" One plash more, quo' Will o' Phaup," is another,— and there are many similar ones. The last mentioned had its origin in one of those Moffat bouses, from which the farmer of Selcouth and Will were returning by night greatly inebriated, the former riding, and Will running by his side. Moffat water being some-what flooded, the farmer proposed taking Laidlaw on the horse behind him. Will sprang on, but, as he averred, never got seated right, till the impatient animal plunged into the water, and the two friends came off, and floated down the river, hanging by one another. The farmer got to his feet first, but in pulling out Will, lost his equilibrium a second time, and plunging headlong into the stream, down he went. Will was then in the utmost perplexity, for, with the drink and ducking together, he was quite benumbed, and the night was as dark as pitch; he ran down the side of the stream to succour his friend, and losing all sight of him, he knew not what to do; but hearing a great plunge, he made towards the place, calling out, " One plash more, sir, and I have you—One plash more, quo' Will o' Phaup !" but all was silent ! " Scots grund ! quo' Will o' Phaup—a man drown'd, and me here !" Will ran to a stream, and took his station in the middle of the water, in hopes of feeling his drowning friend come against his legs ;— but the farmer got safely out by himself.

There was another time at Moffat, that he was taken

in, and had to pay a dinner and drink for a whole large party of gentleman. I have forgot how it happened, but think it was by a wager. He had not only to part with all his money, but had to pawn his whole stock of sheep. He then came home with a heavy heart, told his wife what he had done, and that he was a ruined man. She said, that since he had saved the cow, they would do well enough.

The money was repaid afterwards, so that Will did not actually lose his stock ; but after that he went seldomer to Moffat. He fell upon a much easier plan of getting sport ; for, at that period, there were constantly bands of smugglers passing from the Solway, through the wild region where he lived, towards the Lothians. From these Will purchased occasionally a stock of brandy, and then the gentlemen and farmers came all and drank with him, paying him at the enormous rate of a shilling per bottle, all lesser measures being despised, and out of repute, at Phaup. It became a place of constant rendezvous, but a place where they drank too deep to be a safe place for gentlemen to meet. There were two rival houses of Andersons at that time that never ceased quarrelling, and they were wont always to come to Phaup with their swords by their sides. Being all exceedingly stout men, and equally good swordsmen, it may easily be supposed they were dangerous neighbours to meet in such a wild remote place. Accordingly, there were many quarrels and bloody bouts there as long as the Andersons possessed Phaup ; after which, the brandy system was laid aside. Will twice saved his master's life in these affrays ,——once, when he had drawn on three of the Amoses, tenants of Potburn, and when they had mastered his sword, broken it, and were dragging him to the river by the neckcloth. Will knocked down one, cut his master's neckcloth, and defended him stoutly till he gathered his breath ; and then the two jointly did thrash the Amoses to their heart's satisfaction ! And another time, from the sword of Michael of Tushielaw ; but he could not help the two fighting a duel afterwards, which was the cause of much mischief, and many heartburnings, among these haughty relatives.

Will and his master once fought a battle themselves two, up in a wild glen called Phaup Coom. They differed about a young horse, which the Laird had sent there to graze, and which he thought had not been well treated; and so bitter did the recriminations grow between them, that the Laird threatened to send Will to hell. Will defied him; on which he attacked him furiously with his cane, while the shepherd defended himself as resolutely with his staff. The combat was exceedingly sharp and severe; but the gentleman was too scientific for the shepherd, and hit him many blows about the head and shoulders, while Will could not hit him once, "all that he could thrash on." The latter was determined, however, not to yield, and fought on, although, as he termed it, "the blood began to blind his een." He tried several times to close with his master, but found him so complete in both his defences and offences, that he never could accomplish it, but always suffered for his temerity. At length he "jouked down his head, took a lounder across the shoulders, and, in the mean time, hit his master across the shins." This ungentlemanly blow quite paralyzed the Laird, and the cane dropped out of his hand, on which Will closed with him, mastered him with ease, laying him down, and holding him fast;—but all that he could do, he could not pacify him,—he still swore he would have his heart's blood. Will had then no recourse, but to spring up, and bound away to the hill. The Laird pursued for a time, but he might as well have tried to catch a roebuck; so he went back to Phaup, took his horse in silence, and rode away home. Will expected a summons of removal next day, or next term at the farthest; but Mr Anderson took no notice of the affair, nor ever so much as mentioned it again.

Will had many pitched battles with the bands of smugglers, in defence of his master's grass, for they never missed unloading on the lands of Phaup, and turning their horses to the best grass they could find. According to his account, these fellows were exceedingly lawless, and accounted nothing of taking from the country people whatever they needed in emergencies. The gipsies, too, were then accustomed to traverse the country in bands of from twenty to forty, and were no better than freebooters. But to record every one of Will o Phaup's heroic feats, would require a volume. I shall, therefore, only mention one trait more of his character, which was this—

He was the last man of this wild region, who heard, saw, and conversed with the Fairies; and that not once or twice, but at sundry times and seasons. The sheiling at which Will lived for the better part of his life, at Old Upper Phaup, was one of the most lonely and dismal situations that ever was the dwelling of human creatures. I have often wondered how such a man could live so long, and rear so numerous and respectable a family, in such a habitation. It is on the very outskirts of Ettrick Forest, quite out of the range of social intercourse, a fit retirement for lawless banditti, and a genial one for the last retreat of the spirits of the glen—before taking their final leave of the land of their love, in which the light of the gospel then grew too bright for their tiny moonlight forms. There has Will beheld them riding in long and beautiful array, by the light of the moon, and even in the summer twilight; and there has he seen them sitting in seven circles, in the bottom of a deep ravine, drinking nectar out of cups of silver and gold, no bigger than the dew-cup flower; and there did he behold their wild unearthly eyes, all of one bright sparkling blue, turned every one upon him at the same moment, and heard their mysterious whisperings, of which he knew no word, save now and then the repetition of his own name, which was always done in a strain of pity. Will was coming from the hill one dark misty evening in winter, and, for a good while, imagined he heard a great gabbling of children's voices, not far from him, which still grew more and more audible; it being before sunset, he had no spark of fear, but set about investigating whence the sounds and laughter proceeded. He, at length, discovered that they issued from a deep cleugh not far distant, and thinking it was a band of gipsies, or some marauders, he laid down his bonnet and plaid, and creeping softly over the heath, reached the brink of the precipice, peeped over, and to his utter astonishment, beheld the Fairies sitting in seven circles, on a green spot in the bottom of the dell, where no green spot ever was before. They were apparently eating and drinking; but all their motions were so quick and momentary, he could not well say what they were doing. Two or three at the queen's back appeared to be baking bread. The party consisted wholly of ladies, and their number quite countless—dressed in green pollonians, and grass-green bonnets on their heads. He perceived at once, by their looks, their giggling, and their peals of laughter, that he was discovered. Still fear took no hold of his heart, for it was daylight, and the blessed sun was in heaven, although obscured by clouds; till at length he heard them pronounce his own name twice; Will then began to think it might not be quite so safe to wait till they pronounced it a third time, and at that moment of hesitation it first came into his mind that it was All Hallow Eve! There was no farther occasion to warn Will to rise and run; for he well knew the Fairies were privileged, on that day and night, to do what seemed good in their own eyes. " His hair," he said, " stood all up like the birses on a sow's back, and every bit o' his body, outside and in, prinkled as it had been brunt wi' nettles." He ran home as fast as his feet could carry him, and greatly were his children astonished (for he was then a widower) to see their father come running like a madman, without either his bonnet or plaid. He assembled them to prayers, and shut the door, but did not tell them what he had seen for several years.

Another time he followed a whole troop of them up a wild glen called Entertrony, from one end to the other, without ever being able to come up with them, although

,they never appeared to be more than twenty paces in advance. Neither were they flying from him; for instead of being running at their speed, as he was doing, they seemed to be standing in a large circle. It happened to be the day after a Moffat fair, and he supposed them to be a party of his neighbours returning from it, who wished to lead him a long chase before they suffered themselves to be overtaken. He heard them speaking, singing, and laughing; and being a man so fond of sociality, he exerted himself to come up with them, but to no purpose. Several times did he hail them, and desire them to halt, and tell him the news of the fair; but whenever he shouted, in a moment all was silent, until in a short time he heard the same noise of laughing and conversation at some distance from him. Their talk, although Will could not hear the words of it distinctly, was evidently very animated, and he had no doubt they were recounting their feats at the fair. This always excited his curiosity afresh, and he made every exertion to overtake the party; and when he judged, from the sounds, that he was close upon them, he sent forth his stentorian hollo—" Stop, lads, and tell us the news o' the fair !" which produced the same effect of deep silence for a time. When this had been repeated several times, and after the usual pause, the silence was again broken by a peal of eldrich laughter, that seemed to spread along the skies over his head. Will began to suspect that that unearthly laugh was not altogether unknown to him. He stood still to consider, and that moment the laugh was repeated, and a voice out of the crowd called to him, in a shrill laughing tone, " Ha, ha, ha! Will o' Phaup, look to your ain hearth-stane the night." Will again threw off every encumbrance, and fled home to his lonely cot, the most likely spot in the district for the Fairies to congregate; but it is wonderful what an idea of safety is conferred by the sight of a man's own hearth and family circle.

When Will had become a right old man, and was sitting on a little green hillock at the end of his house, one evening, resting himself there came three little boys up to him, all exactly like one another, when the following short dialogue ensued between Will and them.

" Good e'en t'ye, Will Laidlaw."

" Good e'en t'ye, creatures. Whare ir ye gaun this gate ?"

" Can ye gie us up-putting for the night ?"

" I think three siccan bits o' shreds o' hurchins winna be ill to put up.—Where came ye frae ?"

" Frae a place that ye dinna ken.   But we are come on a commission to you."

" Come away in then, and tak sic cheer as we hae."

Will rose and led the way into the house, and the little boys followed ; and as he went, he said carelessly without looking back, " What's your commission to me bairns ?" He thought they might be the sons of some gentleman, who was a guest of his master's.

" We are sent to demand a silver key that you have in your possession."

Will was astounded ; and standing still to consider of some old transaction, he said, without lifting his eyes from the ground,—

" A silver key ? In God's name, where came ye from ?"

There was no answer, on which Will wheeled round, and round, and round ; but the tiny beings were all gone, and Will never saw them more.   At the name of God, they vanished in the twinkling of an eye.   It is curious that I never should have heard the secret of the silver key, or indeed, whether there was such a thing or not.

But Will once saw a vision which was more unaccountable than this still.   On his way from Moffat one time, about midnight, he perceived a light very near to the verge of a steep hill, which he knew perfectly well on the lands of Selcouth.   The light appeared exactly like one from a window, and as if a lamp moved frequently within. His path was by the bottom of the hill, and the light being almost close at the top, he had at first no thoughts of visiting it ; but as it shone in sight for a full mile, his curiosity to see what it was continued still to increase as he approached nearer.   At length, on coming to the bottom of the steep bank, it appeared so bright and near, that he determined to climb the hill and see what it was. There was no moon, but it was a starry night and not very dark, and Will clambered up the precipice, and went straight to the light, which he found to proceed from an opening into a cavern, of about the dimensions of an ordinary barn. The opening was a square one, and just big enough for a man to creep in. Will set in his head, and beheld a row of casks from one end to the other, and two men with long beards, buff belts about their waists, and torches in their hands, who seemed busy on writing something on each cask. They were not the small casks used by smugglers, but large ones, about one half bigger than common tar-barrels, and all of a size, save two very huge ones at the further end. The cavern was all neat and clean, but there was an appearance of mouldiness about the casks, as if they had stood there for ages. The men were both at the farther end when Will looked in, and busily engaged; but at length one of them came towards him, holding his torch above his head, and, as Will thought, having his eyes fixed on him. Will never got such a fright in his life;—many a fright he had got with unearthly creatures, but this was the worst of all. The figure that approached him from the cavern was of a gigantic size, with grizly features, and a beard hanging down to his belt. Will did not stop to consider what was best to be done, but, quite forgetting that he was on the face of a hill, almost perpendicular, turned round, and ran with all his might. It was not long till he missed his feet, fell, and hurling down with great celerity, soon reached the bottom of the steep, and getting on his feet, pursued his way home in the utmost haste, terror, and amazement; but the light from the cavern was extinguished on the instant—he saw it no more.

Will apprised all the people within his reach, the next morning, of the wonderful discovery he had made; but the story was so like a fantasy or a dream, that most of them were hard of belief; and some never did believe it, but ascribed all to the Moffat brandy. However, they sallied all out in a body, armed with cudgels and two or three rusty rapiers to reconnoitre ; but the entrance into the cave they could not find, nor has it ever been discovered to this day. They observed very plainly the rut in the grass which Will had made in his rapid descent from the cave, and there were also found evident marks of two horses having been fastened that night in a wild cleuch-head, at a short distance from the spot they were searching. But these were the only discoveries to which the investigation led. If the whole of this was an optical delusion, it was the most singular I ever heard or read of. For my part, I do not believe it was ; I believe there was such a cavern existing at that day, and that vestiges of it may still be discovered. It was an unfeasible story altogether for a man to invent ; and, moreover, though Will was a man whose character had a deep tinge of the superstitions of his own country, he was besides a man of probity, truth, and honour, and never told that for the truth, which he did not believe to be so.

## Daft Jock Amos.

DAFT JOCK AMOS was another odd character, of whom many droll sayings are handed down. He was a lunatic ; but having been a scholar in his youth, he was possessed of a sort of wicked wit, and wavering uncertain intelligence, that proved right troublesome to those who took it on them to reprove his eccentricities. As he lived close by the church, in the time of the far-famed Boston, the minister and he were constantly coming in contact, and many of their little dialogues are preserved.

" The mair fool are ye, quo' Jock Amos to the minister," is a constant by-word in Ettrick to this day. It had its origin simply as follows :—Mr Boston was taking his walk one fine summer evening after sermon, and in his way came upon Jock, very busy cutting some grotesque figures in wood with his knife. Jock looking hastily up, found he was fairly caught, and not knowing what to say, burst into a foolish laugh—" Ha ! ha ! ha !

Mr Boston, are you here? Will you coss a good whittle wi' me?"

"Nay, nay, John, I will not exchange knives to-day."

"The mair fool are ye," quo' Jock Amos to the minister.

"But, John, can you repeat the fourth commandment?—I hope you can—Which is the fourth commandment?"

I daresay, Mr Boston, it'll be the ane after the third."

"Can you not repeat it?"

"I am no sure about it—I ken it has some wheeram by the rest."

Mr. Boston repeated it, and tried to show him his error in working with knives on the Sabbath day. John wrought away till the divine added,

"But why won't you rather come to church, John?—what is the reason you never come to church?"

"Because you never preach on the text I want you to preach on."

"What text would you have me to preach on."

"On the nine-and-twenty knives that came back from Babylon."

"I never heard of them before."

"It is a sign you have never read your Bible. Ha, ha, ha, Mr Boston! sic fool sic minister."

Mr Boston searched long for John's text that evening, and at last finding it recorded in Ezra i. 9, he wondered greatly at the acuteness of the fool, considering the subject on which he had been reproving him.

"John, how auld will you be?" said a sage wife to him one day, when talking of their ages.

"O, I dinna ken," said John. "It wad tak a wiser head than me to tell you that."

"It is unco queer that you dinna ken how auld you are," returned he.

"I ken wee nough how auld I am," said John; "but I dinna ken how auld I'll be."

An old man named Adam Linton, once met him running from home in the grey of the morning. "Hey, Jock

Amos," said he, "where are you bound for so briskly this morning?"

"Aha! He's wise that wats that, and as daft wha speers," says Jock, without taking his eye from some object that it seemed to be following.

"Are you running after any body?" said Linton.

"I am that, man," returned Jock; "I'm rinning after the deil's messenger. Did you see ought o' him gaun by?"

"What was he like?" said Linton.

"Like a great big black corbie," said Jock, "carrying a bit tow in his gab. And what do you think?—he has tauld me a piece o' news the day! There's to be a wedding owet by here the day, man—ay, a wedding! I maun after him, for he has gien me an invitation."

"A wedding? Dear Jock, you are raving. What wedding can there be to-day?" said Linton.

"It is Eppy Telfer's man—auld Eppy Telfer to be wed the day; and I'm to be there; and the mister is to be there, and a' the elders. But Tammie, te Cameronian, he darena come, for fear he should hae dance wi' the kimmers. There will be braw wark ere the day, Aedie Linton,—braw wark there the day." And away ran Jock towards Ettrickhouse, hallooing and waving his cap for joy. Old Adam came in, and said to his wife, who was still in bed, that he supposed the moon was at the full, for Jock Amos was "gane quite gie awthegither, and was away shouting to Ettrickhou to Eppy Telfer's wedding."

"Then," said his wife, "if he be ill, she be waur, for they are always affected at the same time and though Eppy is better than Jock in her ordinary way he is waur when the moon-madness comes ower her." (is woman, Eppy Telfer, was likewise subject to lunati ts of insanity, and Jock had a great ill will at her; could not even endure the sight of her.)

The above little dialogue was hardly ended before word came that Eppy Telfer had "put own" herself over night, and was found hanging dead her own little

cottage at daybreak. Mr Bostor
with his servant man and one of hi
in a state of such perplexity and
almost as much dead as alive. Tl
deal, carried to the peak of the Wec
there, and all the while Jock Amo:
in his life met with an entertain:
please him more. While the n
grave, he sat on a stone near by, j
one while, always addressing Epp:
heartily at another.

. After this high fit Jock lost h:
never more recovered them. H
nonentity, and lay mostly in his b
death.

## Willie Candl

ANOTHER notable man of that d:
dart, nicknamed Candlem, one of
house. He was simple, unlettered
sayings that are preserved testify.
married to one Meggie Coltard, a gr(
announced, and the numbers that (
immense. Candlem and his bride v
to be married, and Mr Boston, wh(
perceiving such a motley crowd fol
into the church; and after admil
witnesses, he set his son John, &
Currie, to keep the two doors, ar
from entering. Young Boston le
door, but John Currie stood ma
refusing entrance to all. When
put the question, Are you willing
&c.

. " I wat weel I was thinking s
" Haud to the door, John Currie!'

When the question was put t(
assent like a dumb woman, but this

Candlem.—" What for d'ye no answer, Meggie ?" says he. "Dinna ye hear what the honest man's speering at ye ?"

In due time Willie Candlem and Meggie had a son, and as the custom then was, it was decreed that the first Sabbath after he was born he should be baptized. It was about the Martinmas time, the day was stormy, and the water flooded ; however it was agreed that the baptism could not be put off, for fear of the fairies ; so the babe was well rolled up in swaddling clothes, and laid on before his father on the white mare,—the stoutest of the kimmers stemming the water on foot. Willie Candlem rode the water slowly and cautiously. When about the middle of the stream, he heard a most unearthly yelling and screaming rise behind him ; " What are they squealing at ?" said he to himself, but durst not look back for fear of his charge. After he had crossed the river safely, and a sand-bed about as wide, Willie wheeled his white mare's head about, and exclaimed—" Why, the ne'er a haet I hae but the slough !" Willie had dropped the child into the flooded river, without missing it out of the huge bundle of clothes ; but luckily, one of the kimmers picked him, and as he showed some signs of life, they hurried into a house at Goosegreen, and got him brought round again. In the afternoon he was so far recovered, that the kimmers thought he might be taken up to church for baptism, but Willie Candlem made this sage remark—" I doubt he's rather unfeiroch to stand it ;—he has gotten eneugh o' the water for ae day." On going home to his poor wife, his first address to her was—" Ay, ye may take up your handywark, Meggie, in making a slough open at baith ends. What signifies a thing that's open at baith ends ?"

Another time, in harvest, it came on a rainy day, and the Ettrick began to look very big in the evening. Willie Candlem, perceiving his crop in danger, yoked the white mare in the sledge, and was proceeding to lead his corn out of watermark ; but out came Meggie, and began expostulating with him on the sinfulness of the act,—

"Put in your beast again, like a good Christian man, Willie," said she, "and dinna be setting an ill example to a' the parish. Ye ken, that this verra day the minister bade us lippen to Providence in our straits, and we wad never rue't. He'll take it very ill off your hand, the setting of sic an example on the Lord's day; therefore, Willie, my man, take his advice and mine, and lippen to Providence this time."

Willie Candlem was obliged to comply, for who can withstand the artillery of a woman's tongue? So he put up his white mare, and went to bed with a heavy heart; and the next morning, by break of day, when he arose and looked out, behold the greater part of his crop was gone.—"Ye may take up your Providence now, Meggie! Where's your Providence now? A' down the water wi' my corn! Ah! I wad trust mair to my gude white mare than to you and Providence baith!"

Meggie answered him meekly, as her duty and custom was—"O Willie! dinna rail at Providence, but down to the meadow-head and claim first." Willie Candlem took the hint, galloped on his white mare down to the Ettrick meadows, over which the river spread, and they were covered with floating sheaves; so Willie began and hauled out, and carried out, till he had at least six times as much corn as he had lost. At length one man came, and another, but Willie refused all partition of the spoil. "Ay, ye may take up your corn now where you can find it, lads," said Willie; "I keppit nane but my ain. Yours is gane farther down. Had ye come when I came, ye might have keppit it a'." So Willie drove and drove, till the stackyard was full.

"I think the crop has turn'd no that ill out after a'," said Meggie. "You've been nae the waur o' trusting to Providence."

"Na," rejoined Willie, "nor o' taking your advice, Meggie, and ganging down to kep and claim at the meadow-head."

## CHAP. XIX.

### NANCY CHISHOLM.

JOHN CHISHOLM, farmer of Moorlaggan, was, in the early part of his life, a wealthy and highly respectable man, and associated with the best gentlemen of the country ; and in those days he was accounted to be not only reasonable, but mild and benevolent in his disposition. A continued train of unfortunate speculations, however, at last reduced his circumstances so much, that, though at the time when this tale commences, he still continued solvent, it was well enough known to all the country that he was on the brink of ruin ; and, by an unfortunate fatality, too inherent in human nature ; still as he descended in circumstances, he advanced in pride and violence of temper, until his conduct grew so intolerable, as scarcely to be submitted to even by his own family.

Mr Chisholm had five daughters, well brought up, and well educated ; but the second, whose name was Nancy Chisholm, was acknowledged to be the most beautiful and accomplished of them all. She was so buoyant of spirits, that she hardly appeared to know whether she was treading on the face of the earth, or bounding on the breeze ; and before Nancy was eighteen, as was quite natural, she was beloved by the handsomest lad in the parish, whose proper Christian name was Archibald Gillies, but who, by some patronymic or designation of whose import I am ignorant, was always called Gillespick.

Young Gillies was quite below Nancy in rank, although in circumstances they were by this time much the same. His father being only a small sub-tenant of Mr Chisholm's, the latter would have thought his child degraded, had she been discovered even speaking to the young man. He had, moreover, been bred to the profession of a tailor, which, though an honest occupation, and perhaps more lucrative than many others, is viewed, in the country places of Scotland, with a degree of contempt far exceeding that with which it is regarded in more polished communities. Notwithstanding of all this, Gillespick Gillies, the tailor, had the preference of all others in the heart of pretty Nancy; and, as he durst not pay his addresses to her openly, or appear at Moorlaggan by day, they were driven to an expedient quite in mode with the class to which Gillies belonged, but as entirely inconsistent with that propriety of conduct which ought to be observed by young ladies like those of Moorlaggan—they met by night; that is, about night-fall in summer, and at the same hour in winter, which made it very late in the night.

Now it unluckily had so happened, that Gillies, the young dashing tailor, newly arrived from Aberdeen, had, at a great wedding the previous winter, paid all his attentions to Siobla, Nancy's eldest sister. This happened, indeed, by mere accident, owing to Nancy's many engagements; but Siobla did not know that; and Gillies, being the best dancer in the barn, led her to the head every time, and behaved so courteously, that he made a greater impression on her heart than she was willing to acknowledge. As all ranks mingle at a country wedding, the thing was noted and talked of, both among the low and high; but neither the high nor the low thought or said that young Gillies had made a very prudent choice. She was not, however, the tailor's choice; for his whole heart was fixed on her sister Nancy.

The two slept in one chamber, and it was impossible for the younger to escape to her lover without confiding the secret to Siobla, which, therefore, she was obliged to do; and from that moment jealousy—for jealousy it was, though Miss Siobla called it by another name—began to rankle in her elder sister's bosom. She called Gillies every degrading name she could invent,—a profligate, a libertine,—and to sum up all, she called him *a tailor*, thereby finishing the sum of degeneracy, and crowning the climax of her reproaches.

Nancy was, nevertheless, exceedingly happy with her

handsome lover, who all but adored her. She enjoyed his company perhaps the more on two accounts, one of which she might probably deduce from the words of the wise man, that "stolen waters are sweet, and bread eaten in secret is pleasant;" but another most certainly was, that Gillies having opened her eyes to the true state of her father's affairs, and by this led her to perceive that she was only "a pennyless lass wi' a lang pedigree," she could not help drawing the conclusion, that the tailor was as good as she, that the course she was taking, besides being very agreeable to her own wishes, was the most prudent that could be conceived.

This information preying on Nancy's mind, she could not help communicating it in confidence to one of her sisters, (Siobla, it is to be supposed,) who, believing the report to be a malicious falsehood, went straight to her father with the news, as soon as he arrived from the market. Some vexatious occurrences connected with his depressed fortunes, had put him sorely out of humour that night, and he had likewise been drinking a good deal, which made matters worse; so that when Siobla informed him of the country rumour, that he was about to become a bankrupt, his fury rose to an ungovernable pitch, and, seizing her by the arm, he adjured her forthwith to name her informer, against whom he at the same time vowed the most consummate vengeance. His daughter was frightened, and without hesitation told him that she had learnt the report from her sister Nancy. Nancy was a favourite with old Chisholm, but that circumstance seemed only to inflame him the more; that one so much cherished and beloved should make herself instrumental in breaking his credit, was, he thought, a degree of ingratitude that justified his severest resentment, and with a countenance of the utmost fury, he turned on her, and demanded if what he had heard was true. With a face as pale as death, and trembling lips, she acknowledged that it was. But when desired to name her informer, she remained silent, trembled, and wept. On being further urged, and threatened, she said, hesitatingly, that she did not invent the story; and supposed she had heard it among the servants.

" This will not do, miss," exclaimed her father; " tell me at once the name of your informer; and depend upon it, that person, whoever it is, had better never been born."

Nancy could not answer, but sobbed and wept.

Just at that unlucky moment, a whistle was heard from the wood opposite the window. This was noticed by Mr Chisholm, who looked a little startled, and inquired what or who it was; but no one gave him any answer.

It had been settled between the two lovers, that when Gillies came to see Nancy, he was to whistle from a certain spot in a certain manner, while she was to open the window, and hold the light close to the glass for an instant, that being the token that she heard and understood the signal. In the present dilemma, the performance of her part of the agreement was impracticable; and, of course, when old Chisholm was once more rising into a paroxysm of rage at his daughter, the ominous whistle was repeated.

" What *is* this ?" demanded he, in a peremptory tone. " Tell me instantly; for I see by your looks you know and understand what it is. Siobla, do you know ?"

" Yes, I do," replied Siobla. " I know well enough what it is—I do not hear it so seldom."

" Well, then, inform me at once what it means," said her father.

" It is Nancy's sweetheart come to whistle her out —young tailor Gillies;" answered Siobla, without any endeavour to avert her father's wrath, by giving the information in an indirect way.

" Oho ! Is it thus ?" exclaimed the infuriated father. " And Nancy always answers and attends to this audacious tailor's whistle, does she ?"

" Indeed she does, sir ; generally once or twice every week," replied the young woman, in the same willing tone.

" The secret is then out !" said old Chisholm, in words

that quavered with anger. "It is plain from whence the injurious report has been attained! Too fond father! alas, poor old man! Have matters already come thus low with thee? And hast thou indeed nourished and cherished this favourite child, given her an education fitting her for the highest rank in society, and all that she might throw herself away upon a—a—a tailor!— Begone, girls! I must converse with this degraded creature alone."

When her sisters had left the apartment, Nancy knelt, wept, prayed, and begged forgiveness; but a temporary distraction had banished her father's reason, and he took hold of her long fair hair, wound it round his left hand in the most methodical manner, and began to beat her with his cane. She uttered a scream; on which he stopped, and told her that if she uttered another sound before he had done chastising her, it should be her last; but this causing her to scream only ten times louder he beat her with such violence that he shivered the cane to pieces. He then desisted, calling her the ruin of her sisters, of himself, and all her father's house; opened the door, and was about to depart and leave her, when the tailor's whistle again sounded in his ears, louder and nearer than before. This once more drove him to madness, and seizing a heavy dog-whip that hung in the lobby, he returned into the parlour, and struck his daughter repeatedly in the most unmerciful manner. During the concluding part of this horrid scene, she opened not her mouth, but eyed her ferocious parent with composure, thinking she had nothing but death to expect from his hands.

Alas! death was nothing to the pangs she then suffered, and those she was doomed to suffer! Her father at last ceased from his brutal treatment, led her from the house, threw her from him, with a curse, and closed the door with a force that made the casements of the house clatter.

There never was perhaps a human being whose circumstances in life were as suddenly changed, or more deplorable than Nancy Chisholm's were that night. But it was not only her circumstances in life that were changed: she felt at once that the very nature within her was changed also, and that from being a thing of happiness and joy, approaching to the nature of a seraph, she was now converted into a fiend. She had a cup measured to her which nature could not endure, and its baneful influences had the instant effect of making her abhor her own nature, and become a rebel to all its milder qualities.

The first resolution she formed was that of full and ample revenge. She determined to make such a dreadful retaliation, as should be an example to all jealous sisters and unnatural parents, while the world lasted. Her plan was to wait till after midnight, and then set fire to the premises, and burn her father, her sisters, and all that pertained to them, to ashes. In little more than an instant was her generous nature so far altered, that she exulted in the prospect of this horrid catastrophe.

With such a purpose, the poor wretch went and hid herself until all was quiet; and there is no doubt that she would have put her scheme in execution, had it not been for the want of fire to kindle the house; for as to going into any dwelling, or seeing the face of an acquaintance, in her present degraded condition, her heart shrunk from it. So, after spending some hours in abortive attempts at raising fire, she was obliged to depart, bidding an eternal adieu to all that she had hitherto held dear on earth.

On the approach of daylight, she retired into a thicket, and, at a brook, washed and bathed her bloated arms and face, disentangled and combed her yellow hair with her fingers, and when she thought she was unobserved, drew the train of her gown over her head, and sped away on her journey, whither she knew not. No distinct account of her escape, or of what became of her for some time, can be given; but the whole bent of her inclinations was to do evil; she felt herself impelled to it by a motive she could not account for, but which she had no power or desire to resist. She felt it as it were incumbent on her always to retaliate evil for good,—the most fiendish disposition that the human heart could feel. She had a desire that the Evil One would appear in person that she might enter into a formal contract to do evil. She had a longing to impart to others some share of the torment she had herself endured, and missed no opportunity of inflicting such. Once in the course of her wanderings, she met, in a sequestered place, a little girl, whom she seized, and beat her " within an inch of her life," as she called it. She was at this period quite a vagabond, and a pest wherever she went.

The manner in which she first got into a place was not the least remarkable of her adventures. On first coming to Aberdeen, she went into the house of one Mr Simon Gordon, in the upper Kirkgate, and asked some food, which was readily granted her by the housekeeper ; for, owing to her great beauty and superior address, few ever refused her any thing she asked. She seemed little disposed to leave the house again, and by no means could the housekeeper prevail upon her to depart, unless she were admitted to speak with Mr Gordon.

This person was an old bachelor, rich and miserly ; and the housekeeper was terrified at the very idea of acknowledging to him that she had disposed of the least morsel of food in charity ; far less dared she allow a mendicant to carry her petition into her master's very presence. But the pertinacity of the individual she had now to deal with fairly overcame her fears, and she carried up to Mr Simon Gordon the appalling message, that a " seeking woman," that is, a begging woman demanded to speak with him. Whether it was that Mr Simon's abhorrence of persons of that cast was driven from the field by the audacity of the announcement, I cannot pretend to say ; but it is certain that he remitted in his study of the state of the public funds, and granted the interview. And as wonders when they once commence, are, for the most part, observed to continue to follow each other for a time, he not only astounded the housekeeper by his ready assent to let the stranger have speech of

him : but the poor woman had nearly sunk into the
ground with dismay when she heard him, after the interview was over, give orders that this same wanderer was
to be retained in the house in the capacity of her assistant. Here, however, the miraculous part of this adventure stops ; for the housekeeper, who had previously been
a rich old miser's only servant, did, in the first place, remonstrate loudly against any person being admitted to
share her labours, or her power ; and on finding all that
could be said totally without effect, she refused to remain with her master any longer, and immediately de-
parted, leaving Nancy Chisholm in full possession of the
premises.

Being now in some degree tired of a wandering unset-
tled life, she continued with Mr Gordon, testifying her
hatred of the world rather by a sullen and haughty apathy, than by any active demonstrations of enmity ; and
what was somewhat remarkable, by her attention to the
wants of the peevish and feeble old man, her master, she
gained greatly upon his good-will.

In this situation her father discovered her, after an
absence of three years, during which time his compunc-
tious visitings had never either ceased or diminished from
the time he had expelled her his house, while under the
sway of unbridled passion. He never had more heart for
any thing in the world. All his affairs went to wreck ;
he became bankrupt, and was driven from his ample possessions, and was forced to live in a wretched cottage in
a sort of genteel penury. But all his misfortunes and
disappointments put together did not affect him half so
much as the loss of his darling daughter ; he never doubted that she had gone to the home of her lover, to the
house of old Gillies ; and this belief was one that carried
great bitterness to his heart. When he discovered that
she had never been seen there, his next terror was that
she had committed suicide ; and he trembled night and
day, anticipating all the horrid shapes in which he might
hear that the desperate act had been accomplished.
When the dread of this began to wear away, a still more

frightful idea arose to haunt his troubled imagination——it was that of his once beloved child driven to lead a life of infamy and disgrace. This conclusion was but too natural, and he brooded on it with many repentant tears for the space of nearly two years, when he at last set out with a resolution either to find his lost daughter, or spend the remainder of his life in search of her.

It is painful to think of the scenes that he went through in this harassing and heart-rending search, until he at length discovered her in the house of Mr Simon Gordon. For a whole week he had not the courage to visit her, though he stole looks of her every day; but he employed himself in making every inquiry concerning her present situation.

One day she was sitting, in gay attire, sewing, and singing the following rhyme, in crooning of which she spent a part of every day :

> I am lost to peace, I am lost to grace,
>   I am lost to all that's beneath the sun ;
> I have lost my way in the light of day,
>   And the gates of heaven I will never won.
>
> If one sigh would part from my burning heart,
>   Or one tear would rise in my thirsty eye,
> Through wo and pain it might come again—
>   The soul that fled, from deep injury.
>
> In one hour of grief I would find relief,
>   One pang of sorrow would ease my pain ;
> But joy or wo, in this world below,
>   I can never never know again !

While she was thus engaged, old Chisholm, with an agitated heart and trembling frame, knocked gently at the door, which was slowly and carelessly opened by his daughter ; for she performed every thing as if she had no interest in it. The two gazed on one another for a moment, without speaking ; but the eyes of the father were beaming with love and tenderness, while those of the daughter had that glazed and joyless gleam which too well bespoke her hardened spirit. The old man spread out his arms to embrace her; but she closed the door upon him. He retired again to his poor lodgings, from whence he sent her a letter fraught with tenderness and sorrow, which produced no answer.

There was another besides her father who had found her out before this time, though he had never ventured to make himself known to her; and that was her former lover, Gillespick Gillies, the tailor. He had traced her in all her wanderings, and though it had been once his intention to settle in Edinburgh, yet for her sake, he hired himself to a great clothier and tailor in the city of Aberdeen. After her father's ineffectual application to her, young Gillies ventured to make his appearance; but his reception was far from what he hoped. She was embarrassed and cold, attaching blame to him for every thing, particularly for persuading her out to the woods by night, which had been the means of drawing down her father's anger upon her. He proffered all the reparation in his power; but she would not hear him speak, and even forbade him ever to attempt seeing her again.

The tailor's love was, however, too deeply rooted to be so easily overcome. He would not be said nay, but waited upon her evening and morning; still she remained callous and unmoved, notwithstanding of all his kind attentions.

The frame of her spirit at this period must have been an anomaly in human nature; she knew no happiness, and shunned, with the utmost pertinacity, every avenue leading towards its heavenly shrine. She often said afterwards, that she believed her father's rod had beat an angel out of her, and a demon into its place.

But Gillespick, besides being an affectionate and faithful lover, was a singularly acute youth. He told this perverse beauty again and again that she was acknowledged the flower of all Aberdeen, saving a Miss Marshall, who sat in the College Church every Sunday, to whom some gentlemen gave the preference; and then he always added, "But I am quite certain that were you to appear there dressed in your best style, every one would at once see how much you outshine her." He went over this so often, that Nancy's vanity became interested, and she proffered, of her own accord, to accompany him one day to the College Kirk.

From the time that Gillies got her to enter the church-door again, although she went from no good motive, he considered the victory won, and counted on the certainty of reclaiming his beloved from despair and destruction. All eyes were soon turned on her beauty, but hers sought out and rested on Mary Marshall alone. She was convinced of her own superiority, which added to the elegance of her carriage and gaiety of her looks ; so that she went home exceedingly well pleased with—*the minister's sermon !*

She went back in the afternoon, the next day, and every day thereafter, and her lover noted that she sometimes appeared to fix her attention on the minister's discourse. But one day in particular, when he was preaching on that divine precept, contained in St Luke's Gospel, " Bless them that curse you, and pray for them which despitefully use you," she seemed all the while enrapt by the most ardent feelings, and never for one moment took her eye from the speaker. Her lover perceived this, and kept his eyes steadfastly fixed on her face. At last the reverend divine, in his application of this doctrine to various characters, painted her own case in such a light that it appeared drawn from nature. He then expatiated on the sweet and heavenly joys of forgiveness with such ardour and devotion, that tears once more began to beam in those bright eyes, whose fountains seemed long to have been dried up ; and ere the preacher concluded, she was forced to hide her face, and give free vent to her feelings, weeping abundantly.

Her lover conducted her home, and observed a total alteration in her manner towards him. This change on her seared and hardened spirit, was more, however, than her frame could brook. The next day she was ill, and she grew worse and worse daily ; a strange disease was hers, for she was seized with stubborn and fierce par-

oxysms, very much resembling those possessed of devils
in the dawning of Christianity. It appeared exactly as
if a good spirit and an evil one were contending for the
possession of her person as their tabernacle, none of the
medical faculty being able to account for these extraordinary changes in a natural way. Her lover hired a
sick-nurse, who attended both on her and the old man,
which pleased the latter well, and he thought there was
not such a man in the city of Aberdeen as the young
tailor

Nancy's disease was at length mastered, but it left her
feeble and emaciated, and from that time forth, she showed herself indeed an altered woman. The worthy divine
who first opened her eyes to her lost condition, had visited her frequently in her sickness, and repeated his exhor-
tations. Her lover waited on her every day ; and not
only this, but being, as I before observed, an acute youth,
he carried to the house with him cordials for the old
miser, and told or read him the news from the Stock
Exchange. Nancy was now attached to Gillespick with
the most ardent and pure affection, and more deeply than
in her early days of frolic and thoughtlessness ; for now
her love toward him was mellowed by a ray from heaven.
In few words, they were married. Old Simon Gordon
died shortly after, and left them more than half his fortune, amounting, it was said, to L.11,000 ; a piece of
generosity to which he was moved, not only by the attention shown him in his latter days by the young pair,
but, as he expressed it in his will, "being convinced
that Gillies would take care of the money." This legacy
was a great fortune for an Aberdeen tailor and clothier.
He bought the half of his master's stock and business,
and in consequence of some army and navy contracts,
realized a very large fortune in a short time.

Old Chisholm was by this time reduced to absolute
beggary ; he lived among his former wealthy acquaintances, sometimes in the hall, sometimes in the parlour,
as their good or bad humour prevailed. His daughters,
likewise, were all forced to accept situations as upper

servants, and were, of course, very unhappily placed, countenanced by no class, being too proud to associate with those in the station to which they had fallen. The company of lowlanders that had taken Moorlaggan on Chisholm's failure, followed his example, and failed also. The farm was again in the market, and nobody to bid any thing for it; at length an agent from Edinburgh took it for a rich lady, at half the rent that had been paid for it before; and then every one said, had old John Chisholm held it at such a rent, he would have been the head of the country to that day. The whole of the stock and furniture were bought up from the creditors, paid in ready money, and the discount returned; and as this was all done by the Edinburgh agent, no one knew who was to be the farmer, although the shepherds and servants were hired, and the business of the farm went on as before.

Old Chisholm was at this time living in the house of a Mr Mitchell, on Spey, not far from Pitmain, when he received a letter from this same Edinburgh agent, stating, that the new farmer of Moorlaggan wanted to speak with him on very important business relating to that farm; and that all his expenses would be paid to that place, and back again, or to what other place in the country he chose to go. Chisholm showed Mr Mitchell the letter, who said, he understood it was to settle the marches about some disputed land, and it would be as well for him to go and make a good charge for his trouble, and at the same time offered to accommodate him with a pony. Mr Mitchell could not spare his own saddle-horse, having to go a journey; so he mounted Mr Chisholm on a small shaggy highland nag, with crop ears, and equipped with an old saddle, and a bridle with hair reins. It was the evening of the third day after he left Mr Mitchell's house before he reached Moorlaggan; and as he went up Coolen-aird, he could not help reflecting with bitterness of spirit on the alteration of times with him. It was not many years ago when he was wont to ride by the same path, mounted on a fine horse of his own, with a livery servant behind him; now he rode a little shabby nag, with crop ears and a hair bridle, and even that diminutive creature belonged to another man. Formerly he had a comfortable home, and a respectful family to welcome him; now he had no home, and that family was all scattered abroad. "Alas!" said he to himself, "times are indeed sadly altered with me; ay, and I may affect to blame misfortune for all that has befallen me; but I cannot help being persuaded that the man who is driven by unmanly passions to do that of which he is ashamed both before God and man, can never prosper. Oh, my child! my lost and darling child! What I have suffered for her both in body, mind, and outward estate!"

In this downcast and querulous mood did the forlorn old man reach his former habitation. All was neat and elegant about the place, and there was a chaise standing at the end of the house. When old Chisholm saw this, he did not venture up to the front door, but alighted, and led his crop-eared pony to the back door, at which he knocked, and having stated the errand upon which he came, was, after some delay, ushered into the presence of a courtly dame, who accosted him in proud and dignified language as follows :—

" Your name is Mr John Chisholm, I believe?"

" It is, madam; at your service."

" And you were once farmer hear, I believe?" (A bow.) " Ay. Hem. And how did you lose your farms?"

" Through misfortunes, madam, and by giving too much credit to insufficient parties."

" Ay—so! That was not prudent in you to give so much credit in such quarters—Eh?"

" I have been favoured with a letter from your agent, madam," said Chisholm, to whom this supercilious tone of cross-questioning was far from being agreeable, "and I beg to know what are your commands with me."

" Ay. True. Very right. So you don't like to talk of your own affairs, don't you? No; it seems not. —Why, the truth is, that my agent wished me to employ you as factor or manager of these lands, as my husband and I must live for the greater part of the year at a great distance. We are willing to give a good salary ; and I believe there is no man so fit for our purpose. But I have heard accounts of you that I do not like,—that you were an inexorable tyrant in your own family, abusing and maltreating the most amiable of them in a very unmanly manner. And, I have heard, but I hope not truly, that you drove one daughter to disgrace and destruction."

Here Chisholm turned his face towards the window, burst into tears, and said, he hoped she had not sent for a miserable and degraded old man to torture his feelings by probing those wounds of the soul that were incurable.

" Nay, I beg your pardon, old gentleman. I sent for you to do you a service. I was only mentioning a vile report that reached my ear, in hopes that you could exculpate yourself."

" Alas, madam, I cannot."

" Dreadful ! Dreadful ! Father of heaven, could thy hand frame a being with feelings like this ! But I hope you did not, as is reported,—No—you could not—you did not strike her, did you ?"

" Alas ! alas !" exclaimed the agonized old man.

" What ? Beat her—scourge her—throw her from your house at midnight with a father's curse upon her head ?"

" I did ! I did ! I did !"

" Monster ! Monster ! Go, and hide your devoted and execrable head in some cavern in the bowels of the earth, and wear out the remainder of your life in praying to thy God for repentance ; for thou art not fit to herd with the rest of his creatures !"

" My cup of sorrow and misery is now full," said the old man as he turned, staggering, towards the door. " On the very spot has this judgment fallen on me."

" But stop, sir—stop for a little space," said the lady. " Perhaps I have been too hasty, and it may be you have repented of that unnatural crime already ?"

" Repented ! Ay, God is my witness, not a night or

day has passed over this grey head on which I have not repented : in that bitterness of spirit too, which the chief of sinners only can feel."

" Have you indeed repented of your treatment of your daughter ? Then all is forgiven on her part. And do you, father, forgive me too !"

The old man looked down with bewildered vision, and, behold, there was the lady of the mansion kneeling at his feet, and embracing his knees ! She had thrown aside her long flowing veil, and he at once discovered the comely face of his beloved daughter.

That very night she put into her father's hand the new lease of all his former possessions, and receipts for the stock, crop, and furniture. The rest of the family were summoned together, and on the following Sabbath they went all to church and took possession of their old family seat, every one sitting in the place she occupied formerly, with Siobla at the head. But the generous creature who had thus repaid good for evil, was the object of attraction for every eye, and the admiration of every heart.

This is a true story, and it contains not one moral, but many, as every true portraiture of human life must do ; It shows us the danger of youthful imprudence, of jealousy, and of unruly passions ; but, above all, it shows, that without a due sense of religion there can be no true and disinterested love.

---

# CHAP. XX.

## THE SHEPHERD'S DOG.

A curious story that appeared lately of a dog belonging to a shepherd, named John Hoy, has brought sundry similar ones to my recollection, which I am sure cannot fail to be interesting to those unacquainted with the qualities of that most docile and affectionate of the whole animal creation—the shepherd's dog.

The story alluded to was shortly this. John was at a sacrament of the Covenanters, and being loath to leave the afternoon sermon, and likewise obliged to have his ewes at the bught by a certain hour, gave his dog a quiet hint at the outskirts of the congregation, and instantly she went away, took the hills, and gathered the whole flock of ewes to the bught, as carefully and quietly as if her master had been with her, to the astonishment of a thousand beholders, for the ewes lay scattered over two large and steep hills.

This John Hoy was my uncle; that is, he was married to my mother's sister. He was all his life remarkable for breeding up his dogs to perform his commands with wonderful promptitude and exactness, especially at a distance from him, and he kept always by the same breed. It may be necessary to remark here, that there is no species of animals so varied in their natures and propensities as the shepherd's dog, and these propensities are preserved inviolate in the same breed from generation to generation. One kind will manage sheep about hand, about a bught, shedding, or fold, almost naturally; and those that excel most in this kind of service, are always the least tractable at a distance; others will gather sheep from the hills, or turn them this way and that way, as they are commanded, as far as they can hear their master's voice, or note the signals made by his hand, and yet can never be taught to command sheep close around him. Some excel again in a kind of social intercourse. They understand all that is said to them, or of them, in the family; and often a good deal that is said of sheep, and of other dogs, their comrades. One kind will bite the legs of cattle, and no species of correction or disapprobation will restrain them, or ever make them give it up; another kind bays at the heads of cattle, and neither precept nor example will ever induce them to attack a beast behind, or bite its legs.

My uncle Hoy's kind were held in estimation over the whole country for their docility in what is termed *hirsel-rinning*; that is, gathering sheep at a distance, but they were never very good at commanding sheep about hand. Often have I stood with astonishment at seeing him standing on the top of one hill, and the Tub, as he called an excellent snow-white bitch that he had, gathering all the sheep from another with great care and caution. I once saw her gathering the head of a hope, or glen, quite out of her master's sight, while all that she heard of him was now and then the echo of his voice or whistle from another hill, yet, from the direction of that echo, she gathered the sheep with perfect acuteness and punctuality.

I have often heard him tell an anecdote of another dog, called Nimble: One drifty day, in *the seventy-four*, after gathering the ewes of Chapelhope, he found that he wanted about an hundred of them. He again betook himself to the heights, and sought for them the whole day without being able to find them, and began to suspect that they were covered over with snow in some ravine. Towards the evening it cleared up a little, and as a last resource, he sent away Nimble. She had found the scent of them on the hill while her master was looking for them; but not having received orders to bring them, she had not the means of communicating the knowledge she possessed. But as soon as John gave her the gathering word, she went away, he said, like an arrow out of a bow, and in less than five minutes he beheld her at about a mile's distance, bringing them round a hill, called the Middle, cocking her tail behind them, and apparently very happy at having got the opportunity of terminating her master's disquietude with so much ease.

I once witnessed another very singular feat performed by a dog belonging to John Graham, late tenant in Ashesteel. A neighbour came to his house after it was dark, and told him that he had lost a sheep on his farm, and that if he (Graham) did not secure her in the morning early, she would be lost, as he had brought her far. John said, he could not possibly get to the hill next morning, but if he would take him to the very spot where he lost the sheep, perhaps his dog Chieftain would find her that

night. On that they went away with all expedition, lest
the traces of the feet should cool; and I, then a boy,
being in the house, went with them. The night was pitch
dark, which had been the cause of the man losing his
ewe; and at length he pointed out a place to John, by
the side of the water, where he had lost her. "Chieftain, fetch that," said John, "bring her back, sir." The
dog jumped around and around, and reared himself up
on end, but not being able to see any thing, evidently
misapprehended his master; on which John fell a-cursing
and swearing at the dog, calling him a great many black-
guard names. He at last told the man, that he must
point out the *very track* that the sheep went, otherwise
he had no chance of recovering it. The man led him to
a grey stone, and said, he was sure she took the brae
within a yard of that. "Chieftain, come hither to my foot,
you great numb'd whelp," said John. Chieftain came.
John pointed with his finger to the ground, "Fetch that,
I say, sir, you stupid idiot—bring that back. Away!"
The dog scented slowly about on the ground for some
seconds, but soon began to mend his pace, and vanished
in the darkness. "Bring her back—away, you great
calf!" vociferated John, with a voice of exultation, as the
dog broke to the hill; and as all these good dogs perform
their work in perfect silence, we neither saw nor heard
any more for a long time. I think, if I remember right,
we waited there about half an hour; during which time,
all the conversation was about the small chance that the
dog had to find the ewe, for it was agreed on all hands,
that she might long ago have mixed with the rest of the
sheep on the farm. How that was, no man will ever be
able to decide. John, however, still persisted in waiting
until his dog came back, either with the ewe or without
her; and at last the trusty animal brought the individual
lost sheep to our very foot, which the man took on his
back, and went on his way rejoicing. I remember the
dog was very warm, and hanging out his tongue—John
called him all the ill names he could invent, which the
animal seemed to take in very good part. Such language

seemed to be John's flattery to his dog.   For my part, I
went home, fancying I had seen a miracle, little weeting
that it was nothing to what I myself was to experience
in the course of my pastoral life, from the sagacity of the
shepherd's dog.

My dog was always my companion.   I conversed with
him the whole day—I shared every meal with him, and
my plaid in the time of a shower ; the consequence was,
that I generally had the best dogs in all the country.
The first remarkable one that I had was named Sirrah.
He was beyond all comparison the best dog I ever saw.
He was of a surly unsocial temper—disdained all flattery,
and refused to be caressed ; but his attention to his
master's commands and interests never will again be
equalled by any of the canine race.   The first time that
I saw him, a drover was leading him in a rope; he was
hungry, and lean, and far from being a beautiful cur, for
he was all over black, and had a grim face striped with
dark brown.   The man had bought him of a boy for three
shillings, somewhere on the Border, and doubtless had
used him very ill on his journey.   I thought I discovered
a sort of sullen intelligence in his face, notwithstanding
his dejected and forlorn situation ; so I gave the drover
a guinea for him, and appropriated the captive to myself.
I believe there never was a guinea so well laid out ; at
least I am satisfied that I never laid out one to so good
purpose.   He was scarcely then a year old, and knew so
little of herding, that he had never turned sheep in his life ;
but as soon as he discovered that it was his duty to do so,
and that it obliged me, I can never forget with what
anxiety and eagerness he learned his different evolutions.
He would try every way deliberately, till he found out
what I wanted him to do ; and when once I made him
to understand a direction, he never forgot or mistook it
again.   Well as I knew him, he very often astonished
me, for when hard pressed in accomplishing the task that
he was put to, he had expedients of the moment that
bespoke a great share of the reasoning faculty.   Were I
to relate all his exploits, it would require a volume ; J

shall only mention one or two, to prove what kind of an animal he was.

I was a shepherd for ten years on the same farm, where I had always about 700 lambs put under my charge every year at weaning-time. As they were of the short, or black-faced breed, the breaking of them was a very ticklish and difficult task. I was obliged to watch them night and day for the first four days, during which time I had always a person to assist me. It happened one year that just about midnight the lambs broke loose, and came up the moor upon us, making a noise with their running louder than thunder. We got up and waved our plaids, and shouted, in hopes to turn them, but we only made matters worse, for in a moment they were all round us, and by our exertions we cut them into three divisions; one of these ran north, another south, and those that came up between us, straight up the moor to the westward. I called out, " Sirrah, my man, they're a' away;" the word, of all others, that set him most upon the alert, but owing to the darkness of the night, and blackness of the moor, I never saw him at all. As the division of the lambs that ran southward were going straight towards the fold, where they had been that day taken from their dams, I was afraid they would go there, and again mix with them; so I threw off part of my clothes, and pursued them, and by great personal exertion, and the help of another old dog that I had besides Sirrah, I turned them, but in a few minutes afterwards lost them altogether. I ran here and there, not knowing what to do, but always, at intervals, gave a loud whistle to Sirrah, to let him know that I was depending on him. By that whistling, the lad who was assisting me found me out; but he likewise had lost all trace whatsoever of the lambs. I asked if he had never seen Sirrah? He said, he had not; but that after I left him, a wing of the lambs had come round him with a swirl, and that he supposed Sirrah had then given them a turn, though he could not see him for the darkness. We both concluded, that whatever way the lambs ran at first, they would finally land at the fold where they left their mothers, and without delay we bent our course towards that ; but when we came there, there was nothing of them, nor any kind of bleating to be heard, and we discovered with vexation that we had come on a wrong track.

My companion then bent his course towards the farm of Glen on the north, and I ran away westward for several miles, along the wild tract where the lambs had grazed while following their dams. We met after it was day, far up in a place called the Black Cleuch, but neither of us had been able to discover our lambs, nor any traces of them. It was the most extraordinary circumstance that had ever occurred in the annals of the pastoral life! We had nothing for it but to return to our master, and inform him that we had lost his whole flock of lambs, and knew not what was become of one of them.

On our way home, however, we discovered a body of lambs at the bottom of a deep ravine, called the Flesh Cleuch, and the indefatigable Sirrah standing in front of them, looking all around for some relief, but still standing true to his charge. The sun was then up ; and when we first came in view of them, we concluded that it was one of the divisions of the lambs, which Sirrah had been unable to manage until he came to that commanding situation, for it was about a mile and a half distant from the place where they first broke and scattered. But what was our astonishment, when we discovered by degrees that not one lamb of the whole flock was wanting ! How he had got all the divisions collected in the dark is beyond my comprehension. The charge was left entirely to himself from midnight until the rising of the sun ; and if all the shepherds in the Forest had been there to assist him, they could not have effected it with greater propriety. All that I can say farther is, that I never felt so grateful to any creature below the sun as I did to Sirrah that morning.

I remember another achievement of his which I admired still more. I was sent to a place in Tweeddale, called Stanhope, to bring home a wild ewe that had strayed from home. The place lay at the distance of about fifteen miles, and my way to it was over steep hills, and athwart deep glens ;—there was no path, and neither Sirrah nor I had ever travelled the road before. The ewe was brought in and put into a barn over night ; and, after being frightened in this way, was set out to me in the morning to be driven home by herself. She was as wild as a roe, and bounded away to the side of the mountain like one. I sent Sirrah on a circular route wide before her, and let him know that he had the charge of her. When I left the people at the house, Mr Tweedie, the farmer, said to me, " Do you really suppose that you will drive that sheep over these hills, and out through the midst of all the sheep in the country ?" I said I would try to do it. " Then, let me tell you," said he, " that you may as well try to travel to yon sun." The man did not know that I was destined to do both the one and the other ! Our way, as I said, lay all over wild hills, and through the middle of flocks of sheep. I seldom got a sight of the ewe, for she was sometimes a mile before me, sometimes two ; but Sirrah kept her in command the whole way—never suffered her to mix with other sheep—nor, as far as I could judge, ever to deviate twenty yards from the track by which he and I went the day before. When we came over the great height towards Manor Water, Sirrah and his charge happened to cross it a little before me, and our way lying down hill for several miles, I lost all traces of them, but still held on my track. I came, to two shepherd's houses, and asked if they had seen any thing of a black dog, with a branded face and a long tail, driving a sheep ? No ; they had seen no such thing ; and, besides, all their sheep, both above and below the houses, seemed to be unmoved. I had nothing for it but to hold on my way homeward ; and at length, on the corner of a hill at the side of the water, I discovered my trusty coal-black friend sitting with his eye fixed intently on the burn below him, and sometimes giving a casual glance behind to see if I was coming :—he had the ewe standing there, safe and unhurt.

· When I got her home, and set her at liberty among our own sheep, he took it highly amiss. I could scarcely prevail with him to let her go ; and so dreadfully was he affronted, that she should have been let go free after all his toil and trouble, that he would not come near me all the way to the house, nor yet taste any supper when we got there. I believe he wanted me to take her home and kill her.

He had one very laughable peculiarity, which often created no little disturbance about the house—it was an outrageous ear for music. He never heard music, but he drew towards it ; and he never drew towards it, but he joined in it with all his vigour. Many a good psalm, song, and tune, was he the cause of spoiling ; for when he set fairly to, at which he was not slack, the voices of all his coadjutors had no chance with his. It was customary with the worthy old farmer with whom I resided, to perform family worship evening and morning ; and before he began, it was always necessary to drive Sirrah to the fields, and close the door. If this was at any time forgot or neglected, the moment that the psalm was raised, he joined with all his zeal, and at such a rate, that he drowned the voices of the family before three lines could be sung. Nothing farther could be done till Sirrah was expelled. But then ! when he got to the peat-stack knowe before the door, especially if he got a blow in going out, he *did* give his powers of voice full scope, without mitigation ; and even at that distance he was often a hard match for us all.

Some imagined that it was from a painful sensation that he did this. No such thing. Music was his delight : it always drew him towards it like a charm. I slept in the byre-loft—Sirrah in the hay-nook in a corner below. When sore fatigued, I sometimes retired to my bed before the hour of family worship. In such cases, whenever the psalm was raised in the kitchen, which was but a short distance, Sirrah left his lair ; and laying his ear close to the bottom of the door to hear more distinctly, he growled a low note in accompaniment, till the

sound expired : and then rose, shook his ears, and returned to his hay-nook. Sacred music affected him most;
but in either that or any slow tune, when the tones dwelt
upon the key-note, they put him quite beside himself;
his eyes had the gleam of madness in them ; and he
sometimes quitted singing, and literally fell to barking.
All his race have the same qualities of voice and ear in a
less or greater degree.

The most painful part of Sirrah's history yet remains ;
but in memory of himself, it must be set down. He
grew old, and unable to do my work by himself. I had
a son of his coming up that promised well, and was a
greater favourite with me than ever the other was. The
times were hard, and the keeping of them both was a tax
upon my master which I did not like to impose, although
he made no remonstrances. I was obliged to part with
one of them ; so I sold old Sirrah to a neighbouring shepherd for three guineas. He was accustomed, while I
was smearing, or doing any work about the farm, to go
with any of the family when I ordered him, and run at
their bidding the same as at my own ; but then, when he
came home at night, a word of approbation from me was
recompense sufficient, and he was ready next day to go
with whomsoever I commanded him. Of course, when
I sold him to this lad, he went away when I ordered him,
without any reluctance, and wrought for him all that day
and the next as well as ever he did in his life. But when
he found that he was abandoned by me, and doomed to
be the slave of a stranger for whom he did not care, he
would never again do another feasible turn. The lad
said that he ran in among the sheep like a whelp, and
seemed intent on doing him all the mischief he could.
The consequence was, that he was obliged to part with
him in a short time ; but he had more honour than I had,
for he took him to his father, and desired him to foster
Sirrah, and be kind to him as long as he lived, *for the
sake of what he had been;* and this injunction the old
man faithfully performed.

He came back to see me now and then for months

after he went away, but afraid of the mortification of being driven from the farm-house, he never came there; but knowing well the road that I took to the hill in the morning, he lay down near to that. When he saw me coming, he did not venture near me, but walked round the hill, keeping always about two hundred yards off, and then returned to his new master again, satisfied for the time that there was no more shelter with his beloved old one for him. When I thought how easily one kind word would have attached him to me for life, and how grateful it would have been to my faithful old servant and friend, I could not help regretting my fortune that obliged us to separate. That unfeeling tax on the shepherd's dog, his only bread-winner, has been the cause of much pain in this respect. The parting with old Sirrah, after all that he had done for me, had such an effect on my heart, that I have never been able to forget it to this day ; the more I have considered his attachment and character, the more I have admired them; and the resolution that he took up, and persisted in, of never doing a good turn for any other of my race, after the ingratitude that he had experienced from me, appeared to me to have a kind of heroism and sublimity in it. I am, however, writing nothing but the plain simple truth, to which there are plenty of living witnesses. I then made a vow to myself, which I have religiously kept, and ever shall, never to sell another dog; but that I may stand acquitted of all pecuniary motives, —which indeed those who know me will scarcely suspect me of,—I must add, that when I saw how matters went, I never took a farthing of the stipulated price of old Sirrah. I have Sirrah's race to this day ; and though none of them has ever equalled him as a sheep dog, yet they have far excelled him in all the estimable qualities of sociality and humour.

A single shepherd and his dog will accomplish more in gathering a stock of sheep from a Highland farm, than twenty shepherds could do without dogs; and it is a fact, that, without this docile animal, the pastoral life would be a mere blank. Without the shepherd's dog, the whole of the open mountainous land in Scotland would not be worth a sixpence. It would require more hands to manage a stock of sheep, gather them from the hills, force them into houses and folds, and drive them to markets, than the profits of the whole stock would be capable of maintaining. Well may the shepherd feel an interest in his dog; he it is indeed that earns the family's bread, of which he is himself content with the smallest morsel; always grateful, and always ready to exert his utmost abilities in his master's interest. Neither hunger, fatigue, nor the worst of treatment, will drive him from his side; he will follow him through fire and water, as the saying is, and through every hardship, without murmur or repining, till he literally fall down dead at his foot. If one of them is obliged to change masters, it is sometimes long before he will acknowledge the new one, or condescend to work for him with the same willingness as he did for his former lord; but if he once acknowledge him, he continues attached to him till death; and though naturally proud and high-spirited, in as far as relates to his master, these qualities (or rather failings) are kept so much in subordination, that he has not a will of his own.

My own renowned Hector,* was the son and immediate successor of the faithful old Sirrah; and though not nearly so valuable a dog, he was a far more interesting one. He had three times more humour and whim; and though exceedingly docile, his bravest acts were mostly tinctured with a grain of stupidity, which showed his reasoning faculty to be laughably obtuse.

I shall mention a striking instance of it. I was once at the farm of Shorthope, in Ettrick head, receiving some lambs that I had bought, and was going to take to market, with some more, the next day. Owing to some accidental delay, I did not get final delivery of the lambs till it was growing late; and being obliged to be at my own house that night, I was not a little dismayed lest I should scatter and lose my lambs, if darkness overtook

---

* See the Mountain Bard.

me. Darkness did overtake me by the time I got half way, and no ordinary darkness for an August evening. The lambs, having been weaned that day, and of the wild black-faced breed, became exceedingly unruly, and for a good while I lost hopes of mastering them. Hector managed the point, and we got them safe home; but both he and his master were alike sore forefoughten. It had become so dark, that we were obliged to fold them with candles; and after closing them safely up, I went home with my father and the rest to supper. When Hector's supper was set down, behold he was wanting! and as I knew we had him at the fold, which was within call of the house, I went out and called and whistled on him for a good while; but he did not make his appearance. I was distressed about this; for, having to take away the lambs next morning, I knew I could not drive them a mile without my dog, if it had been to save me the whole drove.

The next morning, as soon as it was day, I arose, and inquired if Hector had come home. No; he had not been seen. I knew not what to do; but my father proposed that he would take out the lambs and herd them, and let them get some meat to fit them for the road; and that I should ride with all speed to Shorthope, to see if my dog had gone back there. Accordingly, we went together to the fold to turn out the lambs, and there was poor Hector sitting trembling in the very middle of the fold door, on the inside of the flake that closed it, with his eyes still steadfastly fixed on the lambs. He had been so hardly set with them after it grew dark, that he durst not for his life leave them, although hungry, fatigued, and cold; for the night had turned out a deluge of rain. He had never so much as lain down, for only the small spot that he sat on was dry, and there had he kept watch the whole night. Almost any other colley would have discerned that the lambs were safe enough in the fold; but Hector had not been able to see through this. He even refused to take my word for it; for he durst not quit his watch, though he heard me calling both at night and morning.

Another peculiarity of his was, that he had a mortal antipathy at the family mouser, which was ingrained in his nature from his very puppyhood; yet so perfectly absurd was he, that no impertinence on her side, and no baiting on, could ever induce him to lay his mouth on her, or injure her in the slightest degree. There was not a day, and scarcely an hour, passed over, that the family did not get some amusement with these two animals. Whenever he was within doors, his whole occupation was watching and pointing the cat from morning to night. When she flitted from one place to another, so did he in a moment; and then squatting down, he kept his point sedulously, till he was either called off or fell asleep.

He was an exceedingly poor taker of meat, was always to press to it, and always lean; and often he would not taste it till we were obliged to bring in the cat. The malicious looks that he cast at her from under his eyebrows on such occasions, were exceedingly ludicrous, considering his utter incapability of wronging her. Whenever he saw her, he drew near his bicker, and looked angry, but still he would not taste till she was brought to it; and then he cocked his tail, set up his birses, and began a-lapping furiously, in utter desperation. His good nature was so immovable, that he would never refuse her a share of what he got; he even lapped close to the one side of the dish, and left her room—but mercy as he did ply!

It will appear strange to hear a dog's reasoning faculty mentioned, as it has been; but I have hardly ever seen a shepherd's dog do any thing without perceiving his reasons for it. I have often amused myself in calculating what his motives were for such and such things, and I generally found them very cogent ones. But Hector had a droll stupidity about him, and took up forms and rules of his own, for which I could never perceive any motive that was not even farther out of the way than the action itself. He had one uniform practice, and a very bad one it was, during the time of family worship,—that just three or four seconds before the conclusion of the prayer, he started to his feet, and ran barking round the apartment like a crazed beast. My father was so much amused with this, that he would never suffer me to correct him for it, and I scarcely ever saw the old man rise from the prayer without his endeavouring to suppress a smile at the extravagance of Hector. None of us ever could find out how he knew that the prayer was near done, for my father was not formal in his prayers; but certes he did know,—of that we had nightly evidence. There never was any thing for which I was so puzzled to discover a reason as this; but, from accident, I did discover it, and, however ludicrous it may appear, I am certain I was correct. It was much in character with many of Hector's feats, and rather, I think, the most *outré* of any principle he ever acted on. As I said, his chief daily occupation was pointing the cat. Now, when he saw us all kneel down in a circle with our faces couched on our paws, in the same posture with himself, it struck his absurd head, that we were all engaged in pointing the cat. He lay on tenters all the time, but the acuteness of his ear enabling him, through time, to ascertain the very moment when we would all spring to our feet, he thought to himself, " I shall be first after her for you all !"

He inherited his dad's unfortunate ear for music, not perhaps in so extravagant a degree, but he ever took care to exhibit it on the most untimely and ill-judged occasions. Owing to some misunderstanding between the minister of the parish and the session clerk, the precenting in church devolved on my father, who was the senior elder. Now, my father could have sung several of the old church tunes middling well, in his own family circle; but it so happened, that, when mounted in the desk, he never could command the starting notes of any but one (St Paul's), which were always in undue readiness at the root of his tongue, to the exclusion of every other semibreve in the whole range of sacred melody. The minister gave out psalms four times in the course of every day's service, and consequently the congregation were treated with St Paul's in the morning, at great length, twice in the course of the service, and then once again at the close—nothing but St Paul's. And, it being of itself a monotonous tune, nothing could exceed the monotony that prevailed in the primitive church of Ettrick. Out of pure sympathy for my father alone, I was compelled to take the precentorship in hand; and, having plenty of tunes, for a good while I came on as well as could be expected, as men say of their wives. But, unfortunately for me, Hector found out that I attended church every Sunday, and though I had him always closed up carefully at home, he rarely failed to make his appearance in church at some time of the day. Whenever I saw him, a tremor came over my spirits; for I well knew what the issue would be. The moment he heard my voice strike up the psalm, " with might and majesty," then did he fall in with such overpowering vehemence, that he and I seldom got any to join in the music but our two selves. The shepherds hid their heads, and laid them down on the backs of the seats wrapped in their plaids, and the lasses looked down to the ground and laughed till their faces grew red. I disdained to stick the tune, and therefore was obliged to carry on in spite of the obstreperous accompaniment; but I was, time after time, so completely put out of all countenance by the brute, that I was obliged to give up my office in disgust, and leave the parish once more to their old friend, St Paul.

Hector was quite incapable of performing the same feats among sheep that his father did; but, as far as his judgment served him, he was a docile and obliging creature. He had one singular quality, of keeping true to the charge to which he was set. If we had been shearing or sorting sheep in any way, when a division was turned out, and Hector got the word to attend to them, he would have done it pleasantly, for a whole day without the least symptom of weariness. No noise or hurry about the fold, which brings every other dog from his business, had the least effect on Hector save that it made him a little troublesome on his own charge, and set him a-running round and round them, turning them in at corners, out of a sort of impatience to be employed as well as his baying neighbours at the fold. Whenever old Sirrah found himself hard set, in commanding wild sheep on steep ground, where they are worst to manage, he never failed, without any hint to the purpose, to throw himself wide in below them, and lay their faces to the hill, by which means he got the command of them in a minute. I never could make Hector comprehend this advantage, with all my art, although his father found it out entirely of himself. The former would turn or wear sheep no other way, but on the hill above them; and though very good at it, he gave both them and himself double the trouble and fatigue.

It cannot be supposed that he could understand all that was passing in the little family circle, but he certainly comprehended a good part of it. In particular, it was very easy to discover that he rarely missed aught that was said about himself, the sheep, the cat, or of a hunt. When aught of that nature came to be discussed, Hector's attention and impatience soon became manifest. There was one winter evening, I said to my mother that I was going to Bowerhope for a fortnight, for that I had more conveniency for writing with Alexander Laidlaw, than at home; and I added, "But I will not take Hector with me, for he is constantly quarrelling with the rest of the dogs, singing music, or breeding some uproar."—"Na, na," quoth she, "leave Hector with me; I like aye best to have him at hame, poor fallow."

These were all the words that passed. The next morning the waters were in a great flood, and I did not go away till after breakfast; but when the time came for tying up Hector, he was wanting.—"The deuce's in that beast," said I; "I will wager that he heard what we were saying yesternight, and has gone off for Bowerhope as soon as the door was opened this morning."

"If that should really be the case, I'll think the beast no canny," said my mother.

The Yarrow was so large as to be quite impassable, so that I had to go up by St Mary's Loch, and go across by the boat; and, on drawing near to Bowerhope, I soon perceived that matters had gone precisely as I suspected. Large as the Yarrow was, and it appeared impassable by any living creature, Hector had made his escape early in the morning, had swam the river, and was sitting, "like a drookit hen," on a knoll at the east end of the house, awaiting my arrival with much impatience. I had a great attachment to this animal, who, with a good deal of absurdity, joined all the amiable qualities of his species. He was rather of a small size, very rough and shagged, and not far from the colour of a fox.

His son, Lion, was the very picture of his dad, had a good deal more sagacity, but also more selfishness. A history of the one, however, would only be an epitome of that of the other. Mr William Nicholson took a fine likeness of this latter one, which that gentleman still possesses. He could not get him to sit for his picture in such a position as he wanted, till he exhibited a singularly fine picture of his, of a small dog, on the opposite side of the room. Lion took it for a real animal, and, disliking its fierce and important look exceedingly, he immediately set up his ears and his shaggy birses, and fixing a stern eye on the picture, in manifest wrath, he would then sit for a whole day, and point his eye at it, without moving away or altering his position.

It is a curious fact, in the history of these animals, that the most useless of the breed have often the greatest degree of sagacity in trifling and useless matters. An exceedingly good sheep-dog attends to nothing else but that particular branch of business to which he is bred. His whole capacity is exerted and exhausted on it, and he is of little avail in miscellaneous matters; whereas, a very indifferent cur, bred about the house, and accustomed to assist with every thing, will often put the more noble breed to disgrace in these paltry services. If one calls out, for instance, that the cows are in the corn, or the hens in the garden, the house-colley needs no other hint, but runs and turns them out. The shepherd's dog knows not what is astir; and, if he is called out in a hurry for such work, all that he will do is to break to the hill, and rear himself up on end, to see if no sheep are running away. A bred sheep-dog, if coming ravening from the hills, and getting into a milk-house, would most likely think of nothing else than filling his belly with the cream. Not so his initiated brother. He is bred at home, to a more civilized behaviour. I have known such lie night and day, among from ten to twenty pails full of milk, and never once break the cream of one of them with the tip of his tongue, nor would he suffer cat, rat, or any other creature, to touch it. This latter sort, too, are far more acute at taking up what is said in a family. There was a farmer of this country, a Mr Alexander Cuninghame, who had a bitch that, for the space of three or four years, in the latter part of her life, met him always at the boundary of his farm, about a mile and a half from his house, on his way home. If he was half a day away, a week, or a fortnight, it was all the same; she met him at that spot, and there never was an instance known of her going to wait his arrival there on a wrong day. If this was a fact, which I have heard averred by people who lived in the house at that time, she could only know of his coming home by hearing it mentioned in the family. The same animal would have gone and brought the cows from the hill when it grew dark, without any bidding, yet she was a very indifferent sheep-dog.

The anecdotes of these animals are all so much alike, that were I but to relate the thousandth part of those I have heard, they would often look very much like repetitions. I shall therefore only mention one or two of the most singular, which I know to be well authenticated.

There was a shepherd lad near Langholm, whose name was Scott, who possessed a bitch, famed over all the West Border for her singular tractability. He could have sent her home with one sheep, two sheep, or any given number, from any of the neighbouring farms; and in the lambing season, it was his uniform practice to send her home with the kebbed ewes just as he got them.—I must let the town reader understand this. A kebbed ewe is one whose lamb dies. As soon as such is found, she is immediately brought home by the shepherd, and another lamb put to her; and this lad, on going his rounds on the hill, whenever he found a kebbed ewe, immediately gave her in charge to his bitch to take home, which saved him from coming back that way again, and going over the same ground he had looked before. She always took them carefully home, and put them into a fold which was close by the house, keeping watch over them till she was seen by some one of the family; and then that moment she decamped, and hasted back to her master, who sometimes sent her three times home in one morning, with different charges. It was the custom of the farmer to watch her, and take the sheep in charge from her; but this required a good deal of caution; for as soon as she perceived that she was seen, whether the sheep were put into the fold or not, she conceived her charge at an end, and no flattery could induce her to stay and assist in folding them. There was a display of accuracy and attention in this, that I cannot say I have ever seen equalled.

The late Mr Steel, flesher in Peebles, had a bitch that was fully equal to the one mentioned above, and that in the very same qualification too. Her feats in taking home sheep from the neighbouring farms into the flesh-market at Peebles by herself, form innumerable anecdotes in that vicinity, all similar to one another. But there is one instance related of her, that combines so much sagacity with natural affection, that I do not think the history of the animal creation furnishes such another.

Mr Steel had such an implicit dependence on the attention of this animal to his orders, that whenever he put a lot of sheep before her, he took a pride in leaving it to herself, and either remained to take a glass with the farmer of whom he had made the purchase, or took another road, to look after bargains or other business. But one time he chanced to commit a drove to her charge at a place called Willenslee, without attending to her condition, as he ought to have done. This farm is five miles from Peebles, over wild hills, and there is no regularly defined path to it. Whether Mr Steel remained behind, or took another road, I know not; but on coming home late in the evening, he was astonished at hearing that his faithful animal had never made her appearance with the drove. He and his son, or servant, instantly prepared to set out by different paths in search of her; but on their going out to the street, there was she coming with the drove, no one missing; and, marvellous to relate, she was carrying a young pup in her mouth! She had been taken in travail on the hills; and how the poor beast had contrived to manage her drove in her state of suffering, is beyond human calculation; for her road lay through sheep the whole way. Her master's heart smote him when he saw what she had suffered and effected; but she was nothing daunted; and having deposited her young one in a place of safety, she again set out full speed to the hills, and brought another, and another, till she brought her whole litter, one by one; but the last one was dead. I give this as I have heard it related by the country people; for though I knew Mr Walter Steel well enough, I cannot say I ever heard it from his own mouth. I never entertained any doubt, however, of the truth of the relation, and certainly it is worthy of being preserved, for the credit of that most docile and affectionate of all animals—the shepherd's dog.

The stories related of the dogs of sheep-stealers are fairly beyond all credibility. I cannot attach credit to those, without believing the animals to have been devils incarnate, come to the earth for the destruction of both the souls and bodies of men. I cannot mention names, for the sake of families that still remain in the country; but there have been sundry men executed, who belonged to this quarter of the realm, for that heinous crime, in my own time; and others have absconded, just in time to save their necks. There was not one of these to whom

I allude who did not acknowledge his dog to be the greatest offender. One young man, in particular, who was, I believe, overtaken by justice for his first offence, stated, that after he had folded the sheep by moon-light, and selected his number from the flock of a former master, he took them out, and set away with them towards Edinburgh. But before he had got them quite off the farm, his conscience smote him, as he said, (but more likely a dread of that which soon followed,) and he quitted the sheep, letting them go again to the hill. He called his dog off them ; and mounting his poney, rode away. At that time he said his dog was capering and playing around him, as if glad of having got free of a troublesome business ; and he regarded him no more, till, after having rode about three miles, he thought again and again that he heard something coming up behind him. Halting, at length, to ascertain what it was, in a few minutes his dog came up with the stolen drove, driving them at a furious rate to keep pace with his master. The sheep were all smoking, and hanging out their tongues, and their driver was fully as warm as they. The young man was now exceedingly troubled ; for the sheep having been brought so far from home, he dreaded there would be a pursuit, and he could not get them home again before day. Resolving, at all events, to keep his hands clear of them, he corrected his dog in great wrath, left the sheep once more, and taking his dog with him, rode off a second time. He had not ridden above a mile, till he perceived that his dog had again given him the slip ; and suspecting for what purpose, he was terribly alarmed as well as chagrined ; for the daylight approached, and he durst not make a noise calling on his dog, for fear of alarming the neighbourhood, in a place where both he and his dog were known. He resolved therefore to abandon the animal to himself, and take a road across the country which he was sure his dog did not know, and could not follow. He took that road ; but being on horseback, he could not get across the enclosed fields. He at length came to a gate, which he closed behind him, and went about half a mile farther, by a zigzag course, to a farm-house where both his sister and sweetheart lived; and at that place he remained until after breakfast time. The people of this house were all examined on the trial, and no one had either seen sheep, or heard them mentioned, save one man, who came up to the young man as he was standing at the stable-door, and told him that his dog had the sheep safe enough down at the Crooked Yett, and he needed not hurry himself. He answered, that the sheep were not his—they were young Mr Thomson's, who had left them to his charge; and he was in search of a man to drive them, which made him come off his road.

After this discovery, it was impossible for the poor fellow to get quit of them; so he went down and took possession of the stolen property once more, carried them on, and disposed of them; and, finally, the transaction cost him his life. The dog, for the last four or five miles that he had brought the sheep, could have no other guide to the road his master had gone, but the smell of his poney's feet.

It is also well known that there was a notorious sheep-stealer in the county of Mid-Lothian, who, had it not been for the skins and sheep's-heads, would never have been condemned, as he could, with the greatest ease, have proved an *alibi* every time on which there were suspicions cherished against him. He always went by one road, calling on his acquaintances, and taking care to appear to every body by whom he was known; while his dog went by another with the stolen sheep; and then on the two felons meeting again, they had nothing more ado than turn the sheep into an associate's enclosure, in whose house the dog was well fed and entertained, and would have soon taken all the fat sheep on the Lothian Edges to that house. This was likewise a female, a jet-black one, with a deep coat of soft hair, but smooth-headed, and very strong and handsome in her make. On the disappearance of her master, she lay about the hills and the places he had frequented; but never attempted to steal a drove by herself, nor yet any thing for her own hand.  She was kept a while by a relation of her master's ; but never acting heartily in his service, soon came to an untimely end.  Of this there is little doubt, although some spread the report that one evening, after uttering two or three loud howls, she had vanished !

END OF THE SHEPHERD'S CALENDAR.

# EMIGRATION.

I know of nothing in the world so distressing as the last sight of a fine industrious independent peasantry taking the last look of their native country, never to behold it more. I have witnessed several of these scenes now, and I wish I may never witness another; for each of them has made tears burst every now and then into my eyes for days and nights, and all the while in that mood of mind that I could think about nothing else. I saw the children all in high spirits, playing together and amusing themselves with trifles, and I wondered if those dear innocents, in after life, would remember any thing at all of the land of their nativity. They felt no regret, for they knew that they had no home but where their parents were, no staff or stay but on them. They were beside them, and attending to all their little wants, and they were happy. How different the looks of the parents! They looked backward toward their native mountains and glades with the most rueful expression of countenance. These looks never can be cancelled from my heart; and I noted always, that the older the men were, their looks were the more regretful and desolate. They thought, without doubt, of the tombs of their parents and friends whose heads they had lain in an honoured grave, and that, after a few years of the toil and weariness collateral with old age, they were going to lay down their bones in a new world, a far distant clime, never to mix their ashes with those that were dearest to them. Alas! the days are gone that I have seen! It is long since emigration from the Highlands commenced; for, when clanship was abolished, as far as government edicts could abolish it, the poor

Highlanders were obliged to emigrate.  But never till
now did the brave and intelligent Borderers rush from their
native country, all with symptoms of reckless despair.  It
is most deplorable.  The whole of our most valuable
peasantry and operative manufacturers are leaving us.
All who have made a little money to freight them over
the Atlantic, and procure them a settlement in America,
Van Dieman's Land, or New South Wales, are hurrying
from us as from a place infected with the plague.  Every
day the desire to emigrate increases, both in amount and
intensity : in some parts of the country the movement
is taking place to an immense extent.  In the industrious
village of Galashiels, fifty-two are already booked for
transportation.  In the town of Hawick, and its subordinate villages, are double that number.  My own brothers, sisters, nephews, and nieces, are all going away ;
and if I were not the very individual that I am, I should
be the first to depart.  But my name is now so much
identified with Scotland and Ettrick Forest, that though I
must die as I have lived, I cannot leave them.

But the little affecting story I set out with the purpose
of telling is not begun yet.  I went the other year to
see some particular friends on board the gallant ship,
Helen Douglas, for the British settlements of America.
Among the rest was Adam Haliday, a small farmer, who
had lost his farm, and whom I had known intimately in
my young days.  He had a wife, and, I think, nine sons
and daughters ; but his funds being short, he was obliged
to leave his two oldest sons behind, until they themselves
could procure the means of following him.  An old pedler, whom I think they named Simon Ainslie, was there
distributing little religious tracts among the emigrants
gratis, and perhaps trying to sell some of his cheap wares.
The captain and he and Mr Nicholson, the owner of the
vessel, myself, and some others, were standing around the
father and sons, when the following interesting dialogue
took place :—

" Now, Aidie, my man, ye're to behave yoursell, and
no be like a woman and greet.  I canna bide to see the

tears comin' papplin' ower thae manly young cheeks; for though you an' Jamie wad hae been my riches, my strength, an' shield in America, in helpin' me to clear my farm, it is out o' my power to take ye wi' me just now. Therefore, be good lads, an' mind the thing that's good. Read your Bibles, tell aye the truth, an' be obedient to your masters; an' the next year, or the next again, you will be able to join your mother an' the bairns an' me, an' we'll a' work thegither to ane anither's hands."

"I dinna want to gang, father," said Adam, "until I can bring something wi' me to help you. I ken weel how ye are circumstanced, an' how ye hae been screwed at hame. But if there's siller to be made in Scotland in an honest way, Jamie an' me will join you in a year or twa wi' something that will do ye good."

By this time poor little James's heart was like to burst with crying. He was a fine boy, about fourteen. His father went to comfort him, but he made matters only the worse. "Hout, Jamie, dinna greet that gate, man, for a thing that canna be helpit," said he. "Ye ken how weel I wad hae likit to hae had ye wi' me, for the leavin' ye is takin' the pith out o' my arm. But it's out o' my power to take ye just now; for, as it is, afore I win to the settlement, I'll no hae a siller sixpence. But ye're young an' healthy an' stout, an' gin ye be a good lad, wi' the blessing o' God, ye'll soon be able to join your auld father an' mother, an' help them."

"But aince friends are partit, an' the half o' the globe atween them, there's but a sma' chance that they ever meet again," said poor James, with the most disconsolate look. "I wad hae likit to hae gane wi' ye, an' helpit ye, an' wrought wi' ye, an' leev'd an' dee'd wi' ye. It's an awfu' thing to be left in a country where ane has nae hame to gang to, whatever befa' him."

The old man burst into tears. He saw the prospect of helpless desolation, that preyed on his boy's heart, in the event of his being laid on a bed of sickness; but he had no resource. The boat came to the quay, in which they were about to step; but word came with her that the vessel could not sail before high tide to-morrow; so the family got one other night to spend together, at which they seemed excessively happy, though lodged in a hay-loft.

Having resolved to sail with the Helen Douglas as far the Point of Cumberland, I attended the next day at the quay, where a great number of people were assembled to take farewell of their friends. There were four boats lying ready to take the emigrants on board. The two brothers embraced their parents and sisters, and were just parting rather decently, when the captain, stepping out of a handsome boat, said to Haliday, " Sir, your two sons are entered as passengers with me, so you need not be in such a hurry in taking farewell of them."

" Entered as passengers!" said Haliday; " why, the poor fellows hae na left themsels a boddle in helpin' to fit out their mother and me; how can they enter themsels as passengers?"

" They are entered, however," said the captain, " and both their fare and board paid to Montreal, from which place you can easily reach your destination; but if any more is required, I am authorized to advance that like-wise."

" An' wha is the generous friend that has done this?" cried Haliday, in raptures, the tears streaming from his eyes. " He has strengthened my arms, and encouraged my heart, and rendered me an independent man—at aince, tell me wha is the kind good man?—was it Mr Hogg?"

The captain shook his head. " I am debarred from telling you, Mr Haliday," said he; " let it suffice that the young men are franked to Montreal. Here are both their tickets, and there are their names registered as *paid*."

" I winna set my fit aff the coast o' Scotland, sir," said Haliday, " until I ken wha has done this generous deed. If he should never be paid mair, he can be nae the waur o' an auld man's prayers night and morning; no,

I winna set a fit into the boat—I winna leave the shore
o' auld Scotland till I ken wha my benefactor is. Can
I gang awa without kenning wha the friend is that has
rendered me the greatest service ever conferred on me
sin' I was born? Na, na! I canna, captain; sae ye may
just as weel tell me at aince."

"Then, since I must tell you, I must," said the captain; "it was no other than that old packman with the
ragged coat."

"God bless him! God bless him!" fell, I think, from
every tongue that was present. The mother of the
young men was first at the old pedler, and clapping her
hands about his neck, she kissed him again and again,
even maugre some resistance. Old Haliday ran and
took the pedler by both hands, and in an ecstasy, mixed
with tears and convulsive laughter, said, "Now, honest
man, tell me your direction, for the first money that I
can either win, or beg, or borrow, shall be sent to reim-
burse you for this. There was never sic a benefit conferred on a poor father an' mother sin' the world stood
up. An' ye sall hae your money, good auld Christian—
ye sall hae your siller."

" Ay, that he sall!" exclaimed both of the young lads.

" Na, na, Aidie Haliday, say nay mair about the payment just now," said the pedler; "d'ye ken, man, I had
sundry verra strong motives for this: in the first place,
I saw that you *could not* do without the lads; and mair
than that, I am coming up amang my countrymen about
New Dumfries an' Loch Eiry, to vend my wares for a
year or twa, an' I wantit to hae ae-house at ony rate where
I wad be sure o' a night's quarters. I'll ca' for my siller,
Aidie, an' I'm sure to get it, or value for't; an' if I dinna
ca' for't, be sure never to send it. It wad be lost by
the way, for there's never ony siller reaches this frae
America."

I never envied any man's feelings more than I did the
old pedler's that day, when all the grateful family were
hanging around him, and every eye turned on him with
admiration.

IV. z

# TWO HIGHLANDERS.

On the banks of the Albany River, which falls into Hudson's Bay, there is, amongst others, a small colony settled, which is mostly made up of emigrants from the Highlands of Scotland. Though the soil of the valleys contiguous to the river is exceedingly rich and fertile, yet the winter being so long and severe, these people do not labour too incessantly in agriculture, but depend for the most part upon their skill in hunting and fishing for their subsistence—there being commonly abundance of both game and fish.

Two young Kinsmen, both Macdonalds, went out one day into these boundless woods to hunt, each of them armed with a well-charged gun in his hand, and a skene-dhu, or Highland dirk by his side. They shaped their course towards a small stream, which descends from the mountains to the N. W. of the river; on the banks of which they knew there were still a few wild swine remaining; and of all other creatures they wished most to meet with one of them, little doubting but that they would overcome even a pair of them, if chance would direct them to their lurking-places, though they were reported to be so remarkable both for their strength and ferocity. They were not at all successful, having neglected the common game in searching for these animals; and a little before sunset they returned homeward, without having shot any thing save one wild turkey. But when they least expected it, to their infinite joy they discovered a deep pit or cavern, which contained a large litter of fine half-grown pigs, and none of the old ones with them. This was a prize indeed; so, without losing a moment, Donald said to the other, ' Mack, you pe te littlest man—creep you in and durk te little sows, and I'll pe keeping vatch at te door." Mack complied without hesitation, gave his gun to Donald, unsheathed his skene-dhu, and crept into the cave head foremost; but after he was all out of sight, save the brogues, he stopped short, and called back, ' But Lord, Tonald, pe shoor to keep out te ould ones.'—Ton't vou pe fearing tat, man,' said Donald.

The cave was deep, but there was abundance of room in the further end, where Mack, with his sharp skene-dhu, now commenced the work of death. He was scarcely well begun, when Donald perceiving a monstrous wild boar advancing upon him, roaring, and grinding his tusks, while the fire of rage gleamed from his eyes. Donald said not a word for fear of alarming his friend; besides, the savage was so hard upon him ere he was aware, he scarcely had time for any thing: so setting himself firm, and cocking his gun, he took his aim; but, that the shot might prove the more certain death, he suffered the boar to come within a few paces of him before he ventured to fire; he at last drew the fatal trigger, expecting to blow out his eyes, brains and all. Merciful heaven!—the gun missed fire, or flashed in the pan, I am not sure which. There was no time to lose—Donald dashed the piece in the animal's face, turned his back, and fled with precipitation. The boar pursued him only for a short space, for having heard the cries of his suffering young ones as he passed the mouth of the den, he hasted back to their rescue. Most men would have given all up for lost. It was not so with Donald—Mack's life was at stake. As soon as he observed the monster return from pursuing him, Donald faced about, and pursued him in his turn; but having, before this, from the horror of being all torn to pieces, run rather too far without looking back, the boar had by that oversight got considerably a-head of him— Donald strained every nerve—uttered some piercing cries—and even for all his haste did not forget to implore assistance from heaven. His prayer was short, but pithy —' O Lord! puir Mack! puir Mack!' said Donald, in a loud voice, while the tears gushed from his eyes. In spite of all his efforts, the enraged animal reached the mouth of the den before him, and entered! It was, however, too narrow for him to walk in on all-four; he was obliged to drag himself in as Mack had done before, and, of course, his hind feet lost their hold of the ground, At this important crisis Donald overtook him—laid hold of his large long tail—wrapped it round both his hands—set his feet to the bank, and held back in the utmost desperation

Mack, who was all unconscious of what was going on above ground, wondered what way he came to be involved in utter darkness in a moment, He waited a little while, thinking that Donald was only playing a trick upon him, but the most profound obscurity still continuing, he at length bawled out, 'Tonald, man, Tonald—phat is it that'll ay pe stoping te light?' Donald was too much engaged, and too breathless, to think of making any reply to Mack's impertinent question, till the latter having waited in vain a considerable time for an answer, repeated it in a louder cry. Donald's famous laconic answer, which perhaps never was, nor ever will be equalled, has often been heard of—'Tonald, man, Tonald—I say phat is it that'll aye pe stoping te light?' bellowed Mack—'Should te tail preak, you'll fin' tat,' said Donald.

Donald continued the struggle, and soon began to entertain hopes of ultimate success. When the boar pulled to get in, Donald held back; and when he struggled to get back again, Donald set his shoulder to his large buttocks, and pushed him in; and in this position he kept him, until he got an opportunity of giving him some deadly stabs with his skene-dhu behind the short rib, which soon terminated his existence.

Our two young friends by this adventure realized a valuable prize, and secured so much excellent food, that it took them several days to get it conveyed home. During the long winter nights, while the family were regaling themselves on the hams of the great wild boar, often was the above tale related, and as often applauded and laughed at.

# WATCHMAKER.

DAVID DRYBURGH was the head watchmaker in the old burgh of Caverton, and a very good watchmaker he was; at least I never knew one who could better make a charge, and draw out a neat and specious bill. Every watch that went to him to clean required a new mainspring at least, and often new jewels for pivots to the fly-wheel, or a new chain or hairspring; or, if the owner had a very simple look, his watch needed all these together.

But experience teacheth fools wisdom. David, for all his good workmanship and handsome charges, never had one sixpence to polish another; so, after due consideration, he said to himself one day, " This will never do! I must have a wife! There is no respectability to be obtained in this world without a wife! No riches, no comfort, without a wife! I'll have one, if there is one to be had in this town for love or money. Money! God bless the mark! I'll not have a lady. No, no; I'll not have a lady; I never could find out what these creatures called ladies were made for. It could not be for mothers of families, for not one of them can nurse a child; and it is a queer thing if our Maker made so many handsome elegant creatures just to strum upon a piano, eat fine meat, and wear braw claes. No, no! Before I married a lady, I would rather marry a tinkler. I'll marry Peg Ketchen. She can put a hand to every thing; and if any body can lay by something for a sore foot or a rainy day, I think Peg's that woman. I'll ask Peg. If she refuse, I have no less than I have."

David went that very evening, and opened his mind to Peg Ketchen. " Peg, I have taken it into my head to have a wife to keep me decent, sober, and respectable, and I'm going to make you the first offer."

"Thank you, sir; I'm singularly obliged to you. Only you may save yourself the trouble of making such an offer to me; for of all characters, a confirmed drunkard is the one that I dread most. You are a Sabbath-breaker; I know that. You are a profane swearer; I know that also. From these I think I could wean you; but a habitual drunkard it is out of the power of woman or man to reclaim. Oh, I would not be buckled to such a man for the world! As lang as Will Dunlop, or Jamie Inglis, or John Cheap, needed a dram, your last penny would go for it."

"It is ower true you say, Peg, my bonny woman. But ye ken I can work weel, an' charge fully as weel; an' gin ye were to take the management o' the *proceeds*, as the writers ca't, I think things wad do better. Therefore, take a walk into the country with me on Sunday."

"Did ever ony leevin' hear the like o' that! preserve us a' to do weel and right; the man's a heathen, an', I declare, just rinnin' to the deil wi' his een open. Wad ye hae me to profane the Sabbath-day, gaun rakin' athwart the country wi' a chap like you? Heigh-wow! I wad be come to a low mete then! What wad the auld wives be sayin' to the lads an I were to do that? I can tell you what they wad be sayin', 'What think ye o' your bonny Peg Ketchen now? When she should hae been at the kirk, like a decent lass, serving her Maker, she has been awa' flirtin' the hale Sunday wi' a drunken profligate, wha bilkit his auld uncle, an' sang himsel' hame frae London wi' a tied-up leg, like a broken sailor.' Ha, ha, Davie! I ken ye, lad."

"Now, your are rather too hard on me, Peg; I am proffering you the greatest honour I have in my power to bestow."

"The greatest *dis*honour, you mean."

"You know I am as good a tradesman as is in Scotland."

"The mair's the pity! And wha's the best drinker i'

Scotland ? For it will lie atween you an' John Henderson
and Will Dunlop ; for, as for Tam Stalker, he's no aince
to be compared wi' you.

"But, Peg, my woman—my dear bonny woman—hear
me speak, will you !"

"No, no, David, I winna hear you speak ; sae dinna
try to lead me into a scrape, for I tell you again, as I
tauld ye already, that of a' characters i' the warld a confirmed drunkard is the most dangerous that a virtuous
young woman can be connectit wi'. Depend on it, the
heat o' your throat will soon burn the claes aff your back ;
an' how soon wad it burn them aff mine too !—for ye
ken, a woman's claes are muckle easier brunt than a man's.
Sae, gang yours ways to the changehouse, an' tak a
dram wi' Will Dunlop ; ye'll be a great deal the better
o't. An', hear ye, dinna come ony mair to deave me wi'
your love, and your offers o' marriage ; for, there's my
hand, I sall never court or marry wi' you. I hae mair
respect for mysel' than that comes to."

Was not Peg a sensible girl ? I think she was. I
still think she must naturally have been a shrewd girl ;
but no living can calculate what a woman will do when
a man comes in question. There is a feeling of dependence and subordination about their guileless hearts, in
reference to the other sex, that can be wound up to any
thing, either evil or good. Peg was obliged to marry
David, after all her virtuous resolutions. The very night
of the wedding he got drunk ; and poor Peg, seeing what
she had brought herself to, looked in his face with the
most pitiful expression, while his drunken cronies made
game of him, and were endless in their jests on "Bene-
dict the married man." Peg saw the scrape she had
brought herself into, but retreat was impracticable : so
she resolved to submit to her fate with patience and resignation, and to make the most of a bad bargain that she
could.

And a bad bargain she has had of it, poor woman,
apparently having lost all heart several years ago, and
submitted, along with three children, to pine out life in

want and wretchedness. The wedding boose increased
David's thirst so materially, that it did not subside, night
or day, for nearly a fortnight, until a kind remonstrance,
mixed with many tears, from his young wife, made him
resolve to turn over a new leaf. So away David went
into the country, and cleaned all the people's clocks early
in the morning before the owners rose, for fear of making
confusion or disturbance in the house afterwards:—
David was very attentive and obliging that way. Of
course the clocks got nothing more than a little oil on
the principal wheels; but the charge was always fair and
reasonable, seldom exceeding five shillings. Then all
the bells in each house required new cranks and new
wires. They needed neither, but only a little oil and
scrubbing up; but these were a source of considerable
emolument. Then he gathered in all the watches of the
country which were not going well, cleaned them all, and
put in a great many nominal mainsprings, and really
would have made a great deal of money, had it not been
for the petty changehouses, not one of which he could
go by; and when he met with a drouthy crony like Captain Palmer, neither of them would rise while they had a
sixpence between them.

But the parish minister of the old burgh of Caverton,
though accounted a very parsimonious gentleman himself,
had a sincere regard for the welfare of his flock, temporal
as well as spiritual; and in his annual visit he charged
every one of them, that when David did any work for
them, they were to pay the wife, and not him. The
greater part of them acquiesced; but Wattie Henderson
refused, and said, " O, poor soul, ye dinna ken what he
has to thole! Ye ken about his drinkin'; but ye ken
little thing about his drouth."

The shifts that David was now put to for whisky were
often very degrading, but still rather amusing. One day
he and Dunlop went in to Mr Mercer's inn, David saying,
" I must try to get credit for a Hawick gill or two here
to-day, else we'll both perish." They went in, and called
for the whisky. Mercer asked David if he had the money

to pay for it? David confessed that he had not, but said Mr Elliot of Dodhope was owing him three-and-sixpence, and as he was in town that day, he would give him an order on him, if he was afraid of the money coming through his hands. Mr Mercer said he would never desire a better creditor than Gideon, and gave them their three gills of whisky; but on going and presenting his order to Mr Elliot, he found that he had never, in his life, been owing David any thing which he had not paid before he left the house.

Another time he met the clergyman, and said to him, "You have been a great deal of money out of my pouch, sir, wi' your grand moral advices. I think you owe me one-and-sixpence about yon bells—would it be convenient to pay me to-day? I have very much need of it."

"And what are you going to do with it, David? I wish I were owing you ten times the sum; I should know whom to pay it to, for you have a wife and family that are worth looking after; but if you tell me the sterling truth of your necessity, perhaps I may pay you."

"Why, the truth is, sir—look yonder: yonder is Will Dunlop and Jamie Inglis, standing wi' their backs against the wa', very drouthy like. I wad like to gie them something, poor chiels, to drink."

"Now, David, as I am convinced you have told me the sterling truth, and as there is no virtue I value higher, there is your eighteen-pence, although I shall tax myself with the payment of it a second time to Peg."

"God bless you, sir!—God bless you! and may you never want a glass of whisky when you are longing as much for it as I am."

Another day he came up with Will Dunlop, and said, "O man, what hae ye on ye? for I'm just spitting sixpences."

"I have just eighteen-pence," said Dunlop, "which I got from my wife to buy a shoulder of mutton for our dinner; and as it is of her own winning, I dare not part with it, for then, you know, the family would want their dinner."

"It is a hard case any way," said David; "but I think the hardest side of it is, for two men, dying of thirst, to lose that eighteen-pence. Give it to me, and I'll try to make a shift."

Dunlop gave it him, and David went away to Wattie Henderson, an honest, good-natured, simple man, and said that his wife had sent him "for a shoulder of mutton for their dinner, and she has limited me to a sum, you see (showing him the money). If you have a shoulder that suits the price, I must have it."

"We can easily manage that, David," said he; "for see, here is a good cleaver; I can either add or diminish." He cut off a shoulder. "It is too heavy for the money, David; it comes to two-and-fourpence."

"I wad like to hae the shoulder keepit hale, sir, as I suspect my sister is to dine with us to day. Will you just allow me to carry the mutton over to the foot of the wynd, and see if Peg be pleased to advance the rest of the price?"

"Certainly," said Mr Henderson; "I can trust your wife with any thing."

David set straight off with the shoulder of mutton to Mrs Dunlop, who declared that she had never got such a good bargain in the flesh-market before; and the two friends enjoyed their three gills of whisky exceedingly. Mr Henderson, wondering that neither the mutton nor the money was returned, sent over a servant to inquire about the matter. Poor Peg had neither ordered nor received the shoulder of mutton; and all that she and her three children had to dine upon, was six potatoes.

"Poor fellow," said Wattie, "if I had kend he had been sae dry, I wad hae wat his whistle to him without ony cheatery."

At length there came one very warm September, and the thirst that some men suffered was not to be borne. David felt that in a short time his body would actually break into chinks with sheer drought, and that some shift was positively required to keep body and soul together. Luckily, at that very time a Colonel Maxwell came to the house of John Fairgrieve, an honest, decent man, who had made a good deal of money by care and parsimony, and lived within two or three miles of Caverton. The colonel came with his dog, his double-barrelled gun, and livery servant, and bargained with John, at a prodigiously high board, for himself and servant. He said, as his liberty of shooting lay all around there, he did not care how much board he paid for a few weeks, only John was to be sure to get him the best in the country, both to eat and drink. He did so—laying in wine and spirits, beef and mutton; and the colonel and his servant lived at heck and manger, the one boozing away in the room, and the other in the kitchen, in both of which every one who entered was treated liberally. In the forenoons the colonel thundered among the partridges; but he never killed any, as he was generally drunk from morning to night, and from night to morning.

At length, John's daughter, Joan, a comely and sensible girl, began rather to smell a rat; and she says to her father one day, " Father, dinna ye think this grand cornel o' your's is hardly sickan a polished gentlemanly man as ane wad expect o' ane o' his rank?"

" I dinna ken, Joan; the man's weel eneuch if he wadna swear sae whiles, whilk I like unco ill. But there's ae thing that's ayont my comprehension : I wish he may be cannie; for dinna ye hear that our cock begins to craw every night about midnight, an' our hens to cackle as gin they war a' layin' eggs thegither, an' feint an egg's amang them a'?"

Joan could not repress a laugh; so she turned her back, and took a hearty one, saying, when she recovered her breath, " I think baith master an' man are very uncivil and worthless chaps."

" If either the ane or the ither hae been unceevil to you, my woman, just tell me sae. Say but the word, an' I'll——"

" Na, na, father ; dinna get intil a passion for naething, I'll take care o' mysell, if ye can but take care o' yoursell. It is that I'm put till't about. Dinna ye think that for a' your outlay ye're unco lang o' fingerin' ony o' their siller?"

John gave a hitch up with his shoulder, as if something had been biting it, rubbed his elbow, and then said, "The siller will answer us as weel when it comes a' in a slump thegither; for then, ye ken, we can pop it into the bank; whereas, if it were coming in every day, or even every week, we might be mootering it away, spending it on this thing an' the ither thing."

"Yes, father; but, consider, if ye shoudna get it ava. Is nae the cornel's chaise an' horses standin' ower at the Blue Bell?"

"Ay, that they are, an' at ten shillings a-day, too. Gin the cornel warna a very rich man, could he afford to pay that sae lang, think ye?"

"Weel, father, take ye my advice. Gang away ower to Mr Mather, o' the Bell, an' just see what the carriage an' horses are like; for I wadna wonder if ye had to arreest them yet for your expenses. Mr Mather's a gayan auld-farrant chap, and, it is said, kens every man's character the first time he hears him speak. He'll tell you at aince what kind o' man your grand cornel is. And by a' means, father, tak a good look o' the carriage an' the horses, that ye may ken them again, like."

John knew that his daughter Joan was a shrewd sensible lassie; so, without more expostulation, he put on his Sunday clothes, went away to the old burgh of Caverton, and called on Mr Mather. No! there were no carriage nor horses there belonging to a Colonel Maxwell, nor ever had been. This was rather astounding news to John; but what astounded him more was a twinkling blink from the wick of Mr Mather's wicked black eye, and an ominous shake of his head. "Pray tell me this, John," said Mr Mather: "does this grand colonel of yours ever crow like a cock, or cackle like a laying hen?"

John's jaws fell down. "It's verra extrordner how ye should hae chanced to speer that question at me, sir," said he; "for the truth is, that, sin' ever that man came to our house, our cock has begun a crawin' at midnight, an' a' our hens a-cackling, as the hale o' them had been layin' eggs, an' yet no an egg amang them a'."

"Ah, John, ye may drink to your expenses and board wages, then ; for I heard of a certain gentleman being amissing out of this town for a while past ; and I likewise heard that he had borrowed a hunting-jacket, a dog, and a gun, from John Henderson."

John went away home in very great wrath, resolved, I believe, to throttle the colonel and his servant both ; but they had been watching his motions that day, and never returned to his house more, neither to crow like cocks, cackle like hens, drink whisky, or pay for their board and lodging.

Tom Brown was very angry at David about this, and reproved him severely for taking in an honest industrious old man. "But, dear man, what could a body do ?" said David. "A man canna dee for thirst if there's ony thing to be had to drink either for love or money."

"But you should have wrought for your drink yoursell, David."

"Wrought for my drink ? An' what at, pray ? A the house bells were gaun janglin' on, like broken pots, in their usual way ; there wasna even the mainspring of a watch wanting. And as for the clocks, they just went on, tick-for-tick, tick-for-tick with the most tedious and provoking monotony. I couldna think of a man, in the whole country, who didna ken my face, but John ; an' I kend he was as able to keep me a wee while as ony other body. An' what's the great matter ? I'll clean his watch an' his clock to him as lang as he lives, an' never charge him ony thing, gin it be na a new mainspring whiles, an' we'll maybe come nearly equal again."

The last time I saw Peg Ketchen—what a change ! From one of the sprightliest girls in the whole country, she is grown one of the most tawdry, miserable-looking objects. There is a hopeless dejection in her looks which I never saw equalled ; and I am afraid, that, sometimes when she has it in her power, she may take a glass herself, and even get a basting for, no man can calculate what a drunken man will do.

Now, though I have mixed two characters together in these genuine and true sketches, my reason for thus publishing them is to warn and charge every virtuous maiden, whatever she does, never to wed with a habitual drunkard. A virtuous woman may reclaim a husband from almost every vice but that; but that will grow upon him to his dying day; and if she outlive him, he will leave her a penniless and helpless widow. It is well known the veneration I have for the fair sex, and I leave them this charge as a legacy, lest I should not be able to address them again.

---

A STORY

# OF THE FORTY-SIX.

One day in July 1746, a tall raw-boned Highlander came into the house of Inch-Croy, the property of Stewart Shaw, Esq., in which there was apparently no person at the time but Mrs Shaw and her three daughters, for the laird was in hiding, having joined the Mackintoshes, and lost two sons at Culloden. This Highlander told the lady of the house that his name was Serjeant Campbell, and that he had been commissioned to search the house for her husband, as well as for Cluny, Loch-Garry, and other proscribed rebels. Mrs Shaw said that she would rather the rudest of Cumberland's English officers had entered her house to search for the prince's friends, than one of the Argyle Campbells—those unnatural ruffians, who had risen against their lawful prince, to cut their brethren's throats.

The Highlander, without being in the least ruffled, requested her to be patient, and added, that at all events the ladies were safer from insult in a countryman's hands than in the hands of an English soldier. The lady denied it, and in the haughtiest manner flung him the keys, saying that she hoped some of hers would yet see the day when the rest of the clans would get their feet on the necks of the Campbells. He lifted the keys, and instantly commenced a regular and strict scrutiny; and just as he was in the act of turning out the whole contents of a wardrobe, the lady in the mean while saying the most cutting things to him that she could invent, he stood straight up, looked her steadily in the face, and pointed to a bed, shaking his hand at the same time. Simple as that motion was, it struck the lady dumb. She grew as pale as death in a moment. At that moment an English officer and five dragoons entered the house.

" O, sir," said Mrs Shaw, " here is a ruffian of a serjeant, who has been sent to search the house, and who, out of mere wantonness and despite, is breaking every thing, and turning the whole house topsy-turvy."

" Desist, you vagabond," said the cornet, " and go about your business. If any of the proscribed rebels are in the house, I'll be accountable for them."

" Nay, nay," said the Highlander, " I am first in commission, and I'll hold my privilege. The right of search is mine, and whoever are found in the house, I claim the reward. And moreover, in accordance with the orders issued at head-quarters, I order you hence."

" Show me your commission then, you Scotch dog; your search-warrant, if you so please?"

" Show me your authority for demanding it first."

" My designation is Cornet Letham of Cobham's dragoons, who is ready to answer every charge against him. Now, pray tell me, sir, under whom you hold your commission?"

" Under a better gentleman than you, or any one who ever commanded you."

" A better gentleman than me, or any who ever commanded me! The first expression is an insult not to be borne. The other is high treason; and on this spot I seize you for a Scotch rebel, and a traitor knave."

With that he seized the tall red-haired loon by the throat, who, grinning, heaved his long arm at him as threatening a blow; but the English officer only smiled contemptuously, knowing that no single man of 'that humiliated country durst lift his hand against him, especially backed as he was by five sturdy dragoons. He was mistaken in this instance, for the Highlander lent him such a blow as felled him in a moment, so that, with a heavy groan, he fell dead on the floor. Five horse-pistols were instantly pointed at the Highlander by the dragoons, but he took shelter behind the press, or wardrobe, and with his cocked pistol in one hand, and drawn broadsword, kept them at bay, for the entrance ben the house was so narrow, that two could not enter at a time, and certain death awaited the first to enter. At length two of them went out to shoot him in at a small window behind, which hampered him terribly, as he could not get far enough forward to guard his entry, without exposing himself to the fire of the two at the window. An expedient of the moment struck him; he held his bonnet by the corner of the wardrobe, as if peeping to take aim, when crack went two of the pistols, his antagonists having made sure of shooting him through the head. Without waiting farther, either to fire or receive theirs, he broke at them with his drawn sword; and the fury with which he came smashing and swearing up the house on them appalled them so horribly, that they all three took to their heels, intending probably to fight him in the open fields. But a heavy dragoon of Cobham's was no match for a kilted clansman six feet high; before they reached the outer door, two of them were cut down, and the third, after a run of about thirty or forty yards. By this time, the two at the west window had betaken them to their horses, and were galloping off. The Highlander, springing on the officer's horse, galloped after them, determined that they should not escape, still waving his bloody sword, and calling on them to stop. But stop they would not; and a better chase never was seen. Peter Grant and Alexander M'Eachen, both in hiding at the time, saw it from Craig-Neart, at a short distance, and described it as unequalled. There went the two dragoons, spurring on for bare life, the one always considerably before the other, and behind all, came the tall Highlander, riding very awkwardly, as might be supposed, and thrashing the hind quarters of his horse with his bloody sword, for lack of spurs and whip. He did not appear to be coming up with them, but nevertheless cherishing hopes that he would, till his horse floundered with him in a bog, and threw him; he then reluctantly gave up the chase, and returned leading his horse by the bridle, having got enough of riding for that day.

The two Highlanders, M'Eachen and Grant, then ran from the rock and saluted him, for this inveterate Highlander was no other than their own brave and admired colonel, John Roy Stewart. They accompanied him back to Inch-Croy, where they found the ladies in the greatest dismay, and the poor dragoons all dead. Mrs Stewart Shaw and her daughters had taken shelter in an outhouse on the breaking out of the quarrel; and that which distressed her most of all was, the signal which the tremendous Highlander made to her; for, beyond that bed, there was a concealed door to a small apartment, in which her husband, and Captain Finlayson, and Loch-Garry, were all concealed at the time, and she perceived that that door was no secret to Serjeant Campbell, as he called himself. When the pursuit commenced, the ladies hastened to apprize the inmates of their little prison of the peril that awaited them, but refused to fly till matters were cleared up, for they said, that one who was cutting down the red coats at such a rate, could scarcely be an enemy to them. We may conceive how delighted they were on finding that this hero was their brave and beloved Colonel Stewart. He knew that they were concealed in that house, and in that apartment; and perceiving, from the height where he kept watch, the party of dragoons come in at the strait of Corry-Bealach, he knew to what place they were bound, and hastened before them, either to divert the search, or assist his friends in repelling the aggressors.

There was now no time to lose.  Mr Shaw, Captain Finlayson, Alexander M'Eachen, and another gentleman, whose name I have lost, mounted as King George's dragoons, effected their escape to Glasgow through a hundred dangers, mostly arising from their own friends.  In particular, the very first night of their flight, in one of the woods of Athol, at the dead of the night, they were surrounded by a party of the Clan-Donnach, and would have been sacrificed, had not Stewart Shaw made an exclamation in Gaelic, which awakened as great an overflow of kindness.  Colonel Roy Stewart and Loch-Garry escaped on foot, and fled towards the wild banks of Loch-Erriched, where they remained in safety till they went abroad with Prince Charles.

It is amazing how well this incident was kept secret, as well as several others that tended to the disgrace of the royalists, owing to the control they exercised over the press of the country; but neither Duke William, nor one of his officers ever knew who the tall red-haired Serjeant Campbell was, who overthrew their six dragoons. The ladies of Inch-Croy did not escape so well, for Cumberland, in requital for a disgrace in which they were nowise influential, sent out another party, who plundered the house and burnt it, taking the ladies into custody, and every thing else that was left on the lands of Inch-Croy and Bally-Beg—an instance of that mean and ungentlemanly revenge for which he was so notorious.

# OF THE MARTYRS.

Red Tam Harkness came into the farm-house of
Garrick, in the parish of the Closeburn, one day, and
began to look about for some place to hide in, when the
goodwife, whose name was Jane Kilpatrick, said to him
in great alarm, "What's the matter, what's the matter,
Tam Harkness?"

"Hide me, or else I'm a dead man : that's the present matter, goodwife," said he. "But yet, when I have
time, if ever I hae mair time, I have heavy news for you.
For Christ's sake, hide me, Jane, for the killers are hard
at hand."

Jane Kilpatrick sprang to her feet, but she was quite
benumbed and powerless. She ran to one press, and
opened it, and then to another; there was not room to
stuff a clog into either of them. She looked into a bed ;
there was no shelter there, and her knees began to plait
under her weight with terror. The voices of the troopers
were by this time heard fast approaching, and Harkness
had no other shift, but in one moment to conceal himself
behind the outer door, which stood open, yet the place
where he stood was quite dark. He heard one of them
say to another, "I fear the scoundrel is not here after all.
Guard the outhouses."

On that three or four of the troopers rushed by him,
and began to search the house and examine the inmates.
Harkness that moment slid out without being observed,
and tried to escape up a narrow glen called Kinrivvah,
immediately behind the house ; but unluckily two
troopers, who had been in another chase, there met
him in the face. When he perceived them he turned
and ran to the eastward ; on which they both fired, which

raised the alarm, and instantly the whole pack were after him. It was afterwards conjectured that one of the shots had wounded him, for, though he, with others, had been nearly surrounded that morning, and twice waylaid, he had quite outrun the soldiers; but now it was observed that some of them began to gain ground on him, and they still continued firing, till at length he fell in a kind of slough east from the farm-house of Locherben, where they came up to him, and ran him through with their bayonets. The spot is called Red Tam's Gutter to this day.

Jane Kilpatrick was one of the first who went to his mangled corpse,—a woful sight, lying in the slough, and sore did she lament the loss of that poor and honest man. But there was more; she came to his corpse by a sort of yearning impatience to learn what was the woful news he had to communicate to her. But, alas, the intelligence was lost, and the man to whose bosom alone it had haply been confided was no more; yet Jane could scarcely prevail on herself to have any fears for her own husband, for she knew him to be in perfectly safe hiding in Glen-Gorar; still Tam's last words hung heavy on her mind. They were both suspected to have been at the harmless rising at Enterkin, for the relief of a favourite minister, which was effected; and that was the extent of their crime. And though it was only suspicion, four men were shot on the hills that morning, without trial or examination, and their bodies forbidden Christian burial.

One of these four was John Weir of Garrick, the husband of Jane Kilpatrick, a man of great worth and honour, and universally respected. He had left his hiding-place in order to carry some intelligence to his friends, and to pray with them, but was entrapped among them and slain. Still there was no intelligence brought to his family, save the single expression that fell from the lips of Thomas Harkness in a moment of distraction. Nevertheless Jane could not rest, but set out all the way to her sister's house in Glen-Gorar, in Crawford-muir, and arrived there at eleven o'clock on a Sabbath evening.

The family being at prayers when she went, and the house dark, she stood still behind the hallan, and all the time was convinced that the voice of the man that prayed was the voice of her husband, John Weir. All the time that fervent prayer lasted the tears of joy ran from her eyes, and her heart beat with gratitude to her Maker as she drank into her soul every sentence of the petitions and thanksgiving. Accordingly, when worship was ended, and the candle lighted, she went forward with a light heart and joyful countenance, her sister embraced her, though manifestly embarrassed and troubled at seeing her there at such a time. From her she flew to embrace her husband, but he stood still like a statue, and did not meet her embrace. She gazed at him—she grew pale, and, sitting down, she covered her face with her apron. This man was one of her husband's brothers, likewise in hiding, whom she had never before seen, but the tones of his voice, and even the devotional expressions that he used, were so like her husband's, that she mistook them for his.

All was now grief and consternation, for John Weir had not been seen or heard of there since Wednesday evening, when he had gone to warn his friends of some impending danger; but they all tried to comfort each other as well as they could, and, in particular, by saying, they were all in the Lord's hand, and it behoved him to do with them as seemed to him good, with many other expressions of piety and submission. But the next morning, when the two sisters were about to part, the one says to the other, "Jane, I cannot help telling you a strange confused dream that I had just afore ye wakened me. Ye ken I pit nae faith in dreams, and I dinna want you to regard it; but it is as good for friends to tell them to ane anither, and then, if ought turn out like it in the course o' providence, it may bring it to baith their minds that their spirits had been conversing with God."

" Na, na, Aggie, I want nane o' your confused dreams. I hae other things to think o', and mony's the time an aft ye hae deaved me wi' them, an' sometimes made me angry."

"I never bade ye believe them, Jeanie, but I likit ay to tell them to you, and this I daresay rase out o' our conversation yestreen. But I thought I was away, ye see, I dinna ken where I was; and I was fear'd an' confused, thinking I had lost my way. And then I came to an auld man, an' he says to me, 'Is it the road to heaven that you are seeking, Aggie?' An' I said, 'Aye,' for I didna like to deny't.

'Then I'll tell you where ye maun gang,' said he, 'ye maun gang up by the head of yon dark, mossy cleuch, an' you will find ane there that will show you the road to heaven;' and I said, 'Aye,' for I didna like to refuse, although it was an uncouth-looking road, and ane that I didna like to gang. But when I gangs to the cleuch head, wha does I see sitting there but your ain goodman, John Weir, and I thought I never saw him look sae weel; and when I gaed close up to him, there I sees another John Weir, lying strippit to the sark, an' a' beddit in blood. He was cauld dead, and his head turned to the ae side; and when I saw siccan a sight, I was terrified, an' held wide off him. But I gangs up to the living John Weir, and says to him, 'Gudeman, how's this?'

'Dinna ye see how it is, sister Aggie?' says he, 'I'm just set to herd this poor man that's lying here.'

'Then I think ye'll no hae a sair post, John,' says I, 'for he disna look as he wad rin far away.' It was a very unreverend speak o' me, sister, but these were the words that I thought I said; an' as it is but a dream, ye ken ye needna heed it.

'Alas, poor Aggie!' says he, 'ye are still in the gall o' bitterness yet. Look o'er your right shoulder, an' you will see what I hae to do.' An' sae I looks o'er my right shoulder, an' there I sees a hail drove o' foxes an' wulcats, an' fumarts an' martins, an' corbey craws, an' a hunder vile beasts, a' stannin round wi' glarin een, eager to be at the corpse o' the dead John Weir; an' then I was terribly astoundit, an' I says to him, 'Gudeman, how's this?'

'I am commissioned to keep these awa', says he. 'Do

ye think these een that are yet to open in the light o'
heaven, and that tongue that has to syllable the praises
of a Redeemer far within yon sky, should be left to become
the prey o' siccan vermin as these !'

' Will it make sae verra muckle difference, John Weir,'
says I, ' whether the carcass is eaten up by these or by
the worms ?'

' Ah, Aggie, Aggie ! worms are worms; but ye little
wat what these are,' says he.  ' But John Weir has war-
red with them a' his life, an' that to some purpose, and
they maunna get the advantage o' him now.'

' But which is the right John Weir ?' says I, ' for here
is ane lying stiff and lappered in his blood, and another
in health and strength and sound mind.'

' I am the right John Weir,' says he.  ' Did you ever
think the goodman o' Garrick could die ?  Na, na,
Aggie ; Clavers can only kill the body, an' that's but the
poorest part of the man.  But where are ye gaun this
wild gate ?'

' I was directed this way on my road to heaven,' says I.

' Ay, an' ye were directed right then,' says he.  ' For
this is the direct path to heaven, and there is no other.'

' That is very extraordinary,' says I.  ' And, pray,
what is the name of this place, that I may direct my sister Jane, your wife, and all my friends, by the same way ?'

' This is Faith's Hope,' says he.''

But behold, at the mention of this place, Jane Kilpatrick of Garrick arose slowly up to her feet and held up
both her hands.  " Hold, hold, sister Aggie," cried she,
" you have told enough.  Was it in the head of Faith's
Hope that you saw this vision of my dead husband."

" Yes ; but at the same time I saw your husband alive."

" Then I fear your dream has a double meaning," said
she.  " For though it appears like a religious allegory,
you do not know that there really is such a place, and
that not very far from our house.  I have often laughed
at your dreams, sister, but this one hurries me from you
to-day with a heavy and a trembling heart."

Jane left Glen-Gorar by the break of day, and took

her way through the wild ranges of Crawford-muir,
straight for the head of Faith's Hope. She had some
bread in her lap, and a little bible that she always carried
with her, and without one to assist or comfort her, she
went in search of her lost husband. Before she reached
the head of that wild glen, the day was far spent, and the
sun wearing down. The valley of the Nith lay spread
far below her, in all its beauty, but around her there
was nothing but darkness, dread, and desolation. The mist
hovered on the hills, and on the skirts of the mist the
ravens sailed about in circles, croaking furiously, which
had a most ominous effect on the heart of poor Jane.
As she advanced farther up, she perceived a fox and an
eagle sitting over against each other, watching something
which yet they seemed terrified to approach ; and right
between them in a little green hollow, surrounded by
black haggs, she found the corpse of her husband in the
same manner as described by her sister. He was stripped
of his coat and vest, which, it was thought, he had thrown
from him when flying from the soldiers, to enable him to
effect his escape. He was shot through the heart with
two bullets, but nothing relating to his death was ever
known, whether he died praying, or was shot as he fled ;
but there was he found lying, bathed in his blood, in the
wilderness, and none of the wild beasts of the forest had
dared to touch his lifeless form.

The bitterness of death was now past with poor Jane.
Her staff and shield was taken from her right hand, and
laid down low in death, by the violence of wicked men.
True, she had still a home to go to, although that home
was robbed and spoiled ; but she found that without *him*
it was no home, and that where his beloved form reposed,
that was the home of her rest. She washed all his
wounds, and the stains of blood from his body, tied her
napkin round his face, covered him with her apron, and
sat down and watched beside him all the live-long night,
praying to the Almighty, and singing hymns and spiritual
songs alternately. The next day she warned her friends
and neighbours, who went with her on the following night,

and buried him privately in the north-west corner of the churchyard of Morton. The following verses are merely some of her own words versified, as she was sitting by his corpse in the wild glen, or rather the thoughts that she described as having passed through her heart.

### JOHN WEIR, A BALLAD.

I canna greet for thee, my John Weir,
   O, I canna greet for thee ;
For the hand o' heaven lies heavy here,
   And this sair weird I maun dree
They harried us first o' cow and ewe,
   With curses and crueltye,
And now they hae shed thy dear life blood,
   An' what's to become o' me ?
I am left a helpless widow here
   O, what's to become o' me ?

I hae born thee seven sons, John Weir,
   And nursed them upon my knee ;
But two are fled to their father's hame,
   Frae the evils awaiting thee ;
Their little green graves lie side by side,
   Like twins in fond ally,
But in beside thy children dear
   Thy dust maun never lie—
Like an outcast o' the earth, John Weir
   In the moorland thou maun lie.

But though thou lie at the back o' the dyke,
   Or in hagg o' the mountain hee,
Wherever thy loved dust remains,
   It is sacred ground to me.
And there will I watch, and there will I pray,
   For tears I now hae nane,
For the injuries done by wicked men
   Have sear'd my simple brain.
Even over thy pale corpse, John Weir,
   I try to weep in vain.

But soon shall our oppressors' sway
   In desolation lie,
Like autumn flowers it shall decay,
   And in its foulness die.
The tyrant's reign, the tyrant's name,
   Whose rule hath never thriven,
The blood of saints hath blotted out
   Both from the earth and heaven—
For this dear blood of thine, John Weir,
   Can never be forgiven.

# ADAM SCOTT.

On a fine summer evening, about the beginning of July, on a year which must have been about the latter end of the reign of Queen Anne, or some years subsequent to that, as Adam Scott, farmer of Kildouglas, was sitting in a small public-house on North Tyne, refreshing himself on brown bread and English beer, and his hungry horse tearing up the grass about the kail-yard dike, he was accosted by a tall ungainly fellow, who entered the hut, and in the broadest Northumberland tongue, inquired if he was bound for Scotland. "What gars ye speer that, an it be your will?" said Scott, with the characteristic caution of his countrymen.

"Because a neighbour and I are agoing that way tonight," said the stranger, "and we knaw neything at all about the rwoad; and mwore than that, we carry soomthing reyther ower valuable to risk the losing of; and as we saw your horse rooging and reyving with the saddle on him, I made bould to call, thinking you might direct us on this coorsed rwoad."

"An' what will you gie me if I guide you safely into Scotland, an' set ye aince mair upon a hee road?" said Scott.

"Woy, man, we'll give thee as mooch bread as thou canst eat, and as mooch beer as thou canst drink—and mwore we cannot have in this moorland," said the man.

"It is a fair offer," said Adam Scott; "but I'll no pit ye to that expense, as I am gaun o'er the fells the night at ony rate; sae, if ye'll wait my bijune, for my horse is plaguit weary, and amaist jaded to death, then we shall ride thegither, and I ken the country weel; but road ye will find nane."

The two men then fastened their horses, and came in and joined Scott; so they called for ale, drank one another's healths at every pull, and seemed quite delighted that they were to travel in company. The tall man, who came in first, was loquacious and outspoken, though one part of his story often did not tally with the other; but his neighbour was sullen and retired, seldom speaking, and as seldom looking one in the face. Scott had at first a confused recollection of having seen him, but in what circumstances he could not remember, and he soon gave up the idea as a false one.

They mounted at length, and there being no path up the North Tyne then nor till very lately, their way lay over ridges and moors, and sometimes by the margin of the wild river. The tall man had been very communicative, and frankly told Scott that they were going into Scotland to try to purchase sheep and cattle, where they expected to get them for next to nothing, and that they had brought gold with them for that purpose. This led on Scott to tell him of his own adventures in that line. He had come to Stagshawbank fair, the only market then for Scots sheep and cattle in the north of England, with a great number of sheep for sale, but finding no demand, he bought up all the sheep from his countrymen for which he could get credit, and drove on to the Yorkshire markets, where he hawked them off in the best manner he could, and was now in fact returning to Scotland literally laden with money to pay his obligations.

After this communication, the tall man always rode before Adam Scott, and the short thick-set sullen fellow behind him, a position which, the moment it was altered, was resumed, and at which Scott began to be a little uneasy. It was still light, though wearing late, for there is little night at that season, when the travellers came to a wild glen called Bell's Burn, a considerable way on the English side of the Border. The tall man was still riding before, and considerably ahead, and as he was mounting the ridge on the north side of Bell's Burn, Adam Scott turned off all at once to the right. The hindermost man drew bridle on seeing this, and asked Scott, " where now ?"

" This way, lads.    This way," was the reply.

The tall man then fell a swearing that that could never be the road to Liddisdale, to which he had promised to accompany them,

" The straight road, honest man—the straight road. Follow me," said Scott.

The tall man then rode in before him and said, " Whoy, man, thou'st either drunk, or gone stooped with sleep, for wilt thou tell me that the road up by Blakehope Shiel, and down the Burnmouth rigg, is nwot the rwoad into Liddisdale ?"

" Ay, man !—ay, man ! How comes this ?" said Scott. " Sae it seems ye are nae sic strangers to the road as ye pretendit ?    Weel, weel, since ye ken that road sae particularly weel, gang your gates, an' take that road. For me, I'm gaun by the Fair-Lone, an' if Willie Jardine's at hame, I'll no gang muckle farther the night."

" The devil of such a rwoad thou shalt go friend, let me tell thee that," said the tall fellow, offering to lay hold of Scott's bridle.    " It is of the greatest consequence to us to get safely over the fell, and since we have put ourselves under thyne care, thou shalt either go with us, or do worse."

" Dare not for your soul to lay your hand on my bridle, sir," said Scott; " for, if you touch either my horse or myself but with one of your fingers, I'll give you a mark to know you by."    The other swore by a terrible oath that he would touch both him and it if he would not act reasonably, and seized the horse rudely by the bridle. Scott threw himself from his horse in a moment, and prepared for action, for his horse was stiff and unwieldy ; and he durst not trust himself on his back between two others, both horses of mettle.    He was armed with a cudgel alone, and as his strength and courage were unequalled at that time, there is little doubt that the tall Englishman would have come down, had not the other, at the moment the bridle was seized, rushed forward and seized his companion by the arm—"Fool! madman!" cried he; "What do you mean? has not the honest man a right to go what way he pleases, and what business have you to stop him? Thou wert a rash idiot all the days of thy life, and thou wilt die one, or be hangit for thy mad pranks. Let go!—for here, I swear, thou shalt neither touch the honest man nor his horse as long as I can hinder thee, and I thinks I should be as good a man as thee. Let us go all by the Fair-Lone, since it is so, and mayhap Mr Jardine will take us all in for the night."

"Whoy, Bill, thou sayest true after all," said the tall man succumbing; "I'm a passionate fool; but a man cannot help his temper. I beg Mr Scwott's pardon, for I was in the wrong. Come, then, let us go by the Fair-Lone with one consent."

Scott was now grieved and ashamed of his jealousy and dread of the men's motives, and that moment, if they had again desired him to have accompanied them over the fell, he would have done it; but away they all rode on the road towards the Fair-Lone, the tall man before as usual, Adam Scott in the middle, and the gruff but friendly fellow behind.

They had not rode above five minutes in this way, Scott being quite reassured of the integrity of his companions, perfectly at his ease, and letting them ride and approach him as they listed, when the hindermost man struck him over the crown with a loaded whip such a tremendous blow as would have felled an ox, yet, as circumstances happened to be, it had not much effect on the bullet head of Adam Scott. When the man made the blow, his horse started and wheeled, and Scott, with a readiness scarcely natural to our countrymen, the moment that he received the blow, knocked down the foremost rider, who fell from his horse like lead. The short stout man had by this time brought round his horse, and Adam Scott and he struck each other at the same moment. At this stroke he cut Adam's cheek and temple very sore; and Adam in return brought down his horse, which fell to the earth with a groan. A desperate combat now ensued, the Englishman with his long loaded whip, and the Scott with his thorn staff. At the second or third stroke, Adam Scott knocked off his antagonist's wig, and then at once knew him for a highwayman, or common robber and murderer, whom he had seen at his trials both at Carlisle and Jeddart. This incident opened Scott's eyes to the sort of company he had fallen into, and despising the rogue's cowardice who durst not attack him before, two to one, but thought to murder him at one blow behind his back, he laid on without mercy, and in about a minute and a half left him for dead. By this time the tall fellow had got up on one knee and foot, but was pale and bloody, on which Scott lent him another knoit, which again laid him flat; and then, without touching any thing that belonged to them, Adam mounted his sorry horse, and made the best of his way homewards.

As ill luck would have it, our farmer did not call at Fair-lone. Indeed, his calling there was only a pretence to try his suspicious companions; for William Jardine and he were but little acquainted, and that little was the reverse of kindness for one another. At that time the Borders were in much disorder, owing to the discontents regarding the late Union, which were particularly cherished there; and there were many bickerings and heart-burnings between the natives on each side of the Marches. To restrain these as much as possible, there were keepers, as they were called, placed all along the Border line, who were vested with powers to examine and detain any suspicious person from either side till farther trial. Of these keepers, or marchmen, Jardine was one; and he being placed in the very entry of that wild pass which leads from Liddisdale and the highlands of Teviotdale into North Tyne, he often found his hands full. He was an intrepid and severe fellow; and having received a valuable present from some English noblemen for his integrity, from that time forth it was noted that he was most severe on the Scots, and blamed them for every thing.

Now Scott ought, by all means, to have called there, and laid his case before the keeper, and have gone with him to the maimed or killed men, and then he would have been safe. He did neither, but passed by on the other side, and posted on straight over moss and moor for Kildouglas. He seems to have been astounded at the imminent danger he had escaped; and after having, as he believed, killed two men, durst not face the stern keeper, and that keeper his enemy; and as a great part of the treasure he carried belonged to others, and not to himself, he was anxious about it, and made all the haste home that he could, that so he might get honestly quit of it.

But alas! our brave farmer got not so soon home as he intended. There is a part of the thread of the narrative here which I remember but confusedly. But it seems, that immediately after Scott left the prostrate robbers, some more passengers from the fair came riding up, and finding the one man speechless and the other grievously mauled, and on inquiring what had happened, the tall man told them in a feeble voice that they had been murdered and robbed by a rascally Scot called Adam Scott of Kildouglas. As the matter looked so ill, some of the men galloped straight to Fair-Lone, and apprized the marchman, who instantly took horse and pursued; and having a privilege of calling one man out of each house, his company increased rapidly. Jardine, well knowing the wild tract that Scott would take, came up with him about midnight at a place called Langside, and there took him prisoner.

It was in vain that our honest yeoman told the keeper the truth of the story—he gained no credit. For the keeper told him, that *he* had no right to *try* the cause; only he, Adam Scott, had been accused to him of robbery and murder, and it was his office to secure him till the matter was inquired into. He assured Scott further, that his cause looked very ill; for had he been an honest man, and attacked by robbers, he would have called in passing, and told him so. Scott pleaded hard to be taken before the Sheriff of Teviotdale; but the alleged crime having been committed in England, he was carried to

Carlisle.   When Scott heard that such a hard fate awaited him, he is said to have expressed himself thus :——
" Aye, man, an' am I really to be tried for my life by
Englishmen for felling twa English robbers?   If that be
the case, I hae nae mair chance for my life than a Scots
fox has amang an English pack o' hounds.   But had I
kend half an hour ago what I ken now, you an' a' your
menzis should never hae taen Aidie Scott alive."

To Carlisle he was taken and examined, and all his
money taken from him, and given in keeping to the
Mayor, in order to be restored to the rightful owners ;
and witnesses gathered in all the way from Yorkshire,
such as the tall man named ;—for as to all that Adam
told in his own defence, his English Judges only laughed
at it, regarding it no more than the barking of a dog.
Indeed, from the time he heard the tall man's evidence,
whom he felled first, he lost hope of life.   That scoundrel
swore that Scott had knocked them both down and robbed them, when they were neither touching him nor
harming him in any manner of way.   And it seemed to
be a curious fact, that the fellow really never knew that
Scott had been attacked at all.   He had neither heard
nor seen when his companion struck the blow, and that
instant having been knocked down himself, he was quite
justifiable in believing that, at all events, Scott had meant
to dispatch them both.   When Adam related how this
happened, his accuser said he knew that was an arrant
lie ; for had his companion once struck, there was not a
head which he would not have split.

" Aha! it is a' that ye ken about it, lad," said Adam ;
" I faund it nae mair than a rattan's tail! I had baith my
night-cap an' a flannen sark in the crown o' my bannet.
But will ye just be sae good as tell the gentlemen wha
that companion o' yours was ; for if ye dinna do it, I can
do it for you.   It was nae other than Ned Thom, the
greatest thief in a' England."

The Sheriff here looked a little suspicious at the witnesses ; but the allegation was soon repelled by the oaths
of two, who, it was afterwards proven, both perjured

themselves. The mayor told Scott to be making provision for his latter end; but, in the mean time, he would delay passing sentence for eight days, to see if he could bring forward any exculpatory proof. Alas! lying bound in Carlisle prison as he was, how could he bring forward proof? For in those days, without a special messenger, there was no possibility of communication; and the only proofs Adam could have brought forward were, that the men forced themselves into his company, and that he had as many sheep in his possession as accounted for the whole of the money. He asked in Court if any person would go a message for him, but none accepted or seemed to care for him. He believed seriously that they wanted to hang him for the sake of his money, and gave up hope.

Always as Adam sold one drove of sheep after another in Yorkshire, he dispatched his drivers home to Scotland, and with the last that returned, he sent word of the very day on which he would be home, when all his creditors were to meet him at his own house, and receive their money. However, by the manœuvres of one rascal, (now one of his accusers,) he was detained in England three days longer. The farmers came all on the appointed day, and found the gudewife had the muckle pat on, but no Adam Scott came with his pockets full of English gold to them, though many a long look was cast to the head of the Black Swire. They came the next day, and the next again, and then began to fear that some misfortune very serious had befallen their friend.

There was an elderly female lived in the house with Scott, called Kitty Cairns, who was aunt either to the goodman or the goodwife, I have forgot which; but Auntie Kitty was her common denomination. On the morning after Adam Scott was taken prisoner, this old woman arose early, went to her niece's bedside, and said " Meggification, hinny! sic a dream as I hae had about Aidie!—an' it's a true dream, too! I could tak my aith to every sentence o't—aye, an' to ilka person connectit wi't, gin I saw him atween the een."

"Oh, auntie, for mercy's sake haud your tongue, for you are garring a' my heart quake! Ower weel do I ken how true your dreams are at certain times!"

"Aye, hinny! an' did you ever hear me say that sic an' sic a dream was true when it turned out to be otherwise? Na, never i' your life. An' as for folk to say that there's nae truth in dreams, ye ken that's a mere meggification. Weel, ye shall hear; for I'm no gaun to tell ye a dream, ye see, nor aught like ane; but an evendown true story. Our Aidie was sair pinched to sell the hinderend o' his sheep, till up comes a braw dashing gentleman, and bids him a third mair than they were worth, wi' the intention o' paying the poor simple Scotchman in base money. But, aha! let our Aidie alane! He begoud to poize the guineas on his tongue, an feint a ane o' them he wad hae till they were a' fairly weighed afore a magistrate; and sae the grand villain had to pay the hale in good sterling gowd. This angered him sae sair that he hired twa o' his ruffians to follow our poor Aidie, and tak a' the money frae him. I saw the haill o't, an' I could ken the twa chaps weel if confrontit wi' them. They cam to him drinkin' his ale. They rade on an' rade on wi' him, till they partit roads, an' then they fell on him, an' a sair battle it was; but Aidie wan, and felled them baith. Then he fled for hame, but the English pursued, an' took him away to Carlisle prison; an' if nae relief come in eight days, he'll be hanged."

This strange story threw the poor goodwife of Kildouglas into the deepest distress; and the very first creditor who came that morning, she made Auntie Kitty repeat it over to him. This was one Thomas Linton, and she could not have repeated it to a fitter man; for, though a religious and devout man, he was very superstitious, and believed in all Auntie's visions most thoroughly. Indeed, he believed farther; for he believed she was a witch, or one who had a familiar spirit, and knew every thing almost either beneath or beyond the moon. And Linton and his brother being both heavy creditors, the former undertook at once to ride to the south, in order, if possible, to learn something of Adam Scott and the money ; and, if he heard nothing by the way, to go as far as Carlisle, and even, if he found him not there, into Yorkshire. Accordingly he sent a message to his brother, and proceeded southward; and at a village called Stanegirthside, he first heard an account that a man called Scott was carried through that place, on the Friday before, to Carlisle jail, accused of robbery and murder. This was astounding news ; and, in the utmost anxiety, Linton pressed on, and reached Carlisle before the examination concluded, of which mention was formerly made; and when Adam Scott asked through the crowded court, if any present would go a message for him into Scotland for a fair reward, and all had declined it, then Thomas Linton stepped forward within the crowd, and said, "Aye, here is ane, Adam, that will ride to ony part in a' Scotland or England for ye ; ride up to Lunnon to your chief in the house o' Lords, afore thae English loons shall dare to lay a foul finger on ye !—An' I can tell you, Mr Shirra, or Mr Provice, or whatever ye be, that you are gaun to get yoursell into a grand scrape, for there never was an honester man breathed the breath o' life than Aidie Scott."

The judge smiled, and said he would be glad to have proofs of that ; and, for Linton's encouragement, made the town-clerk read over the worst part of the evidence, which was very bad indeed, only not one word of it true. But Linton told them, he cared nothing for *their* evidence against a Scot; "for it was weel kend that the Englishers was a' grit leears, an' wad swear to ony thing that suited them ; but let him aince get Adam Scott's plain story, an' *then* he wad ken how matters stood."

He was indulged with a private interview, and greatly were the two friends puzzled how to proceed. The swindler, who really had bought the last ewes from Scott, had put a private mark upon all his good gold to distinguish it from his base metal, and made oath that all that gold was his ; and that he had given it to his servant, whom Scott had robbed, to buy cattle for him in Scotland.

The mark was evident; and that had a bad look; but, when Scott told the true story, Linton insisted on the magistrate being summoned to Court, who saw that gold weighed over to his friend. "And will mysell tak in hand," said he, "not only to bring forward all the farmers from whom Scott bought the sheep, but all the Englishmen to whom he sold them; an' gin I dinna prove him an honest man, if ye gie me time, I sall gie you leave to hang me in his place."

The swindler and robber now began to look rather blank, but pretended to laugh at the allegations of Thomas Linton; but the Scot set up his birses, and told the former that "he could prove, by the evidence of two English aldermen, who saw the gold weighed, that he had paid to his friend the exact sum which he had here claimed; and that, either dead or alive, he should be obliged to produce the body of the other robber, or he who pretended to have been robbed, to show what sort of servants he employed. "I'll bring baith noblemen and lawyers frae Scotland," added he, "who will see justice done to so brave and so worthy a man; an' if they dinna gar you skemps take his place, never credit a Scot again."

Adam Scott's chief being in London, and his own laird a man of no consequence, Linton rode straight off to his own laird, the Earl of Traquair, travelling night and day till he reached him. The Earl, being in Edinburgh, sent for a remarkably clever and shrewd lawyer, one David Williamson, and also for Alexander Murray, Sheriff of Selkirkshire, and to these three Linton told his story, assuring them, that he could vouch for the truth of it in every particular; and after Williamson had questioned him backwards and forwards, it was resolved that something should instantly be done for the safety of Scott. Accordingly, Williamson wrote a letter to the Mayor, which was signed by the Earl, and the Sheriff of Scott's county, which letter charged the Mayor to take good heed what he was about, and not to move in the matter of Scott till Quarter-session day, which was not distant, and then counsel would attend to see justice done to a man, who had always been so highly esteemed. And that by all means he (the Mayor) was to secure Scott's three accusers, and not suffer them by any means to escape, as he should answer for it. The letter also bore a list of the English witnesses who behoved to be there. Linton hastened back with it, and that letter changed the face of affairs mightily. The grand swindler and the tall robber were both seized and laid in irons, and the other also was found with great trouble, From that time forth there remained little doubt of the truth of Scott's narrative; for this man was no other than the notorious Edward Thom, who had eluded the sentence of the law both in Scotland and England, in the most wonderful manner, and it was well known that he belonged to a notable gang of robbers.

It is a pity that the history of that interesting trial is far too long and minute for a tale such as this, though I have often heard it all gone over;—how Williamson astonished the natives with his cross questions, his speeches, and his evidences;—how confounded the Mayor and aldermen were, that they had not discerned these circumstances before;—how Thom, at last, turned king's evidence, and confessed the whole:—how the head swindler was condemned and executed, and the tall robber whipped and dismissed, because he had in fact only intended a robbery, but had no hand in it;—and finally, how Scott was released with the highest approbation; while both magistrates and burgesses of ancient Carlisle strove with one another how to heap most favours on him and his friend Thomas Linton. There were upwards of two hundred Scottish yeomen accompanied the two friends up the Esk, who had all been drawn to Carlisle to hear the trial; and there is little doubt, that, if matters had gone otherwise than they did, a rescue was intended.

Why should any body despise a dream, or any thing whatever in which one seriously believes?

# BARON ST GIO.

---

I HAVE often wondered if it was possible that a person could exist without a conscience. I think not, if he be a reasonable being. Yet there certainly are many of whom you would judge by their actions that they had none ; or, if they have, that conscience is not a mirror to be trusted. In such cases we may suppose that conscience exists in the soul of such a man as well as others, but that it is an erroneous one, not being rightly informed of what sin is, and consequently unable to judge fairly of his actions, by comparing them with the law of God. It is a sad state to be in ; for surely there is no condition of soul more wretched than that of the senseless obdurate sinner, the faculties of whose soul seem to be in a state of numbness, and void of that true feeling of sensibility which is her most vital quality.

I was led into this kind of mood to-night by reading a sort of Memoir of the life of Jasper Kendale, *alias* the Baron St Gio, written by himself, which, if at all consistent with truth, unfolds a scene of unparalleled barbarity, and an instance of that numbness of soul of which we have been speaking, scarcely to be excelled.

Jasper says, he was born at bonny Dalkerran, in the parish of Leeswald ; but whether that is in England, Scotland, or Wales, he does not inform us ; judging in his own simplicity of heart, that every one knows where bonny Dalkerran is as well as he does. For my part I never heard either of such a part or of such a parish ; but from many of his expressions, I should draw the conclusion, that he comes from some place in the West of Scotland.

" My father and mother were unco good religious

focks,'' says he, "but verry poor. At least I think sae,
for we were verry ragged and duddy in our claes, and
often didna get muckle to eat." This is manifestly Scottish, and in the same style the best parts of the narrative
are written; but for the sake of shortening it two-thirds
at least, I must take a style more concise.

When I was about twelve years of age, my uncle got
me in to be stable-boy at Castle-Meldin, and a happy
man I was at this change; for whereas before I got only
peel-an-eat potatoes and a little salt twice a-day at home,
here I feasted like a gentleman, and had plenty of good
meat to take or to leave every day as I listed, and as
suited my appetite, for it suited my constitution wonderfully. I was very thankful for this, and resolved to be a
good, diligent, and obedient servant; and so I was, for
I took care of everything intrusted to me, and, as far as
I could see, every body liked me.

Before I had been a year there the old laird died, and
as I had hardly ever seen him, that did not affect me
much; but I suspected that all things would go wrong
about the house when the head of it was taken away;
that there would be nothing but fasting and mourning,
and every thing that was disagreeable. I was never more
agreeably mistaken, for the feasting and fun never began
about the house till then. The ladies, to be sure, were
dressed in black; and beautiful they looked, so that
wooers flocked about them every day. But there was
one that far outdid the rest in beauty. Her name was
Fanny, the second or third daughter of the family. I
am not sure which, but she was the most beautiful woman
I ever saw in the world. There was a luxuriance of
beauty about her that is quite indescribable, which drew
all hearts and all eyes to her. She was teazed by lovers
of every age and description, but I only know what the
maids told me about these things. They said her behaviour was rather lightsome with the gentlemen; for that
she was constantly teazing them, which provoked them
always to fasten on her for a romp, and that her sisters
were often ill-pleased with her, because she got the most

part of the fun to herself. I know nothing about these things; but this I know, that before the days of mourning were over Miss Fanny vanished—was lost—and her name was said never to have been mentioned up stairs, but with us she was the constant subject of discourse, and one of the maids always put on wise looks, and pretended to know where she was. Time passed on for some months, until one day I was ordered to take my uncle's pair, and drive a gentleman to a certain great market town. (Jasper names the town plain out, which I deem improper.) I did as I was ordered, and my uncle giving the gentleman some charges about me, closed the door, and off we drove. The man was very kind to me all the way, and good to the horses; but yet I could not endure to look at him. He had a still, round, whitish face, and eyes as if he had been half sleeping, but when they glimmered up, they were horribly disagreeable.

We remained in the town two nights and on the following morning I was ordered to drive through the town by his direction. He kept the window open at my back, and directed me, by many turnings, to a neat elegant house rather in the suburbs. He went in. I waited long at the door, and often heard a noise within as of weeping and complaining, and at length my gentleman came out leading Miss Fanny with both hands, and put her into the coach. She was weeping violently, and much altered, and my heart bled at seeing her. There was no one came to the door to see her into the chaise, but I saw two ladies on the stair inside the house. He then ordered me to drive by such a way, which I did, driving the whole day by his direction; and the horses being in excellent keeping, we made great speed; I thought we drove on from twenty to thirty miles, and I knew by the sun that we were going to the eastward, and of course not on the road home. We had for a good while been on a sort of a country road; and at length on a broad common road covered with furze, I was ordered to draw up which, I did. The gentleman stepped first out, and then handed out Miss Fanny; but still not with that sort of respect which I weened to be her due. They only walked a few steps from the carriage, when he stopped, and looked first at one whin bush, then at another, as if looking for something of which he was uncertain. He then led her up to one, and holding her fast by the wrist with one hand, with the other he pulled a dead body covered with blood out of the midst of the bush, and asked the lady if she knew who that was? Such a shriek, I think, was never uttered by a human creature, as that hapless being uttered at that moment, and such may my ears never hear again! But in one instant after, and even I think before she could utter a second, he shot her through the head, and she fell.

I was so dreadfully shocked, and amazed at such atrocity, that I leaped from the seat and ran for it; but my knees had no strength, and the boots hampering me, the ruffian caught me before I had run fifty paces, and dragged me back to the scene of horror. He then assured me, that if I offered again to stir from my horses, he would send me the same way with these culprits whom I saw lying there; and perceiving escape to be impossible I kneeled, and prayed him not to shoot me, and I would stay and do anything that he desired of me. He then re-loaded his pistol, and taking a ready cocked one in each hand, he ordered me to drag the bodies away and tumble them into an old coal-pit, which I was forced to do, taking first the one and then the other. My young mistress was not quite dead, for I saw her lift her eyes, and as she descended the void, I heard a slight moan, then a great plunge, and all was over.

I wonder to this day that he did not send me after them. I expected nothing else; and I am sure if it had not been for the driving of the chaise by himself, which on some account or other he durst not attempt, my fate had been sealed.

He did not go into the chaise, but mounted on the seat beside me, and we drove and drove on by quite another road than that we went, until the horses were completely forespent, and would not raise a trot. I was so terrified for the fellow, that I durst not ask him to stop and corn the horses, but I said several times that the horses were quite done up. His answer was always, " Whip on."

When it began to grow dark, he asked my name, my country, and all about my relations; and in particular about the old coachman at Castle-Meldin. I told him the plain truth on every point, on which he bade me be of good cheer and keep myself free of all suspicions, for as long as I made no mention of what I had seen, no evil should happen to me; and he added, " I daresay you would be a little astonished at what you saw to-day. But I hope you will say, God forgive you !"

" I'll be unco laith to say ony sic thing, man," quo' I, " for I wad be very sorry if he did. I hope to see you burning in hell yet for what ye hae done the day." (These are Jasper's own words.)

" What ! *you* hope to see me there, do you ? Then it bespeaks that you hope to go there yourself," said he.

" If I do not see you there, some will," said I ; for by this time I saw plenty of human faces around us, and lost all fear, so I said what I thought.

" If you have any value for your life," said he, " be a wise boy, and say nothing about it. Can't you perceive that there is no atrocity in the deed—at least not one hundredth part of the sum which you seem to calculate on ? Do you think it was reasonable that a whole family of beautiful and virtuous sisters of the highest rank, should all have been ruined by the indiscretion of one ?"

" That is no reason at all, sir, for the taking away of life," said I. " The law of God did not condemn her for aught she had done ; and where lay your right to lift up your hand against her life ? You might have sent her abroad, if she had in any way disgraced the family, which I never will believe she did."

" True," said he, " I could have secured her person, but who could have secured her pen ? All would have come out, and shame and ruin would have been the consequence. Though I lament with all my heart that such a deed was necessary, yet there was no alternative. Now, tell me this, for you have told me the plain truth hitherto, —did or did you not recognise the body of the dead gentleman ?"

"Yes, I did," said I, frankly. "I knew it for the body of a young nobleman whom I have often seen much caressed at Castle-Meldin."

He shook his head and gave an inward growl, and then said, "since you say so, I must take care of *you!* You are wrong; that is certain; and you had better not say such a thing again. But nevertheless, since you *have* said it, and *may* say it again, I must take care of *you.*"

He spoke no more. We were now driving through a large town; but whether or not it was the one we left in the morning, I could not tell, and he would not inform me. We drew up on the quay where a fine barge with eight rowers, all leaning on their oars, stood ready to receive us. My fine gentleman then desired me to alight, and go across the water with him, for a short space. I refused positively, saying, that I would not leave my horses for any man's pleasure. He said he had a lad there to take care of the horses, and I knew it behoved me to accompany him across. "I'll not leave my horses; that's flat. And you had better not insist on it. I'm not in the humour to be teased much farther," said I.

That word sealed my fate. I was that moment pulled from my seat, gagged by a fellow's great hand, and hurled into the boat by I know not how many scoundrels. There I was bound, and kept gagged by the sailors, to their great amusement. We reached a great ship in the offing, into which I was carried, and cast into a dungeon, bound hands and feet. We sailed next morning, and for three days I was kept bound and gagged but fed regularly. My spirit was quite broken, and even my resolution of being avenged for the death of the lovely Fanny began to die away. On the fourth day, to my inexpressible horror, the murderer himself came down to my place of confinement, and addressed me to the following purport.

"Kendale, you are a good boy—a truthful, honourable, and innocent boy. . I know you are : and I do not like to see you kept in durance this way. We are now far at sea on our way to a foreign country. You must be sensible that you are now entirely in my power, and at my disposal, and that all your dependence must be on me. Swear then to me that you will never divulge the rueful scene, which you witnessed on the broad common among the furze, and I will instantly set you at liberty, and be kind to you. And to dispose you to comply, let me assure you that the day you disclose my secret is your last, and no power on earth can save you, even though I were at the distance of a thousand miles. I have ventured a dreadful stake, and must go through with it, cost what it will."

I perceived that all he had said was true, and that I had no safety but in compliance ; and yearning to be above deck to behold the sun and the blue heavens, I there, in that dismal hole, took a dreadful oath never to mention it, or divulge it in any way, either on board, or in the country to which we were going. He appeared satisfied, and glad at my compliance, and loosed me with his own hand, telling me to wait on him at table, and appear as his confidential servant, which I promised, and performed as well as I could. But I had no happiness, for the secret of the double murder preyed on my heart, and I looked on myself as an accomplice. There was one thing in which my belief was fixed ; that we never would reach any coast, for the ship would to a certainty be cast away, and every gale that we encountered, I prepared for the last.

My master, for so I must now denominate him, seemed to have no fears of that nature. He drank and sung, and appeared as happy and merry as a man so gloomy of countenance could be. He was called Mr Southman, and appeared the proprietor of the ship. We saw no land for seven weeks, but at length it appeared on our starboard side, and when I asked what country it was, I was told it was Carolina. I asked if it was near Jerusalem or Egypt, and the sailors laughed at me, and said that it was just to Jerusalem that I was going, and I think my heart never was so overjoyed in my life.

Honest Jasper has nearly as many chapters describing this voyage, as I have lines, and I must still hurry on in order to bring his narrative into the compass of an ordinary tale, for though I have offered the manuscript complete to several booksellers, it has been uniformly rejected. And yet it is exceedingly amusing, and if not truth, tells very like it. Among other things, he mentions a Mr M'Kenzie from Ross-shire, as having been on board, and from some things he mentions relating to him, I am sure I have met with him.

Suffice it to say, that they landed at what Jasper calls a grand city, named Savannah, which the sailors made him believe was Jerusalem; and when undeceived by his master, he wept. The captain and steward took their orders from Mr Southman, hat in hand, and then he and his retinue sailed up the river in a small vessel, and latterly in a barge, until they came to a fine house on a level plain, so extensive that Jasper Kendale says, with great simplicity, " It looked to me to be bigger nor the whole world."

Here they settled; and here Jasper remained seven years as a sort of half idle servant, yet he never knew whether his master was proprietor of, or steward on, the estates. There is little interesting in this part of the work, save some comical amours with the slave girls, to which Jasper was a little subject, and his master ten times worse, by his account. There is one summing up of his character which is singular. It is in these emphatic words,—" In short, I never saw a better master, nor a worse man."

But there is one thing asserted here which I do not believe. He avers that the one half of all the people in that country are slaves! Absolute slaves, and bought and sold in the market like sheep and cattle! " Then said the high priest, Are these things so?"

At the end of seven years or thereby, there was one day that I was in the tobacco plantation with forty workers, when a gentleman came up to me from the river, and

asked for Mr Southman.   My heart flew to my throat, and
I could scarcely contain myself, for I knew him at once
to be Mr Thomas B———h, the second son at Castle-
Meldin.   There were only two brothers in the family,
and this was the youngest and the best.   We having only
exchanged a few words, he did not in the least recognise
me and indeed it was impossible he could, so I said nothing to draw his attention, but knowing what I knew, I
could not conceive what his mission to my master could
import.   I never more saw him alive ; but the following
mórning, I knew by the countenance of my master that
there was some infernal plot brewing within, for he had
that look which I had never seen him wear but once before.   There was no mistaking it.   It was the cloven
foot of Satan, and indicated certain destruction to some
one.   I had reason to suspect it would be myself, and so
well convinced was I of this, that I had resolved to fly,
and try to get on board some ship.   But I was mistaken.
The bolt of hell struck elsewhere.   The young stranger
disappeared, after staying and being mightily caressed
two days and nights ; and shortly thereafter, his body was
thrown on the shore of the Savannah by the reflux of
the tide, not far below the boundary of my master's estate.   I went, with many others, and saw the body, and
knew it well, and it was acknowledged both by my master
and the house servants, to have been a stranger gentleman that was in that country wanting to purchase land——
that he had been entertained by Mr Southman ; but none
could tell his name.   He had been murdered and robbed,
and his body thrown into the river, and no light whatever
was cast on the circumstances of the crime by the investigation.   The Georgians seemed greatly indifferent about
the matter.   I was never called or examined at all ; and
if I had, I know not what I would have said, I knew nothing of his death, farther than suspicion dictated, but of
the identity of his person I was certain.

   Immediately on this I was sent to an estate far up the
country, on the fine table lands, to assist a Mr Courteny
in managing it.   I took a letter from my master to him,

and was kindly received, and made superintendent of every thing under Mr Courteny. He was a delightful man, and held as delightful a place; but neither did he know whether Mr Southman was the proprietor of these estates, or steward over them, with a power of attorney. He knew they were purchased by one bearing quite another name; but he had exercised all the powers of a proprietor for a number of years, and had been sundry voyages over at Britain. It was a lucrative property, and he was held as a very great man.

Here I remained for three years. Among others of my master's satellites who attended me to that place, there was a German called Allanstein. That man had come with us from England, and was one of them who bound and gagged me in the boat. But he was a pleasant old fellow, and I liked him, and was always kind to him. He was taken very ill; and, on his deathbed, he sent for me, and told me that he and another, whom he would not name, had orders to watch all my motions, and in no wise to suffer me to leave the country, but to shoot me. He said he would never see his master again, and he thought it best to warn me to be on my guard, and remain quietly where I was. He likewise told me that Mr Southman had left America for some time, and he believed for ever. After giving me the charge of his concerns, and a handsome present, poor Allanstein died.

As long as I had no knowledge of this circumstance, I had no desire to leave the country; but the moment I knew I was watched like a wild beast, and liable to be murdered on mere suspicion, I grew impatient to be gone. There was one fellow whom I suspected, but had no means of learning the truth. I turned him out of our employment, but he remained on the estate, and lingered constantly near me. He had likewise come with us from England, and appeared to have plenty of money at command. I contrived, however, to give him the slip, and, escaping into South Carolina, I scarcely stinted night or day till I was at Charlestown, where I got on board the Elizabeth sloop, bound for Liverpool. Then I breathed

freely, accounting myself safe ; and then, also, I was free
from my oath, and at liberty to tell all that I had seen.
The vessel, however, had not got her loading on board,
and we lay in the harbour, at the confluence of the rivers,
two days ; but what was my astonishment to perceive,
after we had heaved anchor, the wretch Arnotti on board
along with me, brown with fatigue in the pursuit, and covered with dust.  I was now certain that he was the remaining person who was sworn to take my life if I should
offer to leave the state, and knew not what to do, as I
was persuaded he would perform it at the risk of his own
life.  I had paid my freight to Britain ; nevertheless, I
went on shore on Sullivan's Island, and suffered the vessel to proceed without me, and was now certain that I
was quite safe, my enemy having gone on with the Elizabeth.  I waited here long before a vessel passed to a
right port, but at length I got one going to the Clyde,
and took my passage in her ; and, after we were fairly
out to sea, behold, there my old friend Arnotti popped
his head once more out of the fore-castle, and eyed me
with a delighted and malicious grin !  I was quite confounded at again seeing this destroying angel haunting
my motions, and said, " What is that murdering villain
seeking here ?"

The seamen stared ; but he replied, sharply, " Vat you
say, Monsieur Ken-dale ?  You say me de moorderour ?
Vat you derr ?  You help de moorderour, and keep him
secret.  Dat is de vay, is it ?"

I then took the captain of the ship by himself, and
told him what I suspected, and that I was certain the
villain would find means of assassinating me.  He at first
laughed at me, and said, he could not think I was so
much of a coward as to be afraid of any single man ; but
perceiving me so earnest, he consented to disarm all the
passengers, beginning with myself, and on none of them
were any arms found save Arnotti, who had two loaded
pistols and a dagger, neatly concealed in his clothes.  He
was deprived of these, and put under a partial confinement, and then I had peace and rest.

For all this severity, the unaccountable wretch tried to strangle Jasper by night, just as they began to approach Ireland; he was, however, baffled, wounded, and tossed overboard, a circumstance afterwards deeply regretted. But Jasper makes such a long story, I am obliged to pass it over by the mere mention of it.

Jasper found his mother still alive, and very frail; his father dead, and his brethren and sisters all scattered, and he could find no one to whom to unburden his mind. He went next to Castle-Meldin, and there also found the young squire dead, and his brother Thomas *lost abroad!* whither he had gone to claim an estate; and the extensive domains were now held by Lord William E——le in right of his wife. The other ladies were likewise all married to men of rank. Old coachee, Jasper's mother's brother, was still living at the Castle, on the superannuated list, and to him Jasper unfolded by degrees his revolting and mysterious tale. The old man could not fathom or comprehend it. The remaining capabilities of his mind were inadequate to the grasp. He forgot one end of it ere he got half way to the other; and though at times he seemed to take deep interest in the incidents, before one could have noted any change in his countenance, they had vanished altogether from his mind.

The two friends agreed on the propriety of acquainting Lord William with the circumstances, and after watching an opportunity for some time, they got him by himself in the shrubbery. I must give this in Jasper's own words.

"When the lord saw my uncle's white head, and the old laced hat held out afore him, as if to beg for a bawbee, he kend be the motion that he wantit to speak till him. So he turns to us, and he says, ' Well, old coachee, what has your stupid head conceived it necessary to say to me to-day? Is the beer of the hall too weak?'

" ' Wod, ye see, my lord, ye see, that's no the thing. But this wee callant here, he tells me sic a story, ye see, that, wod, ye see, I canna believe't, 'at can I nae. He's a sister's son o' mine. Ye'll may be mind o' him when ye were courtin' here? Oogh !'

"'What boy do you speak of, Andrew? Is it this boardly young man?'

"'Ay, to be sure.—Him? Hout! A mere kittlin, ye see. He's my sister Nanny's son, that was married to Joseph Kendale, ye ken. A very honest upright man he was; but this callant has been abroad, ye see, my lord. And—What was this I was gaun to say?"

"'Some story you were talking of.'

"'Ay, wod, that's very true, my lord, an' weel mindit. Ye'll mind your eldest brother weel eneugh? Did ye ever ken what oord o' him?

"'No; I am sorry to say I never did.'

"'And do you mind your sister-in-law, Miss Fanny, the bonniest o' them a'? Oogh? Or did ye ever ken what came o' her?—(Lord William shook his head)— 'There's a chap can tell ye then. Lord forgie us, my lord, didna he murder them baith, an' then trail them away, first the tane and then the tither, an' fling them intil a hole fifty faddom deep, ye see! Oogh? Wasna that the gate o't, callant?'

"Lord William burst out in laughter at the old man's ridiculous accusation; but I stopped him, assuring him, that, although my uncle's mind was unstable and wandering on a subject that affected him so much, I nevertheless had nearly twelve years before, on the 7th day of October, seen that young lady murdered. Aye, led far away out to a wild common, like a lamb to the slaughter, and cruelly butchered in one instant, without having time given her to ask pardon of Heaven. And though I had not seen his brother slain, I had seen him lying slain on the same spot, and was compelled by a charged pistol held to my head, to carry both the bodies, and throw them into a pit.

"I never saw such a picture as the countenance of Lord William displayed. Consternation, horror, and mental pain, were portrayed on it alternately, and it was at once manifest, that, at all events, he had no hand nor foreknowledge of the foul transaction. He asked at first if I was not raving?—if I was in my sound mind? And

then made me recite the circumstances all over again,
which I did, in the same way and order, that I have set
them down here. I told him also of the murder of his
brother-in-law in the country of the Savannah, and that
I was almost certain it was by the same hand. That I
knew the city from which the young lady was abstracted,
and thought I could know the house if taken to it; but I
neither knew the way we went, the way by which we returned, nor what town it was at which I was forced aboard
in the dark, so that the finding out the remains of the hapless pair appeared scarcely practicable. My identity was
proven to Lord William's satisfaction, as well as my disappearance from the Castle at the date specified; but no
one, not even my old uncle, could remember in what
way. The impression entertained was, that I had got
drunk at the town, and been pressed aboard, or persuaded
on board one of his Majesty's ships.

"Lord William charged me not to speak of it to any
other about the Castle, lest the story should reach the
ears of his lady, on whom the effects might be dreadful
at that period. So, taking me with him in the carriage,
we proceeded to the chief town of the county, the one
above mentioned, where he had me examined by the
public authorities; but there my story did not gain implicit credit, and I found it would pass as an infamous
romance, unless I could point out the house from which
the lady was taken, and the spot where the remains were
deposited. The house I could not point out, though I
perambulated the suburbs of the town over and over
again. Every thing was altered, and whole streets built
where there were only straggling houses. Mr Southman's name, as an American planter, was not known; so
that these horrid murders, committed in open day in this
land of freedom, were likely to be passed over without
farther investigation.

"I traversed the country, day after day, and week after week, searching for the broad common covered with
furze, and the old open coal-pit into which I had cast the
bodies of the comely pair. I searched till I became

known to the shepherds and miners on those wastes, but all to no purpose—I could not find even the slightest resemblance in the outlines of the country, which still remained impressed on my memory—till one day I came to an old man casting turf whose face I thought I knew, with whom I entered into conversation, when he at once asked what I was looking for, for he had seen me, he said, traversing these commons so often, without dog or gun, that he wondered what I wanted. I told him all, day and date, and what I was looking for. The old fellow was never weary of listening to the tale of horror, but the impression it made on his feelings scattered his powers of recollection. He had never heard of the lady's name, but he guessed that of the gentleman of his own accord, remembering of his disappearance in that very way. It was understood by his family that he had been called out to fight a duel that morning, he said; but the circumstances were so confused in his memory, that he entreated of me to meet him at the same place the following day, and by that time, from his own recollection, and that of others, he would be able to tell me something more distinctly.

"The next day I came as appointed, when he said he suspected that I was looking for the fatal spot at least thirty miles distant from where it was, for he had learned the place where Lord Richard E———le had been last seen, and by the direction in which he then rode, it was evident the spot where he met his death could not be in that quarter. And that, moreover, if I would pay him well, he thought he could take me to the place, or near it, for he had heard of a spot where a great deal of blood had been shed, which was never accounted for, and where the cries of a woman's ghost had been heard by night.

" I said I would give him five shillings a-day as long as I detained him, which offer he accepted, and away we went, chatting about the 'terrible job,' as he called it. Lord Richard had been seen riding out very early in the morning at full speed with a gentleman, whose description tallied pretty closely with that of the assassin, even at that distance of time. We did not reach the spot that night, after travelling a whole day; but the next morning I began to perceive the landmarks so long remembered, and so eagerly looked for. I was confounded at my stupidity, and never will comprehend it while I live. I now at once recognised the place. The common was partly enclosed and improven, but that part on which the open pits were situated remained the same. I knew the very bush from which I saw the body of the young nobleman drawn, and the spot where, the next moment, his betrothed fell dead across his breast. The traces of the streams of blood were still distinguishable by a darker green, and the yawning pit that received their remains stood open as at that day. I dispatched the old hind in one direction, and I posted off in another, to bring Lord William and all the connexions of the two families together, to examine the remains, and try to identify them. I had hard work to find him, for he had been to all the great trading houses in the west of England to find out the assassin's name. It occurred in none of their books. But there was one merchant, who, after much consideration and search, found a letter, in which was the following sentence : ' My neighbour, Mr Southman, has a large store of the articles, which I could buy at such and such prices.' A list followed, and this was all. That gentleman engaged to write to his correspondent forthwith, as did many others ; and in this state matters stood when I found him.

" A great number repaired to the spot. There were noblemen, knights, surgeons, and divines, and gaping peasants, without number; there were pulleys, windlasses, baskets, coffins, and every thing in complete preparation, both for a search, and the preservation of such remains as might be discovered. I went down with the first to a great depth. It was a mineral pit, and had a strong smell, as of sulphur mixed with turpentine ; and I confess I was far from being at my ease. I was afraid the foul air would take flame ; and, moreover, it was a frightsome thing to be descending into the bowels of the earth in

search of the bones of murdered human beings.  I expected to see some shadowy ghosts ; and when the bats
came buffing out of their holes, and put out our lights, I
was almost beside myself.   We had, however, a lamp of
burning charcoal with us, and at length reached the water
in safety.   It was rather a sort of puddle than water, at
that season, and little more than waist-deep.   We soon
found the bodies, fresh and whole as when flung in, but
they were so loaden with mire as not to be recognisable
until taken to a stream and washed, and then the identity
was acknowledged by every one to whom they were formerly known.   The freshness of the bodies was remarkable, and viewed by the country people as miraculous ;
but I am persuaded, that if they had lain a century in
that mineral puddle, they would have been the same.
The bodies were pure, fair, and soft ; but when handled,
the marks of the fingers remained.

"It was now manifest, that Lord Richard E——le
had been murdered.   He had been shot in the back by
two pistol-bullets, both of which were extracted from the
region of the heart.   And—woe is my heart to relate it !
—it appeared but *too* manifestly that the young lady had
lived for some time in that frightful dungeon !

"Every effort was now made to discover the assassin.
Officers were dispatched to Savannah, with full powers
from government ; high rewards were offered for appre-
hending him, his person described, and these were published through all Europe ; but the culprit could no where
be found.   A singular scene of villany was, however,
elucidated, all transacted by that arch villain, known by
the name of Southman in Georgia, but nowhere else."

The part that follows this, in Mr Kendale's narrative
I do not understand, nor am I aware that it is at all founded on facts.   He says, that some rich merchants of Ger-
many got an extensive grant of lands from King Charles
the First, on the left bank of the Savannah, on condition
of furnishing him with a set number of troops ; that these
merchants sent a strong colony of Germans as settlers to
cultivate the district ; and that after a long struggle with

the natives, and other difficulties, they succeeded in making it a fine country, and a lucrative speculation ; but the original holders of the grant having made nothing but loss of it, and their successors disregarding it, the whole fell into the hands of the trustees, and ultimately into the hands of this infamous rascal, who first sold the whole colony to a company of British gentlemen, received the payment and returned as their manager, and shortly after sold it to the British government, and absconded. I cannot pretend to clear up this transaction, as l know nothing about the settlement of that colony, nor where to find it ; so I must pass on to some other notable events in Jasper's life.

He was now established at Castle-Meldin as housesteward and butler, and, if we take his own account of it, he must have been an excellent servant. " I watched every wish and want of my lord and lady," he says, " both of whom I loved as myself, and I would generally present them with things they wanted before they asked for them. Indeed, I knew the commands of my lady's eye as well as those of her tongue, and rather better." Jasper must have been a most valuable servant, and no one can wonder that he was a favourite. " I had likewise learned to keep books and accounts of all kinds with Mr Courteny, and that with so great accurateness, that at the end of the year I could have made ends meet in the Castle expenses to the matter of a few pounds." What must the world think of such *accurateness* as this ? I have known a gentleman in business go over the whole of his books for a twelvemonth, because they did not balance by threepence. That man Jasper would have taken for a fool, knowing that it is easier to discover that such a sum is wanting than how to make it up.

" I grew more and more into favour, until at length I was treated like a friend, and no more like a menial servant, and the mysterious, but certain circumstances of the murders, which it was impossible to keep concealed, reaching my lady's ear, so much affected her health, which before was delicate, that her physicians strongly recommended a change of climate. Preparations were accordingly made for our departure into the south of Europe, and it was arranged that I should travel with them as a companion, but subordinate so far as to take the charge of every thing ; pay all accounts, hire horses, furnish the table, acting as steward and secretary both. I was to sit at table with my lord, be called Mr Kendale, and introduced to his friends."

The journey through France I must leave out, it being merely a tourist's journal, and not very intelligible. They tarried for some time at Paris, then at Lyons ; at both of which places Mr Kendale met with some capital adventures. They then crossed into Tuscany ; but Mr Kendale seems to have had little taste for the sublime or beautiful, for he only says of the Alps, " It is an horrid country, and the roads very badly laid out." And of the valley of the Arno—" The climate was so good here, and the sky so pure, that my lord resolved to remain in the country till his lady got quite better, as she was coming round every day." At Florence Lord E———le had an introduction to a Count Sonnini, who showed them all manner of kindness, and gave many great entertainments on their account. He was a confidant of the Grand Duke's, and a man of great power both in the city and country, and Mr Kendale is never weary of describing his bounty and munificence. But now comes the catastrophe.

" One day the Count had been showing my lord through the grand cathedral, which is a fine old kirk ; and then through the gallery of the medicines, (the Medicis perhaps,) filled with pictures and statutes, (qu?) many of them a shame to be seen, but which my gentlemen liked the best. The Count Sonnini, perceiving that I did not know where to look, put his arm within mine, and leading me forward, said in his broken English, ' Tell me now, Mashi Ken-dale, vat you do tink of dis Venus ?'—' She is a soncy, thriving-like quean, my lord count,' said I, ' and does not look as she wanted either her health or her meat ; it is a pity she should be in want of clothes.'

" But the next scene was of a different description. On turning from the Duke's palazzo about a gun-shot, the Count says to us, ' I can show you a scene here that the like is not perhaps to be seen in the world. There are none admitted but members, and such as members introduce ; and as I have been admitted, I will claim a privilege which they dare not refuse me.' He then led us through a long gallery paved with marble, and down some flights of steps, I do not know how far, till, coming to a large door, he rung for admittance. A small iron shutter was opened in the door, and a porter demanded the names and qualities of the guests. ' The Count Sonnini and two friends foreigners,' was the reply. The iron shutter sprung again into its place, and we waited long. The Count lost patience and rung again, when the shutter again opened, and a person apparently of high consequence, addressing the Count politely, reminded him that he was asking a privilege which it was out of the society's power to grant ; and entreating him to rest satisfied till some future day, that he and his friends could be introduced in the usual form. My lord entreated to be gone, but the Count was a proud man, and aware of his power and influence, and go he would not, but requested to see the Marquis Piombino. The Marquis came, when the Count requested him, in a tone that scarcely manifested the brooking of a refusal, to introduce him and his two friends. The Marquis hesitated—returned again to consult the authorities, and finally we were admitted, though with apparent reluctance. This was a gambling house on a large scale, in which hundreds of people were engaged at all manner of games, while the money was going like slate stones.

" I cannot describe it, nor will I attempt it. It was splendidly lighted up, for it had no windows, and the beams of the sun had never entered there. There were boxes all around, and a great open space in the middle for billiards, and a promenade. My lord and the Count began betting at once, to be like others, but my attention was soon fixed on one object, and that alone ; for at one of the banking tables I perceived the identical Mr Southman, seated on high as a judge and governor. I saw his eyes following my lord through the hall with looks of manifest doubt and trepidation, but when the Count and he vanished into one of the distant boxes, and the villain's looks dropped upon me almost close beside him, I shall never forget the fiendish expression of horror legible in his countenance. With the deep determined look, indicative of self-interest, and that alone, in despite of all other emotions of the soul, there was at this time one of alarm, of which I had never witnessed a trait before. It was that of the Arch-fiend, when discovered in the garden of Eden.

" He could attend no farther to the banking business, for I saw that he dreaded I would go that instant and give him up. So, deputing another in his place, he descended from his seat, and putting his arm in mine, he led me into an antechamber. I had no reason to be afraid of any danger, for no arms of any kind are allowed within that temple of vice and extravagance. But I have something cowardly in my constitution, else I know not how it happened, but I *was* afraid. I was awed before that monster of iniquity, and incapable of acting up to the principles which I cherished in my heart.

" He began by testifying his surprise at seeing me in that country; and at once inquired in what capacity I had come. I answered ingenuously, that I had come as the friend and travelling companion of Lord William E——le. 'That is to say, you were informed of my retreat, and are come in order to have me apprehended?' said he.

" I declared that we had no such information, and came with no such intent ; and was proceeding to relate to him the import of our journey, when he interrupted me. ' I know of all that has taken place in England,' said he, 'relating to that old and unfortunate affair, and have read the high rewards offered for my apprehension. You have been the cause of all this, and have banished me from society. Yet you know I preserved your life when it was in my power, and very natural for me to have taken it. Yea, for the space of seven years your life was in my power every day and every hour.'

" ' I beg pardon, sir,' said I, ' my life was never in your power further than it was in the power of every other assassin. As long as I do nothing that warrants the taking of my life, I deny that my life is in any man's power, or in that of any court on earth.'

" ' Very well,' said he, ' we shall not attempt to settle this problematical point at present. But I have showed you much kindness in my time. Will you promise me this,—that for forty-eight hours you will not give me up to justice? I have many important things to settle. But it would be unfair to deprive you of your reward, which would be a fortune to you. Therefore, all that I request of you is to grant me forty-eight hours before you deliver me up to justice. After that period I care not how soon. I shall deliver up myself, and take my chance for that part of it. Will you promise me this?'

" ' I will,' said I. ' There is my hand on it.' I was conscious I was doing wrong, but I *could* not help it. He thanked me, shook my hand, and squeezed it, and said he expected as much from my generous nature, adding, ' It is highly ungenerous of the E——les this procedure,—d——bly ungenerous of them and their friends. But they do not know all. I wish they did, which they never will, nor ever can now.'

" ' No,' said I, ' they do not know that you robbed and murdered their kinsman and brother, Mr Thomas of Castle-Meldin.'

" He stared me in the face—his lip quivered—his shrivelled cheek turned into a ghastly paleness, and his bloodshot eye darted backward as it were into the ventricles of the brain. ' Hold your peace, sir ; I never robbed the person of man or woman in my life !' said he, vehemently.

" ' True, the dead body might have been robbed, though not by your hands, yet by your orders,' said I. ' And that you murdered him, or caused him to be murdered,

I know as well as that I now see you standing before me.'

"'It will haply puzzle you to prove that,' said he; 'but no more of it. Here is a sealed note, which you may open and peruse at your leisure. It will convince you more of my innocence than any thing I can say.'— And so saying, he went up to his deputy at the bank, and conferred with him a few minutes, and then went as if into one of the back boxes, and I saw no more of him.

"I was sensible I had done wrong, but yet knew not well how I could have done otherwise, being ignorant of the mode of arresting culprits in that strange country. I resolved, however, to keep my word, and at the same time take measures for the fulfilment of my duty. But the first thing I did was to open the note, which was to convince me of my old master's innocence; and behold it was a blank, only enclosing a cheque on a house in Leghorn for a thousand gold ducats.

"I was quite affronted at this. It was such a quiz on my honesty as I had never experienced. But what could I do? I could do nothing with it but put it up in my pocket, and while I was standing in deep meditation how to proceed, I was accosted by an old gentleman, who inquired if I had been a former acquaintance of the Baron's?

"'Of the Baron's? what Baron?' said I.

"'De Iskar,' said he, 'Baron Guillaume de Iskar, the gentleman who addressed you so familiarly just now?'

"I replied that I was an old acquaintance, having known him many years in a distant quarter of the world.

"'That will be viewed as a singular incident here,' said he; 'and will excite intense curiosity, as you are the only gentleman that ever entered Florence who knows any thing where he has sojourned, or to what country he belongs. And I do assure you, he does not miss to lie under dark suspicions; for, though he has the riches of an empire, none knows from whence they flow, and he is never seen save in this hall; for as to his own house, no stranger was ever known to enter it.'

"'I am engaged to be there, however,' said I; 'and,

supposing that every one would know his direction, I forgot to take it from himself.'

" ' His house is not a hundred yards from where we stand,' said he ; ' and has a private entrance to this suite of rooms ; but as for his outer gate, it is never opened.

" This being the very information I wanted, I left the garrulous old gentleman abruptly, and went in search of my master, to whom I related the fact, that I had discovered the mysterious assassin of his three relatives, and requested him to lose no time in procuring a legal warrant from the Grand Duke, and the other authorities, for his apprehension. The interest of the Count Sonnini easily procured us all that was required, and what assistance we judged requisite for securing the delinquent ; but yet, before the forms were all gone through, it was the evening of the next day. In the mean time, the Count set spies on the premises to prevent the Baron's escape, for he seemed the most intent of all for securing him, and engaged all who hired horses and carriages in the city, to send him information of every one engaged for thirty successive hours, for I was still intent on redeeming my pledge. At midnight, we were informed that two coaches were engaged from the Bridge hotel, at two in the morning, but where they were to take up the passengers was not known. I had four policemen well mounted, and four horsemen of the guard, and myself was the ninth. Signor Veccia, the head of the police, had the command, but was obliged to act by my directions. At the hour appointed the carriages started from the hotel. We dogged them to the corner of the Duke's palazzo, where a party of gentlemen, muffled up in cloaks, entered hastily, and the carriages drove off in different directions, one towards Costello, and the other towards Leghorn. We knew not what to do. Veccia got into a great rage at me, and swore most fearfully, for he wanted to take up the whole party at once on suspicion, but I would not consent to it ; for I always acted wrong, although at present I believed myself to be standing on a point of high honour.

" ' I must follow this one,' said Veccia; 'because it
will soon be out of the Duke's territories; and if the
party once reach the Church's dominions, I dare not
touch one of them. Take you four horsemen. I'll take
three; and do you follow that carriage till you ascertain,
at least, who is in it. I shall keep close sight of this,
for here the offender is sure to be, though I do not know
him.'

" We then galloped off, in order to keep within hearing of the carriage-wheels, but it was with the greatest
difficulty we could trace them, short as their start had
been; for they had crossed at the lowest bridge, and then
turned up a lane at a right angle; and this circuitous way
of setting out almost convinced me that the Baron was
in that carriage. At a place called Empoli, on the left
bank of the Arno, a long stage from Florence, we missed
them, and rode on. They had turned abruptly into a
court, and alighted to change the horses, while we kept
on the road towards Leghorn for four miles, before we
learned that no carriage had passed that way. This was
a terrible rebuff. We had nothing for it but to take a
short refreshment, and return to Empoli, where we learned that the carriage with two muffled gentlemen in it,
had set out to the southward with fresh horses, and was
an hour and a half a-head of us. A clean pursuit now
ensued, but not for twenty miles did we come again in
sight of the carriage, and then it was going on again with
fresh horses, at the rate of from ten to twelve miles an
hour. My time was now expired, and I was at full liberty to give one of the greatest wretches, who ever
breathed the breath of life, up to justice. But how to
reach him, there lay the difficulty; for the guardsmen
would not leave their own horses, and were beginning to
get rather cross at so long and so vain a pursuit.

" I gave each of our horses a bottle of wine, which
recruited their spirits remarkably; and neither did I spare
the best of wine upon their riders. After a run of I
daresay seventy and odd miles, (considering the round-
about ways we took,) we fairly run the old fox to earth.

at an old town called Peombyna, or some such name; and just as he and his friend stepped out of the carriage, there were the guards, policemen, and I, entering the court. He rushed into the hotel. I gave the word and followed; but at the very first entry to the house, the number of entries confused me, and I lost him. Not so the policemen; inured to their trade, they kept watch outside, and it was not long till one of them gave the alarm in the back settlements, the Baron having escaped by a window. I was with the policemen in a minute, for I flew out of the same window; and the back of the hotel being toward the cliff that surrounds the town all toward the island of Elba, he had no other retreat but into that. I think he was not aware of what was before him, for he was at least an hundred and fifty yards before us; but when he came to the point of the promontory he looked hastily all around, and perceiving no egress, he faced around, presenting a large horse pistol in every hand. We were armed with a pistol each, and sabres. I would nevertheless gladly have waited for the coming up of our assistants, now when we had him at bay. But whether from fondness of the high reward, or mere temerity, I know not, only certain it is Cesario the policeman would not be restrained. I rather drew back, not caring to rush on a desperate man with two cocked pistols presented, and pistols of such length, too, that they would have shot any man through the body at thirty yards distance, while ours were mere crackers. But Cesario mocked me, and ran forward, so that I was fain to accompany him. Mr Southman, *alias* Guillaume Suddermens Baron de Iskar, stood there undaunted, with a derisive grin, presenting his two huge pistols. We held out our two little ones, still advancing. Luckily I was on the right hand, as behoved the commander of the expedition, and of course opposed to his left hand pistol, which lessened my chance of being shot. For all that, I could not for my life help sidling half behind Cesario the policeman. When we came, as far as I remember, close upon him, even so close as seven or eight yards, he

and Cesario fired both at the same instant. The latter fell.
I rushed onward ; and, not having time to change hands, he
fired his pistol almost close on my face. As the Lord graci-
ously decreed, he missed. 'Now, wretch, I have you!' cried
I ; 'therefore yield, and atone for all your horrid crimes !'

"My three armed assistants came running along the
verge of the cliff which draws to a point; and escape being impossible, he, without so much as shrinking, took a
race, and leaped from the top of that fearful precipice. I
believe he entertained a last hope of clearing the rock
and plunging into the tide; but I being close upon him,
even so close as to have stretched out my hand to lay
hold of him, saw his descent. He had not well begun
to descend, ere he uttered a loud scream; yet it was a
scream more of derision than terror. We perceived that
he had taken a wrong direction, and that he had not
cleared the whole cliff. A jutting point touched him,
and, as I thought, scarcely touched him, ere he plunged
head foremost into the sea.

" He made no effort to swim or move, but floated seaward
with his head down below water. I cried to my assistants to save his life, for the sake of all that was dear to
the relations of the murdered persons. But they were
long in finding their way behind those fearful rocks, for
though there was a cut stair, they did not know of it, and
before they got him to land, he was 'past speaking ;' for
his left loin was out of joint, and his back-bone broken.
We carried him to the hotel, and took all the pains of
him we could, for I had great hopes of a last confession,
explaining his motives for putting so many innocent persons of high rank to death. The satisfaction was, however, denied me. As long as he knew me, he only
shewed a ferocity indicative of hatred and revenge. The
next morning he died, and the motives which urged him
on to the murders he committed, must in part remain a
mystery till the day of doom.

" It was said in England that the circumstance of his
having got a carriage, horses, and servant from Castle-
Meldin indicated a commission from one or another of

that family. I think differently; and that he got these on false pretences. That he was a wooer of Miss Fanny's, and the favoured one by the family, I afterwards satisfactorily ascertained; but on what account he exacted so dreadful a retribution, both of the lady herself and the favoured lover, it is in vain endeavouring to calculate with any degree of certainty, for the moving principles of his dark soul were inscrutable.

"That the young and gallant Lord E——le was foully betrayed to his death, was afterwards satisfactorily proved. A stranger, suiting Mr Southman's description, called on him and spent the greater part of the day with him, and the two seemed on the most friendly terms. Toward evening a gentleman called with a note to Lord E——le. and requested an answer. This was a challenge, a forged one doubtless, signed Ashley or Aspley, it could not be distinguished which, requesting a meeting at an early hour of the morning, on some pretended point of honour. The young lord instantly accepted the challenge, and naturally asked his associate to accompany him as second; so the two continued at the wine over night, and rode out together at break of day. So that it is quite apparent he had taken the opportunity of shooting him behind his back, while waiting in vain on the common for their opponents. The death of the lovely Fanny, and that of her amiable brother, as they exceed other acts in cruelty, so they do in mystery. But it became probable that all these murders formed only a modicum of what that unaccountable wretch had perpetrated.

"His body, and that of poor Cesario the too brave policeman, we took back with us in the carriage to Florence, but what became of the gentleman who fled along with the Baron, was never known. He was probably an accomplice; but we were too long in thinking of him.

"The story, which I was called to relate before the Grand Duke, created a horrible interest in Florence, while every circumstance was corroborated by my lord and lady. The travelling trunk belonging to the deceased was opened. It contained great riches, which were claimed by the Arch-duke as the property of the state. I thought my assistants and I had the best right to them, but I said little, having secured a thousand gold ducats before. We, however, got a share of this likewise.

"In his house was found a young lady of great beauty, whom he had brought up and educated, and two female domestics; but they only knew him as the Baron de Iskar (or rather Ischel, as they pronounced it,) and little could be elicited from them save that there were often nightly meetings in his house. But when his strong-box was opened, the keys of which were found in his trunk, such store of riches and jewels of all descriptions never before appeared in Florence. It had been the depository of all the brigands in Italy, if not of Europe, for there were trinkets in it of every nation. Among other things, there were twenty-seven English gold watch-es, and a diamond necklace which had once belonged to the Queen of France, valued at L.500,000. The state of Tuscany was enriched, and a more overjoyed man than Duke Ferdinand I never saw. And it having been wholly in and through my agency that he obtained all this trea-sure, his commendations of me were without bounds. He indeed gave me some rich presents, but rather, as I thought, with a grudge, and a sparing hand; but to make amends for his parsimony, he created me a peer of the Duchy, by the title of Baron St Gio, with the heritage of an old fortalice of that name.

"It would not do for me to serve any more my be-loved lord and lady, for it would have been laughable to have heard them calling 'Sir Baron,' or 'My Lord St Gio, bring me so and so;' therefore was I obliged to hire a separate house of my own wherein to see my friends, although I lived most with my benefactors. I had besides another motive for this, which was to marry the beautiful young ward of the late Baron de Iskar, whom I conceived to be now left destitute. Her name was Rose Weiland, of Flemish extract, and natural qualities far above com-mon; so we were married with great feasting and re-joicing, about a month before we left Florence."

It turned out that this lovely Fleming, Rose Weiland, now lady St Gio, who was thus left destitute, proved herself to have had some good natural qualities. She had helped herself liberally of the robber's store, for she had one casket of jewels alone which her husband admits to have been worth an earldom. Riches now flowed on our new baron, for besides all that he amassed at Florence and all that his spouse brought him, he exacted the full of the offered reward from his benefactors, which amounted to a great sum. He brought his lady to Lancashire, but she disliked the country, and they retired to Flanders, and there purchased an estate. She was living so late as 1736, for she was visited in the summer of that year by Lady Helen Douglas, and the Honourable Mrs Murray, at her villa on the Seine, above Brussels. Into her hands she put several curiosities of former days, and among others her deceased husband's MS. from which I have extracted these eventful incidents.

----

THE

# MYSTERIOUS BRIDE.

A GREAT number of people now-a-days are beginning broadly to insinuate that there are no such things as ghosts, or spiritual beings visible to mortal sight. Even Sir Walter Scott is turned renegade, and, with his stories made up of half-and-half, like Nathaniel Gow's toddy, is trying to throw cold water on the most certain, though most impalpable, phenomena of human nature. The bodies are daft. Heaven mend their wits! Before they had ventured to assert such things, I wish they had been where I have often been; or, in particular, where the

Laird of Birkendelly was on St Lawrence's Eve, in the year 1777, and sundry times subsequent to that.

Be it known, then, to every reader of this relation of facts that happened in my own remembrance, that the road from Birkendelly to the great muckle village of Balmawhapple, (commonly called the muckle town, in opposition to the little town that stood on the other side of the burn,)—that road, I say, lay between two thorn hedges, so well kept by the Laird's hedger, so close, and so high, that a rabbit could not have escaped from the highway into any of the adjoining fields. Along this road was the Laird riding on the Eve of St Lawrence, in a careless, indifferent manner, with his hat to one side, and his cane dancing a hornpipe on the curtch of the saddle before him. He was moreover, chanting a song to himself, and I have heard people tell what song it was too. There was once a certain, or rather uncertain, bard, ycleped Robert Burns, who made a number of good songs; but this that the Laird sung was an amorous song of great antiquity, which, like all the said bard's best songs, was sung one hundred and fifty years before he was born. It began thus :

> " I am the Laird of Windy-wa's,
> I cam nae here without a cause,
> An' I hae gotten forty fa's
>   In coming o'er the knowe, joe.
> The night it is baith wind and weet;
> The morn it will be snaw and sleet;
> My shoon are frozen to my feet;
>   O, rise an' let me in, joe !
>     Let me in this ae night," &c. &c.

This song was the Laird singing, while, at the same time, he was smudging and laughing at the catastrophe, when, ere ever aware, he beheld, a short way before him, an uncommonly elegant and beautiful girl walking in the same direction with him. " Aye," said the Laird to himself, " here is something very attractive indeed ! Where the deuce can she have sprung from ? She must have risen out of the earth, for I never saw her till this breath. Well, I declare I have not seen such a female figure—I wish I had such an assignation with her as the Laird of Windy-wa's had with his sweetheart."

As the Laird was half-thinking, half-speaking this to himself, the enchanting creature looked back at him with a motion of intelligence that she knew what he was half-saying, half-thinking, and then vanished over the summit of the rising ground before him, called the Birky Brow. " Aye, go your ways !" said the Laird ; "I see by you, you'll not be very hard to overtake. Yon cannot get off the road, and I'll have a chat with you before you make the Deer's Den."

The Laird jogged on. He did not sing the " Laird of Windy-wa's" any more, for he felt a sort of stifling about his heart ; but he often repeated to himself, " She's a very fine woman !—a very fine woman indeed—and to be walking here by herself! I cannot comprehend it."

When he reached the summit of the Birky Brow he did not see her, although he had a longer view of the road than before. He thought this very singular, and began to suspect that she wanted to escape him, although apparently rather lingering on him before. " I shall have another look at her, however," thought the Laird ; and off he set at a flying trot. No. He came first to one turn, then another. There was nothing of the young lady to be seen. " Unless she take wings and fly away, I shall be up with her," quoth the Laird ; and off he set at the full gallop.

In the middle of his career he met with Mr M'Murdie of Aulton, who hailed him with, "Hilloa! Birkendelly ! where the deuce are you flying at that rate?"

" I was riding after a woman," said the Laird, with great simplicity, reining in his steed.

" Then I am sure no woman on earth can long escape you, unless she be in an air balloon."

" I don't know that. Is she far gone ?"

" In which way do you mean ?"

" In this."

" Aha-ha-ha! Hee-hee-hee!" nichered M'Murdie, misconstruing the Laird's meaning.

" What do you laugh at, my dear sir? Do you know her, then?"

" Ho-ho-ho! Hee-hee-hee! How should I, or how can I, know her, Birkendelly, unless you inform me who she is?"

" Why, that is the very thing I want to know of you. I mean the young lady whom you met just now."

" You are raving, Birkendelly. I met no young lady, nor is there a single person on the road I have come by, while you know, that for a mile and a half forward your way, she could not get out of it."

" I know that," said the Laird, biting his lip, and looking greatly puzzled; " but confound me if I understand this; for I was within speech of her just now on the top of the Birky Brow there; and, when I think of it, she could not have been even thus far as yet. She had on a pure white gauze frock, a small green bonnet and feathers, and a green veil, which, flung back over her left shoulder, hung below her waist; and was altogether such an engaging figure, that no man could have passed her on the road without taking some note of her.—Are you not making game of me? Did you not really meet with her?"

" On my word of truth and honour, I did not. Come, ride back with me, and we shall meet her still, depend on it. She has given you the go-by on the road. Let us go; I am only going to call at the mill about some barley for the distillery, and will return with you to the big town."

Birkendelly returned with his friend. The sun was not yet set, yet M'Murdie could not help observing that the Laird looked thoughtful and confused, and not a word could he speak about any thing save this lovely apparition with the white frock and the green veil; and lo, when they reached the top of the Birky Brow, there was the maiden again before them, and exactly at the same spot where the Laird first saw her before, only walking in the contrary direction.

" Well, this is the most extraordinary thing that I ever knew!" exclaimed the Laird.

" What is it, sir ?" said M'Murdie.

" How that young lady could have eluded me," returned the Laird ; " see, here she is still."

"I beg your pardon, sir, I don't see her. Where is she ?"

" There, on the other side of the angle ; but you are short-sighted. See, there she is ascending the other eminence in her white frock and green veil, as I told you. —What a lovely creature !"

" Well, well, we have her fairly before us now, and shall see what she is like at all events," said M'Murdie.

Between the Birky Brow and this other slight eminence, there is an obtuse angle of the road at the part where it is lowest, and, in passing this, the two friends necessarily lost sight of the object of their curiosity. They pushed on at a quick pace—cleared the low angle—the maiden was not there ! They rode full speed to the top of the eminence from whence a long extent of road was visible before them—there was no human creature in view ! M'Murdie laughed aloud ; but the Laird turned pale as death, and bit his lip. His friend asked at him good-humouredly, why he was so much affected. He said, because he could not comprehend the meaning of this singular apparition or illusion ; and it troubled him the more, as he now remembered a dream of the same nature which he had had, and which terminated in a dreadful manner.

" Why, man, you are dreaming still," said M'Murdie ; " but never mind. It is quite common for men of your complexion to dream of beautiful maidens, with white frocks and green veils, bonnets, feathers, and slender waists. It is a lovely image, the creation of your own sanguine imagination, and you may worship it without any blame. Were her shoes black or green ?—And her stockings, did you note them ? The symmetry of the limbs, I am sure you did! Good-bye ; I see you are not disposed to leave the spot. Perhaps she will appear to you again."

So saying, M'Murdie rode on towards the mill, and Birkendelly, after musing for some time, turned his beast's head slowly round, and began to move towards the great muckle village.

The Laird's feelings were now in terrible commotion. He was taken beyond measure with the beauty and elegance of the figure he had seen; but he remembered, with a mixture of admiration and horror, that a dream of the same enchanting object had haunted his slumbers all the days of his life; yet, how singular that he should never have recollected the circumstance till now! But farther, with the dream there were connected some painful circumstances, which, though terrible in their issue, he could not recollect so as to form them into any degree of arrangement.

As he was considering deeply of these things, and riding slowly down the declivity, neither dancing his cane, nor singing the "Laird of Windywa's," he lifted up his eyes, and there was the girl on the same spot where he saw her first, walking deliberately up the Birky Brow. The sun was down; but it was the month of August, and a fine evening, and the Laird, seized with an unconquerable desire to see and speak with that incomparable creature, could restrain himself no longer, but shouted out to her to stop till he came up. She beckoned acquiescence, and slackened her pace into a slow movement. The Laird turned the corner quickly, but when he had rounded it, the maiden was still there, though on the summit of the Brow. She turned round, and, with an ineffable smile and curtsy, saluted him, and again moved slowly on. She vanished gradually beyond the summit, and while the green feathers were still nodding in view and so nigh, that the Laird could have touched them with a fishing-rod, he reached the top of the Brow himself. There was no living soul there, nor onward, as far as his view reached. He now trembled every limb, and, without knowing what he did, rode straight on to the big town, not daring well to return and see what he had seen for three several times; and, certain he would see it again when the shades of evening were deepening, he deemed it proper and prudent to decline the pursuit of such a phantom any farther.

He alighted at the Queen's Head, called for some brandy and water, quite forgot what was his errand to the great muckle town that afternoon, there being nothing visible to his mental sight but lovely fairy images, with white gauze frocks and green veils. His friend, Mr M'Murdie, joined him; they drank deep, bantered, reasoned, got angry, reasoned themselves calm again, and still all would not do. The Laird was conscious that he had seen the beautiful apparition, and, moreover, that she was the very maiden, or the resemblance of her, who, in the irrevocable decrees of Providence, was destined to be his. It was in vain that M'Murdie reasoned of impressions on the imagination, and

"Of fancy moulding in the mind,
Light visions on the passing wind."

Vain also was a story that he told him of a relation of his own, who was greatly harassed by the apparition of an officer in a red uniform, that haunted him day and night, and had very nigh put him quite distracted several times; till at length his physician found out the nature of this illusion so well, that he knew, from the state of his pulse, to an hour when the ghost of the officer would appear; and by bleeding, low diet, and emollients, contrived to keep the apparition away altogether.

The Laird admitted the singularity of this incident, but not that it was one in point; for the one, he said, was imaginary, and the other real; and that no conclusions could convince him in opposition to the authority of his own senses. He accepted of an invitation to spend a few days with M'Murdie and his family; but they all acknowledged afterwards that the Laird was very much like one bewitched.

As soon as he reached home, he went straight to the Birky Brow, certain of seeing once more the angelic phantom; but she was not there. He took each of his former positions again and again, but the desired vision would in nowise make its appearance. He tried every day, and every hour of the day, all with the same effect, till he grew absolutely desperate, and had the audacity to kneel on the spot, and entreat of Heaven to see her. Yes, he called on Heaven to see her once more, whatever she was, whether a being of earth, heaven, or hell!

He was now in such a state of excitement that he could not exist; he grew listless, impatient, and sickly; took to his bed, and sent for M'Murdie and the doctor; and the issue of the consultation was, that Birkendelly consented to leave the country for a season, on a visit to his only sister in Ireland, whither we must accompany him for a short space.

His sister was married to Captain Bryan, younger of Scoresby, and they two lived in a cottage on the estate, and the Captain's parents and sisters at Scoresby Hall. Great was the stir and preparation when the gallant young Laird of Birkendelly arrived at the cottage, it never being doubted that he came to forward a second bond of connection with the family, which still contained seven dashing sisters, all unmarried, and all alike willing to change that solitary and helpless state for the envied one of matrimony—a state highly popular among the young women of Ireland. Some of the Misses Bryan had now reached the years of womanhood, several of them scarcely; but these small disqualifications made no difference in the estimation of the young ladies themselves; each and all of them brushed up for the competition, with high hopes and unflinching resolutions. True, the elder ones, tried to check the younger in their good-natured, forthright, Irish way; but they retorted, and persisted in their superior pretensions. Then there was such shopping in the county-town! It was so boundless, that the credit of the Hall was finally exhausted, and the old squire was driven to remark, that "Och and to be sure it was a dreadful and tirrabell concussion, to be put upon the equipment of seven daughters all at the same moment, as if the young gentleman could marry them all! Och, then, poor dear shoul, he would be after finding that one was sufficient, if not one too many. And therefore, there was no occasion, none at all, at all, and that there was not, for any of them to rig out more than one."

It was hinted that the Laird had some reason for complaint at this time; but as the lady sided with her daughters, he had no chance. One of the items of his account was, thirty-seven buckling-combs, then greatly in vogue. There were black combs, pale combs, yellow combs, and gilt ones, all to suit or set off various complexions; and if other articles bore any proportion at all to these, it had been better for the Laird and all his family that Birkendelly had never set foot in Ireland.

The plan was all concocted. There was to be a grand dinner at the Hall, at which the damsels were to appear in all their finery. A ball was to follow, and note be taken which of the young ladies was their guest's choice, and measures taken accordingly. The dinner and the ball took place; and what a pity I may not describe that entertainment, the dresses, and the dancers, for they were all exquisite in their way, and *outré* beyond measure. But such details only serve to derange a winter evening's tale such as this.

Birkendelly having at this time but one model for his choice among womankind, all that ever he did while in the presence of ladies, was to look out for some resemblance to her, the angel of his fancy; and it so happened, that in one of old Bryan's daughters named Luna, or more familiarly, Loony, he perceived, or thought he perceived, some imaginary similarity in form and air to the lovely apparition. This was the sole reason why he was incapable of taking his eyes off from her the whole of that night; and this incident settled the point, not only with the old people, but even the young ladies were forced, after every exertion on their own parts, to " yild the pint to their sister Loony, who certainly was nit the mist genteelest nor mist handsomest of that guid-lucking fimily."

The next day Lady Luna was dispatched off to the

cottage in grand style, there to live hand and glove with her supposed lover. There was no standing all this. There were the two parrocked together, like a ewe and a lamb, early and late; and though the Laird really appeared to have, and probably had, some delight in her company, it was only in contemplating that certain indefinable air of resemblance which she bore to the sole image impressed on his heart. He bought her a white gause frock, a green bonnet and feathers, with a veil, which she was obliged to wear thrown over her left shoulder; and every day after, six times a-day, was she obliged to walk over a certain eminence at a certain distance before her lover. She was delighted to oblige him; but still when he came up, he looked disappointed, and never said, "Luna, I love you; when are we to be married?" No, he never said any such thing, for all her looks and expressions of fondest love; for, alas, in all this dalliance, he was only feeding a mysterious flame, that preyed upon his vitals, and proved too severe for the powers either of reason or religion to extinguish. Still time flew lighter and lighter by, his health was restored, the bloom of his cheek returned, and the frank and simple confidence of Luna had a certain charm with it, that reconciled him to his sister's Irish economy. But a strange incident now happened to him which deranged all his immediate plans.

He was returning from angling one evening, a little before sunset, when he saw Lady Luna awaiting him on his way home. But instead of brushing up to meet him as usual, she turned, and walked up the rising ground before him. "Poor sweet girl! how condescending she is," said he to himself, "and how like she is in reality to the angelic being whose form and features are so deeply impressed on my heart! I now see it is no fond or fancied resemblance. It is real! real! real! How I long to clasp her in my arms, and tell her how I love her; for, after all that is the girl that is to be mine, and the former a vision to impress this the more on my heart."

He posted up the ascent to overtake her. When at the top she turned, smiled, and curtsied. Good heavens!

it was the identical lady of his fondest adoration herself, but lovelier, far lovelier than ever. He expected every moment that she would vanish as was her wont; but she did not—she awaited him, and received his embraces with open arms. She was a being of real flesh and blood, courteous, elegant, and affectionate. He kissed her hand, he kissed her glowing cheek, and blessed all the powers of love who had thus restored her to him again, after undergoing pangs of love such as man never suffered.

"But, dearest heart, here we are standing in the middle of the highway," said he; "suffer me to conduct you to my sister's house, where you shall have an apartment with a child of nature having some slight resemblance to yourself." She smiled, and said, "No, I will not sleep with Lady Luna to-night. Will you please to look round you, and see where you are." He did so, and behold they were standing on the Birky Brow, on the only spot where he had ever seen her. She smiled at his embarrassed look, and asked if he did not remember aught of his coming over from Ireland. He said he thought he did remember something of it, but love with him had long absorbed every other sense. He then asked her to his own house, which she declined, saying she could only meet him on that spot till after their marriage, which could not be before St Lawrence's Eve come three years. "And now," said she, "we must part. My name is Jane Ogilvie, and you were betrothed to me before you were born. But I am come to release you this evening, if you have the slightest objection."

He declared he had none; and, kneeling, swore the most solemn oath to be hers for ever, and to meet her there on St Lawrence's Eve next, and every St Lawrence's Eve until that blessed day on which she had consented to make him happy, by becoming his own for ever. She then asked him affectionately to exchange rings with her, in pledge of their faith and truth, in which he joyfully acquiesced; for she could not have then asked any conditions, which, in the fulness of his heart's love, he would not have granted; and after one fond and affectionate kiss, and repeating all their engagements over again they parted.

Birkendelly's heart was now melted within him, and all his senses overpowered by one overwhelming passion. On leaving his fair and kind one, he got bewildered, and could not find the road to his own house, believing sometimes that he was going there, and sometimes to his sister's, till at length he came, as he thought, upon the Liffey, at its junction with Loch Allan; and there, in attempting to call for a boat, he awoke from a profound sleep, and found himself lying in his bed within his sister's house, and the day sky just breaking.

If he was puzzled to account for some things in the course of his dream, he was much more puzzled to account for them now that he was wide awake. He was sensible that he had met his love, had embraced, kissed, and exchanged vows and rings with her, and, in token of the truth and reality of all these, her emerald ring was on his finger, and his own away; so there was no doubt that they had met,—by what means it was beyond the power of man to calculate.

There was then living with Mrs Bryan an old Scots. woman, commonly styled Lucky Black. She had nursed Birkendelly's mother, and been dry nurse to himself and sister; and having more than a mother's attachment for the latter, when she was married, old Lucky left her country, to spend the last of her days in the house of her beloved young lady. When the Laird entered the breakfast parlour that morning, she was sitting in her black velvet hood, as usual, reading " The Fourfold State of Man " and being paralytic and somewhat deaf, she seldom regarded those who went out or came in. But chancing to hear him say something about the ninth of August, she quitted reading, turned round her head to listen, and then asked, in a hoarse tremulous voice, "What's that he's saying? What's the unlucky callant saying about the ninth of August? Aih? To be sure it is St Lawrence's Eve, although the tenth be his day

It's ower true, ower true! ower true for him an' a' his kin, poor man! Aih? What was he saying then?"

The men smiled at her incoherent earnestness, but the lady, with true feminine condescension, informed her, in a loud voice, that Allan had an engagement in Scotland on St Lawrence's Eve. She then started up, extended her shrivelled hands, that shook like the aspen, and panted out, " Aih, aih? Lord preserve us! whaten an engagement has he on St Lawrence Eve? Bind him! bind him! shackle him wi' bands of steel, and of brass, and of iron!—O, may He whose blessed will was pleased to leave him an orphan sae soon, preserve him from the fate which I tremble to think on!"

She then tottered round the table, as with supernatural energy, and seizing the Laird's right hand, she drew it close to her unstable eyes, and then perceiving the emerald ring chased in blood, she threw up her arms with a jerk, opened her skinny jaws with a fearful gape, and uttering a shriek, that made all the house yell, and every one within it to tremble, she fell back lifeless and rigid on the floor. The gentlemen both fled, out of sheer terror; but a woman never deserts her friends in extremity. The lady called her maids about her, had her old nurse conveyed to bed, where every means were used to restore animation. But, alas! life was extinct! The vital spark had fled for ever, which filled all their hearts with grief, disappointment, and horror, as some dreadful tale of mystery was now sealed up from their knowledge, which in all likelihood, no other could reveal. But to say the truth, the Laird did not seem greatly disposed to probe it to the bottom.

Not all the arguments of Captain Bryan and his lady, nor the simple entreaties of Lady Luna, could induce Birkendelly to put off his engagement to meet his love on the Birky Brow on the evening of the 9th of August; but he promised soon to return, pretending that some business of the utmost importance called him away. Before he went, however, he asked his sister if ever she had heard of such a lady in Scotland as Jane Ogilvie.

Mrs Bryan repeated the name many times to herself, and said, that name undoubtedly was once familiar to her, although she thought not for good, but at that moment she did not recollect one single individual of the name. He then showed her the emerald ring that had been the death of old Lucky Black; but the moment the lady looked at it, she made a grasp at it to take it off by force, which she had very nearly effected. "O, burn it, burn it!" cried she; "it is not a right ring! Burn it!"

"My dear sister, what fault is in the ring?" said he. "It is a very pretty ring, and one that I set great value by."

"O, for Heaven's sake, burn it, and renounce the giver!" cried she. "If you have any regard for your peace here, or your soul's welfare hereafter, burn that ring! If you saw with your own eyes, you would easily perceive that that is not a ring befitting a Christian to wear."

This speech confounded Birkendelly a good deal. He retired by himself and examined the ring, and could see nothing in it unbecoming a Christian to wear. It was a chased gold ring, with a bright emerald, which last had a red foil, in some lights giving it a purple gleam, and inside was engraven "*Elegit*," much defaced, but that his sister could not see; therefore he could not comprehend her vehement injunctions concerning it. But that it might no more give her offence, or any other, he sewed it within his vest, opposite his heart, judging that there was something in it which his eyes were withholden from discerning.

Thus he left Ireland with his mind in great confusion, groping his way, as it were, in a hole of mystery, yet with the passion that preyed on his heart and vitals more intense than ever. He seems to have had an impression all his life that some mysterious fate awaited him, which the correspondence of his dreams and day visions tended to confirm. And though he gave himself wholly up to the sway of one overpowering passion, it was not without some yearnings of soul, manifestations of terror, and so much earthly shame, that he never more mentioned his love, or his engagements, to any human being, not even to his friend M'Murdie, whose company he forthwith shunned.

It is on this account that I am unable to relate what passed between the lovers thenceforward. It is certain they met at the Birky Brow that St Lawrence's Eve, for they were seen in company together; but of the engagements, vows, or dalliance, that passed between them, I can say nothing; nor of all their future meetings, until the beginning of August 1781, when the Laird began decidedly to make preparations for his approaching marriage; yet not as if he and his betrothed had been to reside at Birkendelly, all his provisions rather bespeaking a meditated journey.

On the morning of the 9th, he wrote to his sister, and then arraying himself in his new wedding suit, and putting the emerald ring on his finger, he appeared all impatience, until towards evening, when he sallied out on horseback to his appointment. It seems that his mysterious inamorata had met him, for he was seen riding through the big town before sunset, with a young lady behind him, dressed in white and green, and the villagers affirmed that they were riding at the rate of fifty miles an hour! They were seen to pass a cottage called Mosskilt, ten miles farther on, where there was no highway, at the same tremendous speed; and I could never hear that they were any more seen, until the following morning, when Birkendelly's fine bay horse was found lying dead at his own stable door; and shortly after, his master was likewise discovered lying a blackened corpse on the Birky Brow, at the very spot where the mysterious, but lovely dame, had always appeared to him. There was neither wound, bruise, nor dislocation, in his whole frame; but his skin was of a livid colour, and his features terribly distorted.

This woful catastrophe struck the neighbourhood with great consternation, so that nothing else was talked of. Every ancient tradition and modern incident were raked

together, compared, and combined; and certainly a most
rare concatenation of misfortunes was elicited. It was
authenticated that his father had died on the same spot
that day twenty years, and his grandfather that day forty
years, the former, as was supposed, by a fall from his
horse when in liquor, and the latter, nobody knew how;
and now this Allan was the last of his race, for Mrs Bryan
had no children.

It was moreover now remembered by many, and
among the rest by the Rev. Joseph Taylor, that he had
frequently observed a young lady, in white and green,
sauntering about the spot on a St Lawrence's Eve.

When Captain Bryan and his lady arrived to take
possession of the premises, they instituted a strict inquiry into every circumstance; but nothing farther than
what was related to them by Mr M'Murdie could be
learned of this Mysterious Bride, besides what the Laird's
own letter bore. It ran thus:—

"DEAREST SISTER,

"I shall before this time to-morrow, be the most
happy, or most miserable, of mankind, having solemnly
engaged myself this night to wed a young and beautiful
lady, named Jane Ogilvie, to whom it seems I was betrothed before I was born. Our correspondence has
been of a most private and mysterious nature; but my
troth is pledged, and my resolution fixed. We set out
on a far journey to the place of her abode on the nuptial
eve, so that it will be long before I see you again.

"Yours till death,

"ALLAN GEORGE SANDISON.
"*Birkendelly, August* 8th, 1781."

That very same year, an old woman, named Marion
Haw, was returned upon that, her native parish, from
Glasgow. She had led a migratory life with her son—
who was what he called a bell-hanger, but in fact a tinker
of the worst grade—for many years, and was at last
returned to the muckle town in a state of great destitu-

tion. She gave the parishioners a history of the Mysterious Bride, so plausibly correct, but withal so romantic, that every body said of it, (as is often said of my narratives, with the same narrow-minded prejudice and injustice,) that it was *a made story.* There were, however, some strong testimonies of its veracity.

She said the first Allan Sandison, who married the great heiress of Birkendelly, was previously engaged to a beautiful young lady, named Jane Ogilvie, to whom he gave any thing but fair play ; and, as she believed, either murdered her, or caused her to be murdered, in the midst of a thicket of birch and broom, at a spot which she mentioned ; that she had good reasons for believing so, as she had seen the red blood and the new grave, when she was a little girl, and ran home and mentioned it to her grandfather, who charged her as she valued her life never to mention that again, as it was only the nombles and hide of a deer, which he himself had buried there. But when twenty years subsequent to that, the wicked and unhappy Allan Sandison was found dead on that very spot, and lying across the green mound, then nearly level with the surface, which she had once seen a new grave, she then for the first time ever thought of a Divine Providence ; and she added, " For my grandfather, Neddy Haw, he dee'd too ; there's naebody kens how, nor ever shall."

As they were quite incapable of conceiving, from Marion's description, any thing of the spot, Mr M'Murdie caused her to be taken out to the Birky Brow in a cart, accompanied by Mr Taylor, and some hundreds of the townsfolks ; but whenever she saw it, she said, " Aha. birkies ! the haill kintra's altered now. There was nae road here then ; it gaed straight ower the tap o' the hill. An' let me see—there's the thorn where the cushats biggit ; an' there's the auld birk that I aince fell aff an' left my shoe sticking' i' the cleft. I can tell ye, birkies, either the deer's grave, or bonny Jane Ogilvie's, is no twa yards aff the place where that horse's hind feet are standin' ; sae ye may howk, an' see if there be ony remains."

The minister, and M'Murdie, and all the people, stared at one another, for they had purposely caused the horse to stand still on the very spot where both the father and son had been found dead. They digged, and deep, deep below the road, they found part of the slender bones and skull of a young female, which they deposited decently in the churchyard. The family of the Sandisons is extinct—the Mysterious Bride appears no more on the Eve of St Lawrence—and the wicked people of the great muckle village have got a lesson on Divine justice written to them in lines of blood.

---

NATURE'S

# MAGIC LANTERN.

It is well known, that, in warm summer mornings, the valleys among our mountains are generally filled with a dense white fog, so that, when the sun rises, the upper parts of the hills are all bathed yellow sheen, looking like golden islands in a sea of silver. After one ascends through the mist to within a certain distance of the sunshine, a halo of glory is thrown round his head, something like a rainbow, but brighter and paler. It is upright or slanting, as the sun is lower or higher; but it uniformly attends one for a considerable space before he reaches the sunshine. One morning, at the time when I was about nineteen years of age, I was ascending a hill-side towards the ewe-buchts, deeply absorbed in admiration of the halo around me, when suddenly my eyes fell upon a huge dark semblance of the human figure, which stood at a very small distance from me, and at first appeared to my affrighted imagination as the enemy of mankind. Without taking a moment to consider, I rushed from the spot, and never drew breath till I had got safe amongst the ewe-milkers. All that day, I felt very ill at ease ; but next morning, being obliged to go past the same spot at the same hour, I resolved to exert, if possible, a little more courage, and put the phenomenon fairly to the proof. The fog was more dense than on the preceding morning, and when the sun arose, his brilliancy and fervour were more bright above. The lovely halo was thrown around me, and at length I reached the haunted spot without diverging a step from my usual little footpath ; and at the very place there arose the same terrible apparition which had frightened me so much the morning before. It was a giant blackamoor, at least thirty feet high, and equally proportioned, and very near me. I was actually struck powerless with astonishment and terror. My first resolution was, if I could keep the power of my limbs, to run home and hide myself below the blankets, with the Bible beneath my head. But then again, I thought it was hard to let my master's 700 ewes go eild for fear of the de'il. In this perplexity (and I rather think I was crying) I took off my bonnet, and scratched my head bitterly with both hands ; when, to my astonishment and delight, the de'il also took off his bonnet, and scratched his head with both hands—but in such a style : Oh, there's no man can describe it ! His arms and his fingers were like trees and branches without the leaves. I laughed at him till I actually fell down upon the sward ; the de'il also fell down and laughed at me. I then noted, for the first time that he had two colley dogs at his foot, bigger than buffaloes. I arose, and made him a most graceful bow, which he returned at the same moment—but such a bow for awkwardness I never saw ! It was as if the Tron Kirk steeple had bowed to me. I turned my cheek to the sun as well as I could, that I might see the de'il's profile properly defined in the cloud. It was capital ! His nose was about half a yard long, and his face at least three yards ; and then he was gaping and laughing so, that one would have thought he might have swallowed the biggest man in the country.

It was quite a scene of enchantment. I could not leave it. On going five or six steps onward, it vanished; but, on returning to the same spot, there he stood, and I could make him make a fool of himself as much as I liked; but always as the sun rose higher, he grew shorter, so that, I think, could I have staid, he might have come into a respectable size of a de'il at the last.

I have seen this gigantic apparition several times since, but never half so well defined as that morning. It requires a certain kind of background which really I cannot describe; for, though I visited the place by day a hundred times, there was so little difference between the formation of that spot and the rest of the hill, that it is impossible to define it without taking a mathematical survey. The halo accompanies one always, but the gigantic apparition very seldom. I have seen it six or seven times in my life, always in a fog, and at sun-rising; but, saving these two times, never well defined, part being always light, and part dark.

One-and-twenty years subsequent to this, I was delighted to read the following note, translated, I think, from a German paper, concerning the Bogle of the Broken, an aërial figure of the very same description with mine, which is occasionally seen on one particular spot among the Hartz mountains, in Hanover. It was taken from the diary of a Mr Hawe, and I kept a copy of it for the remembrance of auld lang syne. I shall copy a sentence or two from it here; and really it is so like mine, that one would almost be tempted to think the one was copied from the other.

" Having ascended the Broken for the thirtieth time, I was at length so fortunate as to have the pleasure of seeing the phenomenon. The sun rose about four o'clock, and the atmosphere being quite serene toward the east, his rays could pass without any obstruction over the Hinrichshohe. In the south-west however, a brisk wind carried before it thin transparent vapours. About a quarter past four, I looked round to see if the atmosphere would permit me to have a free prospect to the south-west, when I observed, at a very great distance, a human figure, of a monstrous size. A violent gust of wind having nearly carried away my hat, I clapped my hand to it, by moving my arm towards my head, and the colossal figure did the same, on which the pleasure that I felt cannot be described ; for I had made already many a weary step, in the hopes of seeing this shadowy image, without being able to gratify my curiosity.

"I then called the landlord of the Broken (the neighbouring inn), and having both taken the same position which I had taken alone, we looked, but saw nothing. We had not, however, stood long, when two such colossal figures were formed over the above eminence. We retained our position, kept our eyes fixed on the same spot, and in a little time the two figures again stood before us, and were joined by a third. Every movement that we made, these figures imitated, but with this difference, that the phenomenon was sometimes weak and faintly defined, and sometimes strong and dark."

I can easily account for the latter part of the phenomenon ; for it could only be when the clouds of haze, or, as he calls them, " thin transparent vapours," were passing, that the shadows in the cloud could possibly be seen. But how there should have been *three* of them, and not either four, or only two, surpasses my comprehension altogether. It is quite out of nature ; and I am obliged to doubt either Mr Hawe's word or the accuracy of his optics.

Among the other strange sights which I have seen among the hills, I reckon one of the most curious to have been a double shadow of myself, at a moment when only the real sun was above the horizon. One morning, in April 1785, I was walking on the MoorBrae of Berry Knowe, gathering the ewes, when, to my utter astonishment, I perceived that I had two shadows. I immediately looked to the east, where the sun had just risen above the horizon, expecting to see two suns. But no—there was but one. There was not even one of those

mock suns called by us weather-gaws. Yet there was I
going to a certainty with two shadows—the one upright,
and well defined, and the other tall, dim, and leaning
backward, something like a very tall awkward servant
waiting upon and walking behind a little spruce master.
The tall one soon vanished, as I turned the hill into
a glen called Carsen's Cleuch; but I never forgot the
circumstance; and after I became an old man, I visited
the very spot, as nearly as I could remember, again and
again, thinking that the reflection of the sun from some
pool or lake which I had not perceived, might have
caused it; but there was no such thing. I never mentioned the circumstance to any living being before, save
to Sir D. Brewster, who, of all men I ever met with,
is the fondest of investigating every thing relating to
natural phenomena : he pretended to account for it by
some law of dioptrical refraction, which I did not understand.

But what I am now going to relate will scarcely procure credit, though, on the word of an honest man, it is
literally true. I once saw about two hundred natural
apparitions at one time, and altogether. One fine summer morning, as I was coming along the Hawkshaw rigg
of Blackhouse, I perceived on the other side of Douglas
Burn, in a little rich glen called Brakehope, a whole drove
of Highland cattle, which I thought could not be fewer
than ten scores. I saw them distinctly—I never saw
any beasts more distinctly in my life. I saw the black
ones, and the red ones, some with white faces, and four
or five spotted ones. I saw three men driving them, and
turning them quietly in at corners. They were on each
side of the burn of Brakehope, and quite from the drove
road. I was once thinking of going to them myself, but
I wanted my breakfast, was very hungry, and had no
charge of that part of the farm : so I hastened home, and
sent off the shepherd who had charge of it, to drive the
drove of cattle from his best land. His name was Robert
Borthwick. He seized a staff in high chagrin at the
drivers, and ran off; and Messrs William and George

Laidlaw both accompanied him, with good cudgels in their hands. They were both alive and well to testify the truth of my report: at least, when they went to Brakehope there were no cattle there, nor man, nor dogs, nor even sheep ! There was not a living creature in the bottom of the glen where I had seen the drove, nor the mark of a cow's hoof. I was of course laughed at as a dreamer and seer of visions ; for, in fact, after inquiring at our neighbours, we found that there was not a drove of Highland cattle at that time in the district. I was neither a dreamer nor a seer of visions. I was in the highest health and spirits. It was between eight and nine o'clock on a fine summer morning of mingled clouds and sunshine. I was chanting a song to myself, or perhaps making one, when I first came in view of the drove. I was rather more than half a mile from it, but not three quarters of a mile ; and as there never was a man had clearer sight than I had, I could not be mistaken in the appearance. In justification of myself, I must here copy two or three sentences from my note-book ; but from whence taken, I do not know.

" On Sunday evening, the 28th ultimo, as Anthony Jackson, farmer, aged forty-five, and Matthew Turner, the son of William Turner, farmer, aged fifteen years, while engaged in inspecting their cattle grazing in Hava-rah Park, near Ripley, part of the estate of Sir John Ingleby, Bart., they were suddenly surprised by a most extraordinary appearance in the park. Turner, whose attention was first drawn to the spectacle, said, ' Look, Anthony, what a quantity of beasts !' ' Beasts !' cried Anthony ; ' Lord bless us, they are not beasts, they are men !'

" By this time the body was in motion, and the spectators discovered that it was an army of soldiers dressed in a white military uniform, and that in the centre stood a personage of commanding aspect, clothed in scarlet. After performing a number of evolutions, the corps began to march in perfect order to the summit of a hill, passing the spectators only at the distance of about one hundred yards. No sooner had the first detachment, which seemed to consist of several hundreds, and extended four deep over an enclosure of thirty acres, attained the hill, than another assemblage of men, far more numerous than the former, arose and marched without any apparent hostility after the military spectres. These were dressed in a dark uniform, and, at the top of the hill, both parties joined, and formed what the spectators called an L, and, passing down the opposite side of the hill, disappeared. At this time a volume of smoke, like that vomited by a park of artillery, spread over the plain, and was so impervious, as for two minutes to hide the cattle from Jackson and Turner. They were both men of character and respectability, and the impression made on their minds was never erased."

In addition to this, I may mention, that, during the last continental war, all the military and volunteers in Ireland were hurried to the north to defend the country against a spectre fleet, which had no existence in those seas. And I find, likewise, in my note-book, the following extraordinary account, which I think was copied long ago from a book called "A Guide to the Lakes of Cumberland." I was always so fond of those romantic and visionary subjects, that I have added thousands of *lees* to them, but in this I shall not deviate one word from the original writer's narrative.

"Souter Fell is nearly nine hundred yards high, barricaded on the north and west sides with precipitous rocks, but somewhat more open on the east, and easier of access. On this mountain occurred the extraordinary phenomena, that, towards the middle of the last century, excited so much consternation and alarm—I mean the visionary appearances of armed men, and other figures, the causes of which have never in the smallest degree received a satisfactory solution, though, from the circumstances hereafter mentioned, there seems reason to believe that they are not entirely inexplicable.

"On a summer's morning of 1743, as David Stricket, then servant to J. Wren of Wilton Hall, the next house to Blakehills, was sitting at the door with his master, they saw the figure of a man with a dog, pursuing some horses along the side of Souter Fell, a place so steep that no horse can travel on it. They appeared to run at an amazing pace till they got out of sight at the lower end of the Fell.

" The next morning, Stricket and his master ascended the steep side of the mountain, in full expectation that they should find the man lying dead, as they were persuaded that the swiftness with which he ran must have killed him. They expected likewise to find several dead horses, and a number of horse-shoes among the rocks, which they were sure the horses could not but throw, galloping at such a furious rate. They were, however, disappointed, for there appeared not the least vestige of either man or horse, not so much as the mark of a horse's hoof on the turf, or among the small stones on the steep. Astonishment, and a degree of fear perhaps, for some time induced them to conceal the circumstances ; but they at length disclosed them, and as well might be supposed, were only laughed at for their credulity.

" The following year, 1744, on the 23d of June, as the same David Stricket, who at the time lived with Mr William Lancaster's father, of Blakehills, was walking a little above the house, about seven in the evening, he saw a troop of horsemen riding on the side of Souter Fell, in pretty close ranks, and at a brisk pace. Mindful of the ridicule which had been excited against him the preceding year, he continued to observe them in silence for some time ; but being at last convinced that the appearance was real, he went into the house, and informed Mr Lancaster that he had something curious to show him. They went out together, but before Stricket had either spoken or pointed out the place, his master's son had himself discovered the aërial troopers ; and when conscious that the same appearances were visible to both, they informed the family, and the phenomena were alike seen by all.

" These visionary horsemen seemed to come from the

lower part of Souter Fell, and became visible at a place called Knott. They then moved in regular troops along the side of the Fell, till they came opposite to Blakehills, when they went over the mountain. Thus they described a kind of curvilineal path, and both their first and last appearances were bounded by the top of the mountain.

" The pace at which these shadowy forms proceeded, was a regular swift walk, and the whole time of the continuance of their appearance was upwards of two hours; but farther observation was then precluded by the approach of darkness. Many troops were seen in succession; and frequently the last, or the last but one, in a troop, would quit his position, gallop to the front, and then observe the same pace with the others. The same changes were visible to all the spectators, and the view of the phenomena was not confined to Blakehills only, but was seen by every person at every cottage within the distance of a mile. The number of persons who witnessed the march of these aërial travellers was twenty-six."

It would therefore appear that my vision of a drove of Highland cattle, with their drivers, was not altogether an isolated instance of the same phenomena. It is quite evident that we must attribute these appearances to particular states of the atmosphere, and suppose them to be shadows of realities; the airy resemblance of scenes passing in distant parts of the country, and by some singular operation of natural causes thus expressively imaged on the acclivities of the mountains.

Lightning Source UK Ltd.
Milton Keynes UK
UKOW05f1859050116

265874UK00009B/165/P